TERRY WAITE
AND OLLIE NORTH

TERRY WAITE
AND OLLIE NORTH

THE UNTOLD STORY OF
THE KIDNAPPING–
AND THE RELEASE

GAVIN HEWITT

LITTLE, BROWN AND COMPANY
Boston Toronto London

First Edition

Credits for insert photographs: *page i* top and bottom
© Popperfoto; *ii* © AP PHOTO; *iii* top and bottom ©
Popperfoto; *iv* top © AP PHOTO, bottom © Popperfoto;
v © Popperfoto; *vi* © AP PHOTO; *vii* top and bottom
© the author; *viii* all © the author.

ISBN 0-316-35990-4

Library of Congress Cataloging-in-Publication information
is available.

10 9 8 7 6 5 4 3 2 1

HAD

Published simultaneously in Canada
by Little, Brown and Company (Canada) Limited

Printed in the United States of America

CONTENTS

PROLOGUE

Six months after Terry Waite had been taken hostage, I was in Washington doing the rounds. The visit took in the State Department, countless think tanks where former Administration officials reside in exile and those anonymous companies beyond the Beltway where erstwhile Pentagon and Intelligence officials turn former access into profit. Through these revolving doors of influence I sought information on what had befallen the envoy of the Archbishop of Canterbury.

The intention was to make a film for BBC *Panorama* but the omens were inauspicious. Waite had disappeared into the black hole of Beirut. By 1987 most Western governments had severed their links with the Western part of the Lebanese capital. What fragments of information emerged amounted to little more than rumour.

The American Administration, like its predecessor, had nearly been brought down by the issue of hostages. By the summer after Waite's capture, hostages had been relegated to the 'take note' file. Initiatives were dead; buried by the revelation that the Reagan Administration had traded arms for hostages. The accepted wisdom was that hostages paid few political dividends. A silence had fallen on official Washington, with no one seeming to know whether Terry Waite was dead or alive.

I was concluding yet another fruitless conversation with a senior Administration official, who had only seen me reluctantly, when he said, 'Our treatment of Waite was shameful.' 'Why?' I asked with some surprise. 'Go ask Ollie North,' he said with a rueful smile and without elaboration.

North, at the time, was the star witness of the Congressional enquiry into what had become known as the Iran–

Contra affair. He was corralled by lawyers and the court-room lay ahead. The man who knew the secrets of this alleg-edly shameful episode was himself beyond reach.

I had resigned myself to leaving Washington intrigued but none the wiser when I met a former State Department official who wanted to talk. He, in his own way, had been a minor victim of the Iran–Contra affair. But he wanted assurances that nothing would be broadcast or published before Terry Waite was a free man again. The information could easily be misunderstood by the captors in Beirut. It was an under-taking I readily gave, both to him and the scores of contacts that were to follow, including Waite's office at Lambeth Palace.

The official told me how Oliver North and others in the Administration had used Terry Waite without his knowing, thereby exposing him to captivity and the accusation that he was a spy for the Americans. Later, the Waite affair would be described to me as 'the last piece of unexploded ordnance of the Reagan era'. A lawyer in the Special Prosecutor's office, with responsibility for investigating this matter, said there was no more sensitive subject than 'Waite'.

So I came to understand that inside the greatest political scandal in the United States of the last decade lay another drama with its own cast of characters and its own particular tragedy. There were political questions, certainly. Who in the Administration had known and authorized the dealings with the envoy from Canterbury? But this was essentially a human drama involving two individuals.

Oliver North and Terry Waite were both Christians; one born-again, the other a devout Anglican. They were brought together in pursuit of a common goal; innocent men held captive in Beirut. For Oliver North, it was a mission ordained by his Commander-in-Chief; a task he was to attend to with Marine zeal. It would make him careless of others, even those he liked and respected. 'Secret operations,' he was to say, 'are at essence a lie.' The tragedy for Terry Waite was that he became a victim of the very deception that was intended to free the hostages.

But this was not a simple story of deceit and betrayal. The two men liked and respected each other; there was a chemistry between them. Even after Waite had been in captivity for four and a half years Oliver North told me that he expected to renew his friendship with Terry Waite when he was released. A grand illusion. Possibly.

When the idea of a book was first mooted, I was initially reluctant. The story seemed best left to the principal players themselves. But, in time, I came to be persuaded that the tangled relationship between a Colonel in the White House and an envoy of the Archbishop of Canterbury was more that just a cameo in a great political drama. It was a story of how nations and individuals can become victims of grand obsessions that set aside caution and restraint with grim consequences.

I had also come to know and respect most of those who had worked closely with Terry Waite. I had watched them suffer from the knowledge that he was enduring a terrible ordeal which they were helpless to end. Their determination to struggle for his release, often against political advice, was worthy of record.

So, the book was written. It is but an initial account of how a man who set out to free others became a hostage himself. For in time, Terry Waite, who has suffered the hell of captivity, must tell his own story.

ON THE EDGE OF THE TARMAC

As he waited to have his bags searched at London's Heathrow airport, other passengers shouted words of encouragement. Security officials wished him well. Tourists reached for their cameras. Terry Waite was a man made famous by freeing hostages.

He had arrived at the airport with an entourage of reporters. It was as if the envoy of the Archbishop of Canterbury had acquired his own press corps. In previous times, envoys glided unnoticed between capitals, their anonymity deemed essential to their trade. Now, in the age of publicity, an envoy embarking on secret negotiations was seen off with a televisual fanfare – a local hero stepping out to haggle with religious zealots and kidnappers.

It was 14 November 1985, and Terry Waite was about to make his first trip to Beirut, a place he would later describe as 'giving anarchy a bad name'. In the past, he had worked exclusively for the release of British hostages. Now he was going to the Lebanon on behalf of captive Americans. They were more than simply a handful of unfortunate individuals; they had become the test of character of the presidency of Ronald Reagan. On taking office, Reagan had promised there would be 'no hiding place' for terrorists. His words were being mocked by a group of Lebanese extremists, and the release of the hostages had become an imperative of his presidency.

Waite had already boarded his Middle East Airlines flight when a plane from Washington landed, several hours late. Oliver North raced up the jetty and ran down the moving walkway of the airport's third terminal. An official from the State Department was a few feet behind him. North went to the head of the queue at passport control.

'I'm from the White House,' he explained breathlessly. 'I have to see Terry Waite before he leaves for the Lebanon. His plane is due to depart in a few minutes.' North showed his White House identification pass to a rather bemused immigration official who, after some hesitation, accepted his story and waved him through.

'Ollie just persuaded them,' said Parker Borg, the official travelling with him. 'He made them feel it was the most important event in the world.'

Oliver North was Deputy Assistant Director for Political—Military Affairs on the National Security Council staff. Through a willingness to work marathon hours he had become one of the more important White House officials. One of his tasks was liaising with the relatives of the American hostages, but over time he had assumed operational control of efforts to free the men held in the Lebanon. His business suit barely disguised his background. His hair wasn't much longer than during his days in the Marines. His face was drawn, spare, but his eyes burned with commitment.

The two men hurried along the connecting bridge to Terminal 2, which handles the non-British Airways flights to Europe and the Middle East. North went straight to the desk of Middle East Airlines.

'I have to talk to Terry Waite,' he announced. 'I represent the US government.'

'The plane has already boarded,' the check-in agent told him, 'and it's left the gate.'

North was insistent and asked to see the Duty Manager. When he arrived, North suggested he call Waite on the plane. 'It's essential to his mission that I speak with him,' he said, looking the man directly in the eyes. It was part of North's charm that people believed him.

A message was passed to Waite that a Mr North from Washington was at the gate. Did he want to speak with him? Waite agreed at once. A cart was sent to the aircraft steps and Waite was driven to the edge of the tarmac. Oliver North and Parker Borg were waiting amidst the clutter of baggage retrieval trucks.

'Oliver, how nice to see you,' said Terry Waite. He was the only person who called North 'Oliver'. To everyone else he was plain 'Ollie'. 'Oliver' amused the White House official; it sounded very English, even aristocratic.

North produced from his pocket a photograph; it was a head and shoulders portrait of a man with a beard, a prominent nose and determined eyes. North asked Waite to study it. The picture, North explained, was of Imad Mugniyah, the man whom intelligence officials regarded as being behind the kidnapping of American hostages. Mugniyah was, in his view, dangerous and capricious – the most wanted terrorist in the world. If Waite met him, during his forthcoming trip, he would be dealing with the man whose word would be needed to release the Americans. North admitted that, despite Mugniyah's fearsome reputation, they knew little about him. Washington would be interested in anything Waite might learn. The Anglican envoy looked again at the picture. It was the face of hundreds of Moslem fighters in Lebanon.

North also spoke about a group of prisoners in Kuwait, whom the captors in Beirut wanted released in exchange for the American hostages. The men had been convicted of planting bombs in Kuwait City. The United States position, he said, was resolute and unchanged. It opposed concessions to terrorists and was not prepared to put any pressure on Kuwait. But it would help Terry Waite's negotiations with the captors, North acknowledged, if he promised to take up the cases of the Kuwaiti prisoners on a humanitarian basis.

The three men spoke for about twenty minutes and shook hands.

'God bless you, Terry,' said North.

It was a curious encounter. North and Borg booked themselves on the first available flight back to Washington. They had flown across the Atlantic for a brief tarmac meeting. As North's diary shows, he and Waite had spoken on the telephone four days earlier. The US stand on the Kuwaiti prisoners was hardly new; it certainly didn't require a last-minute dash to London.

'It was no way of doing business,' admitted Parker Borg, who had accompanied North out of bureaucratic etiquette. He was Assistant Director of the Office of Counter-terrorism at the State Department and had a direct interest in the hostage issue. As to the purpose of the tarmac meeting, he shrugged and smiled.

The encounter was a cameo in the dramas that North liked to create. He would frequently fly through the night to see a contact and be back at his desk in Washington the next day, his colleagues unaware of his travels. He inhabited a world of intrigue: 'Clandestine meetings, in exotic settings, with the cast of *Casablanca*,' as one of those concerned with the hostages described it. Fact and fantasy were divided by a gossamer thread. 'North had a pronounced sense of the theatrical,' said Eugene Douglas, who was President Reagan's Ambassador at Large for Refugees, and friendly with both Terry Waite and Oliver North. He knew about many of their meetings, including the one on the tarmac. 'This was vaudeville, a comic act,' he said, '*The Goon Show* run riot.'

Yet North was a man of contradictions. Theatricality cohabited with shrewdness. The trip to London may have been extravagant and unnecessary, but it flattered Terry Waite that an official from the White House should make the journey. Imperceptibly, without his knowing, it drew the Anglican envoy into an unofficial network which North was creating: a network outside the control of government. In being shown the picture of Mugniyah, Waite was also being asked to pass on any scrap of intelligence that his trip might inadvertently produce – a dangerous step for an envoy.

In the past, Terry Waite's missions had been relatively straightforward. Now he was operating in a zone of ambiguity where the line between working for the release of American hostages and working for the American government was blurred; where his access to groups in the Lebanon attracted intelligence officials. As a Church envoy, his only protection was his independence. He had to talk to governments, but he couldn't afford to be seen as acting on their behalf. Maintaining that distinction would be vital to ensuring his survival and the good name of the Anglican Church. In time, he would become so well known that his mission and the reputation of the Church would become inextricably linked.

Over an eighteen-month period Waite was to work closely with Oliver North, reassured by the knowledge that he was dealing with an official from the White House. They met nearly twenty times and, according to one of Waite's closest colleagues, they had nearly thirty telephone conversations. It wasn't just a professional relationship between officials from two institutions, one a Church, the other a government. The two men saw in each other reflections of themselves. Both were drawn to adventure, to playing the heroic role. They would, in their different ways, become preoccupied by the challenge. For North it was a question of pride, American pride; the captors had thrown down a gauntlet. For Waite it was about trust; the hostage families had invested hope in him.

Waite became intrigued by North and his access to the hidden levers of power. It was an interest which his friends noticed. 'Terry Waite was fascinated, in an ever-deepening way with the arts of government,' observed Ambassador Eugene Douglas,

> that a whole world exists with vast resources at their call; that people can pick up a phone or instrument or press a button [and that things can] happen outside the normal visible realm of citizens or mortals . . . Here he was, ordinary Terry Waite, envoy of a Church, setting out to help hostages without having any knowledge aforehand, finding himself in liaison with the government of the United States, being taken into their confidence on where they think hostages are and what's happening. Of course he's fascinated.

What Waite was less aware of, in those early meetings, was that the hostage issue had created a morality of its own where normal standards were becoming corrupted by the political necessity to get the men released. North belonged to a Manichean world which divided neatly into good and bad. The captors in Beirut were dark, uncivilized forces that had to be defeated. Any action that brought about their downfall and the release of the hostages could be justified. As North said, 'I'd have offered the Iranians a free trip to Disneyland if we could have gotten the Americans home for it.'

The relationship between North and Waite was a sideshow to what became known as the Iran–Contra affair. Yet it was illustrative of the West's failure to develop a coherent strategy for dealing with hostage taking. Values became corrupted, ideals blemished, laws broken and individuals exploited.

Terry Waite shuttled between the captors in Beirut and Oliver North, believing that his status as an envoy of the Church would somehow keep him immune. It didn't. His tragedy was that when he realized how he had been used it was too late. His reputation had been tarnished. The only way he could see of salvaging his good name was to return to Beirut, a journey that would end in his own captivity.

2

THE GENTLE GIANT

Terry Waite belonged to that amorphous group of emissaries and intermediaries who are always in attendance on the rim of international affairs. In Britain he was known for having prised prisoners out of the revolutionary regimes of Iran and Libya. The British had taken to him. He was their kind of hero: a Church layman, an amateur pitted against dictators and extremists. He even looked rather dishevelled, as if he had taken the part at the last moment. At six foot eight inches he was uncomfortably tall, his beard was unkempt and he carried a battered suitcase which might have been favoured by an ageing schoolmaster.

Waite was frequently mistaken for either a clergyman or the Archbishop of Canterbury's bodyguard. His actual job was Secretary for Anglican Communion Affairs, with a salary of £16,000 a year. When the post was created for him in 1980 no one was entirely certain what his duties would be. The role of envoy was unseen. Indeed, the Anglican Church had no record of involvement in international affairs unrelated to Church business. Terry Waite became a kind of advance man for the Archbishop, setting up overseas visits to the outposts of the Anglican Communion.

He had been in the job less than a year when three British missionaries were detained in Iran and accused of spying. The country was at the height of its revolutionary turmoil. Ayatollah Khomeini's Islamic State was in its infancy, obsessed with cleansing the country of the past. Supporters of the Shah were being rooted out from their comfortable houses in North Tehran. At night, self-appointed vigilantes in camouflage jackets would search cars for enemies of the Revolution. The US embassy had been seized and renamed 'the nest of spies', and its staff taken hostage. Documents found inside the embassy building convinced the militants that the United States was plotting against the Khomeini regime.

The British missionaries were caught up in this revolutionary paranoia. One of them, Jean Waddell, had been tied up, held under a blanket and shot by two men who broke into her apartment. She underwent an emergency operation, but before she could leave the country a member of the Church made an accusation against her and she was accused of spying. She was taken to the notorious Evin prison, which had been used by the Shah's secret police as a place of torture. It would fast assume a similar reputation under the Ayatollah.

The Archbishop of Canterbury, Dr Runcie, realized that approaches by the British Foreign Office were unlikely to be productive. If the United States was the Great Satan, then in Iranian eyes Britain was the Devil's spawn. Dr Runcie chose to appeal to Ayatollah Khomeini directly, addressing him as a fellow religious leader. 'I greet you in the name of one God,' he wrote. He asked the Iranian leader to meet his envoy, Terry Waite.

In December 1980, Waite arrived in Tehran. To the Revolutionary guards at the airport he had all the appearance of a religious leader. With his flowing black cassock, dangling cross and prophet's beard he looked more like a priest from the Greek Orthodox Church than a layman from the Church of England. Secular diplomacy had been supplanted by a piece of Christian theatre. The mullahs had closed their ears to the governments of the West, condescending only to deal with believers, fellow People of the Book. So petitioners to the Islamic State were encouraged to parade their faith much as the mullahs flaunted theirs. Terry Waite was to reveal a flair for the dramatic, and his Iranian audience would be duly impressed.

Beyond wishing to see Khomeini, Waite was intent on demonstrating to the Iranian authorities that he was a representative of the Christian Church and quite separate from the British government. Soon after his arrival he called up the few Anglicans left in Iran. He had brought greetings from the Archbishop, he told them, and suggested they hold a service.

Waite turned up at St Paul's church in Tehran still wearing his black cassock and carrying a giant cross. As he started to preach, the back door of the church burst open and in walked five Revolutionary guards with automatic weapons. He stopped preaching and walked down the aisle to greet them. He told them he was glad they had come and sat them down in the front row. One of them was carrying a tape recorder. The sermon had become an audition. Much to the surprise of the congregation, he decided to start again from the beginning. It was through the recommendations of these guards that he was able to visit the missionaries in prison and make contact with those in the Iranian leadership who controlled the fate of the British prisoners.

The missionaries were delightfully resilient. Life in Evin jail reminded Jean Waddell of an English boarding school. The two other British prisoners were Dr John and Audrey Coleman, medical missionaries who had worked for over twenty years in Iran. They celebrated their thirty-fourth wedding anniversary while in detention. 'We were able to have a cake,' said Dr Coleman, 'and invite some of the Revolutionary soldiers. We regarded these soldiers like our sons. My wife used to mend their clothes and many of them were in tears when we left the prison.'

Within a few months the missionaries were free. Terry Waite's high-profile visit had encouraged the Iranian leadership to re-examine their cases and see for themselves that the charges were ludicrous. The Foreign Office had been impressed by Waite's mediation. 'Foxy but friendly' was the verdict of one official. In his negotiations Waite was patient, direct and understanding of the other side's grievances. 'Very few people,' he said, 'give way totally to evil. There's nearly always a good and reasonable side in there somewhere. You have to try and draw that out and build on it.'

He was also unashamedly himself, open, warm and gregarious – the boyish adventurer barely concealed. He challenged the Revolutionary guards to a bout of arm wrestling. 'The guards looked at me,' he later recounted, 'as if to say, "You're a big fellow," so I suggested some arm wrestling.

Two or three of them took me on but they didn't win once.'
The papers in Britain loved it. They wrote of the 'gentle
giant' taming the Revolutionary guards.

The release of the three missionaries wasn't as straightforward as was reported. Privately, the British government
had been talking to the Iranian leadership through Mr Leif
Leifland, a Swedish career diplomat. It was agreed that the
body of an Iranian terrorist killed after a bomb had exploded
at the Queen's Garden Hotel in London the previous May
should be returned to Iran. Mr Leifland was also able to
convey to the Iranians that if the obstacle of the British
missionaries was removed, then Britain would allow the sale
of spare parts for the Iranian army's Chieftain tanks. Terry
Waite's skilful mission had enabled both governments to dis-
pose of an embarrassing problem without being seen to
compromise.

The freeing of the missionaries transformed Terry Waite
into a personality in Britain. All the right ingredients were
present. An ordinary individual, unaffected, unknown, had
charmed Islamic Revolutionaries with common sense, integrity and a dash of humour. The media, in their endless quest
for heroes, had found a candidate rich in solid British virtues.
Praise was lavish, excessive and dangerous. A year later he
was awarded the MBE, an honour he received at
Buckingham Palace on crutches, having been injured in a
biking accident.

From being an obscure aide to the Archbishop, Terry
Waite found himself in demand. Charities sought his
endorsement, ailing churches wanted him to fill their pews
and newspapers wanted stories, anecdotes, anything that had
his name on it. In one article he claimed to be able to see
into the future. In a dream he had seen the Archbishop of
Uganda, Janani Luwum, surrounded by flames. Afterwards
he had a 'disturbing feeling' that something had happened
to Luwum. A short while later he learnt that the archbishop
had been murdered. On another occasion, while driving with
his wife, he had a vision of a car accident. He described it to
her. They rounded a bend in the road and there was a crash
exactly as he had described it. 'I don't know why I should
have these experiences. It's an odd feeling,' he said.

Three years later, in 1984, Britain and Libya had fallen out. A gunman had opened fire from inside the Libyan People's Bureau in London at an anti-Qadaffi demonstration. Yvonne Fletcher, a young policewoman, was killed. The British public was outraged and the building was surrounded by armed police, but the government was constrained in its actions by the knowledge that the eight thousand Britons working in Libya were potential hostages. The Libyans were eventually expelled from the country and Britain severed diplomatic relations. Libya retaliated by detaining four Britons and accusing them of spying.

Three months later, the Archbishop of Canterbury decided to take up their cases. After the death of the policewoman it was politically impossible for the British government even to be seen talking to the Libyans, but the Church was able to discuss humanitarian issues such as the welfare of prisoners. During the latter part of 1984 and the beginning of the following year, Terry Waite was to visit Libya three times.

It was a frustrating mission that required patience, skill and humour. When he arrived in Tripoli on one of his visits he was asked by the Deputy Foreign Minister whether he had had a comfortable journey on the Libyan Airlines flight.

Waite remarked that he had found it hard to fit his six foot eight inches into an economy-size seat.

'Our People's Society tries to make everyone equal, so we have no first-class seats,' replied the Minister.

'That may be man's intention, but it is certainly not God's design,' said Waite with a smile.

'Ah, but didn't you notice,' said the official quickly, 'the plane is of American design.' The two men laughed and the ice was broken.

At Christmas Waite was received by Colonel Qadaffi in his Bedouin tent. The Anglican envoy greeted him in a few words of Arabic which he had hastily mastered in London. Qadaffi, referring to it being Christmas, impishly said that Jesus of Nazareth ranked as one of the three great prophets of Islam.

Waite chose not to argue. 'Christmas,' he agreed, 'is an important occasion to Christians. It is a festival not just of love but of justice.'

The Libyan leader allowed himself a slight smile. He had not missed the reference to the fact that some of the Britons had been detained without trial for eight months.

Waite then presented him with what he called 'a small Christmas gift'. It was a book on Aristotle and the Arabs. 'It speaks of the influence of Greek thought on the Arabs in the seventh and eighth centuries,' Waite told the Libyan leader. Qadaffi was flattered and began speaking, at great length, about Islamic–Christian relations in Africa. Waite had learnt the importance of listening sympathetically to Third World leaders and their view of history. As Qadaffi warmed to his subject, Waite craned forward, his head inclined attentively.

During the meeting, a note was passed to the Libyan leader, who remarked that mail in Libya took about six months to reach its destination.

'You have an efficient postal service here, I see,' said Waite drolly.

The Libyan leader laughed. He revelled in these public encounters with the supplicants from the West, spicing their conversation with flattery and humble requests.

Afterwards Waite was able to claim a success. 'Colonel Qadaffi said that out of respect for the Church and my mission, if it were in his power, he would release the four men now.'

The Libyan leader left the final decision to the People's Congress. It met on 8 January 1985 in a circus ring, and Terry Waite was asked to address it.

'Politics were made by men,' he told his listeners, 'but mercy, compassion and justice come from God.' The speech was cleverly pitched. The tenets of which he spoke were Christian, but were equally true to Islam.

The Congress was impressed and ordered the release of the four Britons, but they attached certain conditions. The Anglican Church must work for the release of Libyans held in prison in the UK; Britain should hand over anti-Qadaffi 'stray dogs' to the Libyan authorities; and Britain should see that anti-Libyan propaganda was stopped and that the Church set up a 'helpline' for Libyans who claimed they were being badly treated by the British authorities.

Terry Waite avoided giving any undertakings to the

Libyans, although in the following months he did visit a number of Libyans held in British prisons. Officials at the State Department in Washington believe that the British government indicated privately to Qadaffi that it would at least look at some of the Libyan grievances.

For Waite it was a triumph. The Prime Minister praised him for his 'patience and skill'. The editorials were effusive. 'How does he do it?' asked one paper. 'Partly, it is personality. Though a humble Anglican, Mr Waite is blessed with a commanding presence.' 'He is gaining the reputation,' wrote another, 'of taking on impossible missions and succeeding.' 'He has established himself as one of the most public Christians of his times,' added yet another paper, 'a man whose influence for peace on earth and goodwill towards his fellow men is beyond doubt.' Awards followed: man of the year, the Templeton prize for humanitarian work and a variety of honorary degrees.

Such recognition had come unexpectedly. Terry Waite had grown up in Styal, Cheshire. It was Old England preserved: the village church, the mill and the Ship Inn where, in an upstairs room, he had attended confirmation classes to the accompaniment of bar-room laughter from downstairs. His father was the village policeman and the family lived in a police house. His mother taught in the Sunday school. It was a secure, intimate world. There was the village, and beyond its boundaries unbroken countryside. Aged four, Terry would wait at his garden gate and tag along with an old man to morning service. When, one day, he went on his own his family was not alarmed. Free from the alienation and suspicion of the cities, the community trusted itself.

Terry Waite left school in the late 1950s at sixteen and joined the Grenadier Guards, the first regiment of the Household Infantry. His height would have made him an ideal guardsman. But, soon afterwards, he was in hospital with a mystery illness. He had come out in a rash and the doctors were baffled. When it subsided he returned to the regiment, only for the rash to reappear. Eventually they found out that he was allergic to the dye in the khaki uniform. His army career was at an end.

He was kept in hospital for a further tests. While there he

was visited by officers from the Church Army, an organization similar to the Salvation Army. Waite liked their commitment and enrolled at their training college. The Church Army, with its ranks and uniform, eased his disappointment at having to abandon a military career. Training was austere and disciplined, with an emphasis on mission. It suited him well. During the summer, recruits had to pull a two-wheeled cart around the seaside resorts, aiding local parishes and holding beach meetings. They had a pulpit amidst the deckchairs, an accordion straining against the transistor radios, Christian puppets out-performing Punch and Judy, games evenings competing with the dance halls and hymns battling with pub revelries – the Church versus the world. It was a gentle, undemonstrative evangelism that formed part of the tapestry of the English seaside in the fifties.

Terry Waite rarely spoke about his faith. The mission itself was practical, concerned and therefore Christian. He was never attracted to being ordained, having to bare his beliefs from a pulpit. He chose, instead, to enter full-time service as an Anglican lay worker, becoming one of the Church's unknown toilers. He advised the Bishop of Bristol on adult education; trained Ugandans for the Anglican ministry; advised a Catholic teaching order in Rome and, in 1980, became an aide to the Archbishop of Canterbury. But by 1985, after his visits to Libya, he was better known in Britain than his employer. Newspapers, while singing his praises, would deign to include a reference to the Archbishop with such headlines as 'Primate's miracle worker'.

Some of Terry Waite's old friends hadn't been surprised by his encounters with Revolutionary guards and his meetings with Qadaffi. The Reverend Philip Turner had worked with him in Uganda and had noticed his love of adventure. 'Terry is a very, very complicated man and I think he's a bit of a gambler and he likes danger. I don't mean this in a bad sense . . . but I think he really likes a certain edge on things.'

'I think the key to this man,' wrote a friend and former diplomatic correspondent, 'is that he belongs to another century. I think myself of the pages of John Bunyan and *Pilgrim's Progress*. I also think of the novels of Henty, of British young men going into dangerous situations in Africa, derring-do and all that.'

Others detected a deep longing to play a significant role. Eugene Douglas, the Reagan Administration's Ambassador at Large for Refugees, formed the impression that Terry Waite, although richly praised, felt excluded by the establishment, by dint of his background. Douglas himself had been to Columbia University and graduated, easily, into government. 'I knew Presidents, met with Heads of State, and had friends in the diplomatic service. Terry wanted to be like that.'

The missions to Iran and Libya had given Terry Waite a new vision. He began to see the Anglican Church playing a role in international affairs, in the manner of the International Red Cross. With so many doors in the Moslem world closed to normal diplomacy, he saw the Church as the only institution capable of maintaining a dialogue with radical Islamic regimes. The vision was tempting. It lifted Waite above the mundanities of Church life, and for the Archbishop it offered respite from the flow of criticisms that the Church was losing its faith, its voice and its congregation.

While Waite was negotiating with the Libyans he had been approached by the Presbyterian Church in the United States on behalf of one of their ministers held hostage in Lebanon. Although he was too busy to become involved at once, he wanted to help. It was exactly the kind of situation where he thought the Church should act. But working on behalf of American hostages was to prove a very different assignment. From being well known in Britain he would be transformed into an international figure. During the next eighteen months he would provide headlines for news magazines, become a familiar personality on the nightly news in America, be sought after by talk shows, grant countless news conferences and earn the curiosity of reporters just by turning up in a country. But 'hostages' was a dangerous word in the American political lexicon; they had undone reputations in the past and there were those who were determined that the United States would not be humiliated again. It was a perilous assignment for an Anglican envoy.

3

AN AMERICAN HOSTAGE APPEALS

Benjamin Weir had been a missionary in Lebanon for thirty-one years. He had seen the country flourish and disintegrate. Beirut had been the Paris of the Middle East, a playground where you could ski in the mountains in the morning and swim in the Mediterranean in the afternoon. The West saw it as an outpost of civilization in a region it little understood. Then in 1976 the illusion snapped. The religious and political rivalries surfaced in the form of armed militias. The civil war had begun. The dominant Christian community found itself battling against resentful Moslems and Palestinians, bent on changing the structure of power. The conflict quickly descended into savagery as massacres repaid massacres. Outside powers tried to impose their own order. There was a *Pax Syriana*, a *Pax Israeli* and a *Pax Americana*. All were to fail. Beirut stubbornly continued to be one of the most dangerous cities in the world, pock-marked by battle and inhabited by gunmen.

Most of the foreigners gradually slipped away. Only a small band remained. Some never lost their affection for the country despite its terror and barbarity. To others, the unfolding tragedy became a cause in itself. Among these were two American missionaries, Benjamin and Carol Weir.

Benjamin Weir was a quiet, thoughtful man; his metal-rimmed glasses and his disappearing hair gave him the appearance of a middle-aged scholar. He was a man at peace with himself, out of place in a city of strident, angry faces. He had first worked as a Presbyterian minister in the Shi'ite Moslem town of Nabatiye. Later, he and his wife Carol had begun teaching at the Near East School of Theology in Beirut. Too much of their lives had been invested in the country for them to leave.

By May 1984 an anarchy prevailed that was more frightening than the clashes across the Green Line between the Christians and the Moslems. Armed gangs roamed Moslem West Beirut. Some of them belonged to recognizable militias, but others had no loyalties except to themselves or their hidden paymasters. For foreigners there was an added danger: Westerners were being taken hostage. Already that year three Americans had been snatched off the streets, and one of those was the CIA Station Chief. Every time Benjamin and Carol Weir ventured outside their apartment they knew they were taking a risk.

On 8 May 1984, they set out to walk the few streets to the ecumenical seminary where they worked. They had only gone a short distance when a car pulled up behind them. Two men got out and said something. Benjamin Weir didn't understand the words and asked, 'What do you want?'

'I want you,' the man shouted, and began pulling Benjamin Weir towards the car. They both knew at once it was a kidnap attempt and began screaming.

Benjamin Weir later wrote,

I tried to resist, but the man was much younger and stronger than I was. He twisted my necktie and pulled me toward the car. I braced my hands on both sides of the open back door, but he gave me a tremendous shove from behind and forced me into the back seat. A man with a black beard jumped into the front passenger seat and pointed an automatic weapon at my head while the driver put the car in motion. The man who had seized me forced me down on the floor of the car and pulled a sack over me, keeping his hand on my back. By now the car was speeding along. I realized I was at the mercy of my assailants, helpless, unable to escape.

Carol Weir instinctively rushed to a police station. They stared at her open-mouthed. Nine years of civil war had left them powerless, a uniformed irrelevance. No one sought their help any more. So the police commander was summoned.

'Don't worry,' he assured her. 'We'll have your husband back soon.'

He boasted of roadblocks that covered the city. They did exist, and they even stopped cars, but the militias ignored them much as they did the few traffic lights that continued to function.

Carol Weir had brought up her four children amidst the chaos of Lebanon. She reminded her friends of an American pioneer – strong in faith, redoubtable and inured to setbacks. After her visit to the police she went to the American embassy and insisted on a meeting with the Ambassador. He was in the United States at the time and she was taken instead to the Deputy Chief of Mission. Later, she was to write about her encounter.

'What do you expect?' the official asked. 'Hasn't the embassy suggested that all non-essential Americans leave? We can't keep our own personnel safe from kidnapping.'

Carol Weir was taken aback and retorted, 'The kidnapping of Americans is a response to our foreign policy.'

'You don't expect us to change our foreign policy, do you?' he enquired testily.

So began a difficult and frequently fractious relationship with American officials. In her frustration she was to look elsewhere for help in securing the release of her husband.

It was 1984 and election year in the United States. The Reagan administration did not want to admit it had a new hostage crisis. Four years earlier Jimmy Carter had had to go to the polls with fifty-three Americans held hostage in Iran and the people had punished him, unable and unwilling to forgive the humbling of American power. As Ronald Reagan began his re-election campaign, the last thing he wanted was for the yellow ribbons, a symbol of absent relatives, to start going up again across America, as had happened during the hostage crisis of 1980.

He had come to power promising to revive the American dream. America, he reassured the people, was still a city set on a hill, with its best years yet to come. He had promised a global crusade against the mullahs, the mobs, the terrorists – those who had kicked sand in the eyes of America. 'Let terrorists beware,' he had declared shortly after his inauguration. 'Our policy will be one of swift and effective retribution.' With the people about to vote, administration officials wanted to play down the importance of a handful of Americans held hostage in Lebanon.

There was another consideration. Officials at the State Department believed that the United States had handled the last hostage crisis incorrectly. Each night the evening news would remind America of how many days its fellow citizens had been held captive in Iran. It placed almost impossible pressure on the President, while at the same time strengthening the bargaining position of the hostage takers. This time some officials were urging a low-key approach, in which the value of the hostage was effectively reduced by the lack of public concern shown.

This more sober strategy coincided with a changing assessment of Lebanon's importance to the United States. By 1984 the administration was tiring of its Lebanese involvement. American lives had been sacrificed and nothing gained. In April the previous year a bomb had exploded at the American embassy, killing sixty-three people and injuring over a hundred. It had been hidden inside a car which had then been driven at the embassy wall; the Shi'ite driver was only too happy to die as a martyr. For the Americans, worse was to follow. In October of that year a Mercedes truck crammed with explosives was driven into the Marine compound in Beirut: 241 servicemen were killed.

The bombings destroyed America's will to continue playing a role in Lebanon. The country was deemed marginal to US interests. Its diplomatic presence was reduced and most of the diplomats moved to the relative safety of Christian East Beirut. Americans were advised against staying in the country.

So when, in May 1984, Carol Weir turned to the administration to help find her husband she was disappointed. America's appetite for action had been dulled by failure. During that summer she stayed on in Beirut, wanting to be near her husband. Progress was slow. She sought out various Middle Eastern officials, including the Syrian Foreign Minister. Everywhere she was received politely, but was offered nothing except sympathy.

In July, the American embassy received a videotape showing her husband in captivity. His beard was shaggy and his hair long; Carol Weir thought him pale and drawn. On the tape he said he was being held in exchange for seventeen men imprisoned in Kuwait. They had carried out bombings against the American and French embassies in Kuwait in December 1983, in which five people were killed and more than sixty wounded. Three of those convicted of the bombings had been given death sentences. They belonged to an Iraqi opposition group called the Da'Wa or the 'Call', who wanted to overthrow the Iraqi government and replace it with an Islamic regime similar to that in Iran. But three of the bombers were Lebanese Shi'ites, and one of them, who was also under sentence of death, was related to the captors in Beirut. For the first time Carol Weir realized that there might be a specific motive behind the seizure of her husband, and not just general hostility to the West.

In New York, the Presbyterian Church assigned its Associate Director, Fred Wilson, to liaise with the administration. He was a minister of the Church, softly spoken but stubbornly determined, and wary of government. Carol Weir asked him to get her an appointment with the Secretary of State, but George Shultz initially declined to meet her. Wilson did see Richard Murphy, Assistant Secretary for Near Eastern and South Asian Affairs, but he was not encouraging. They didn't know where Benjamin Weir was or who was holding him. The investigation was likely to be lengthy and tough.

'By the end of August,' said Carol Weir, 'I was finding the long wait increasingly difficult.'

Then someone in the Church recalled that an envoy of the Archbishop of Canterbury, by the name of Terry Waite, had been successful in getting British missionaries out of Iran. In September 1984 Fred Wilson telephoned Waite in his office at Lambeth Palace in London. Wilson was encouraged. Although Waite was preoccupied with the four Britons held in Libya, he asked for details of Benjamin Weir's case and promised that when he became free he would be happy to help.

Carol Weir's determination was growing with her frustration. She appealed to the Reverend Jesse Jackson and Muhammad Ali, black Americans who were seen in parts of the Third World as fighters against American oppression. Statements were issued by the two men and appeals made, but they were like voices in a fog which started boldly, became distorted and were finally swallowed up.

In early 1985 the Presbyterian Church lost patience with what they considered to be the bureaucratic inertia of Washington. Officials could not even agree who was behind the kidnappings. Some thought it was Iran, others favoured Syria, while yet others thought it was simply the work of a local militia trying to barter for the freedom of their imprisoned relatives. In order to make the hostages an issue in Washington, Carol Weir and Fred Wilson realized they would have to mobilize American public opinion. They were assisted by the seizure of two more Americans in Beirut. On 8 January 1985, Martin Jenco, a Catholic priest and head of the city's Catholic Relief Services, was taken. Although Carol Weir was sad at hearing the news, she knew it would help her cause. Three months later it was the turn of Terry Anderson, chief Middle East correspondent for Associated Press. He had many friends among the declining press corps in Beirut, and AP had important contacts in Washington.

That spring Carol Weir began crossing the United States, holding press conferences and meetings and making television appearances. Her campaigning had its effect. Hers was the voice of an ordinary American complaining about failure in Washington. It was a charge with which many Americans could sympathize. At the end of her first news conference she said emotionally, 'Do I have to wait four hundred and forty-four days for Ben's release?' That was the period that the American hostages in Iran had been held. Carol Weir was goading the administration into acknowledging that it had a new hostage crisis.

On 21 March she finally got an appointment with the Secretary of State, George Shultz. She asked him what he was doing about the captors' demands concerning the prisoners in Kuwait. Mr Shultz was firm. The administration would never interfere with another government, particularly if it were resisting terrorist blackmail.

Mrs Weir then suggested that the United States should negotiate directly with the captors. Mr Shultz said that such people heard voices from God and were deranged. It was impossible to talk with them.

Carol Weir disagreed. They were not lunatics. They were people with grievances against the United States. Mr Shultz became angry and pounded the table. He referred to the festival of Ashura, at which, in order to demonstrate their willingness to sacrifice themselves, Shi'ite Moslems flagellate their backs with knives until the blood runs. These people, he said, were pagan and primitive. Even though Mrs Weir's son, who was at the meeting, tried to explain the significance of Ashura, it was apparent that they were getting nowhere. They left Washington discouraged.

The Church now decided to prime its congregations and the powerful Christian communities across America. Thousands of postcards were sent to the White House, demanding action on the hostages. Although President Reagan wouldn't meet Carol Weir, his staff acknowledged that they had had to hire three more secretaries to deal with the extra mail. Awareness that the United States had another hostage crisis began to grow, but there were other factors that were beginning to change the attitude of the administration.

One of the hostages taken in 1984 had been William Buckley, CIA Station Chief in Lebanon, who was vital to America's intelligence-gathering operations in the Middle East. In an earlier bombing the CIA had lost Robert Eames, one of its most experienced operators; Buckley had been sent to Beirut to revive the Agency's intelligence network. His kidnapping was not only a further setback; Buckley was said to have been carrying documents listing CIA 'assets' in the region.

The then CIA Director, William Casey, made the release of Buckley one of the Agency's top priorities. Satellites were repositioned to spy on Beirut, and the CIA doubled its capacity to monitor telephone conversations coming out of Beirut and Damascus. Casey even made a trip to Damascus to talk to Syrian intelligence. He was accompanied by the Syrian businessman Omram Adham and travelled on an Argentine passport. Considering the hostility between Syria and the United States, the meeting was not unfriendly – but it produced no results.

Casey also considered putting pressure on the Kuwaitis to release the seventeen prisoners accused of bombing the French and American embassies, which was one of the main demands of the captors. It was a measure of his desperation that he should consider giving in to blackmail. The State Department opposed him. The idea, they argued, would undermine the United States' policy of opposing concessions to terrorists. By the spring of 1985, Casey's determination had been strengthened by reports that Buckley was being tortured. The CIA Director had the ear of President Reagan, and the issue of the hostages in Lebanon began to assume greater importance.

It was also the case that as new hostages were taken it became harder to ignore their plight. No longer could they be disregarded as isolated kidnappings. There was public speculation that Iran and Syria might be behind them – the very states that the administration had identified as the sponsors of international terrorism. President Reagan could not continue to wage his war against the terrorists while appearing impotent in the Lebanon. Some commentators drew attention to Syria's close links to the Soviet Union. America, they argued, could be facing a Soviet-inspired plan to make the Middle East unsafe for Americans by encouraging hostage taking. The evidence was flimsy but the mood was changing. America was being challenged, and to an administration that prided itself on its toughness, that was enough.

During the early part of 1985 Terry Waite had stayed in touch with Fred Wilson. On 10 May, while passing through New York on his way back from Australia, Waite agreed to meet Carol Weir at the headquarters of the Episcopal Church in Manhattan. He was shown a letter which Benjamin Weir had written to the Presbyterians in February, in which he complained that the US government was not doing anything to secure the release of the prisoners in Kuwait. 'I am assured,' he wrote, 'that once those prisoners are set free I and others will be released at the same time.' He added that his captors were opposed to interference by any third party, including Syria. 'If such interference is attempted I am told that our lives are in extreme danger and that the place where we are held will be blown up with us.'

Despite the implicit warning that the captors didn't want to deal with any outside mediators, Carol Weir and Fred Wilson urged Terry Waite to become the negotiator on behalf of the Church. Twice before they had considered taking on someone who could make contacts independent of government. Waite agreed in principle, although he told them he would need the formal approval of the Archbishop of Canterbury. The two Presbyterians were delighted. They found Waite reassuring, familiar with their dilemma. He stressed that he had no political view but worked as an independent humanitarian – a phrase which, in time, would become his calling card.

Terry Waite hadn't worked on behalf of Americans before and needed introductions in Washington. Although he had few contacts in the United States he did have friends in the Episcopal Church. The Episcopalians belong to the Anglican Communion and share the same faith, the same traditions and much of the same liturgy as the Church of England.

Compared to the Catholic or Baptist Churches, the Episcopal Church is small in size, but it is well supported by officials in government. It had particularly strong links with the Reagan administration, and it retained its reputation of being the Church of the Establishment. 'It was the instinct of most Episcopalians,' wrote James Reichley in his *Religion in US Public Life*, 'to align themselves with the party of order, which in England caused their Anglican cousins to be regarded as "the Tory Party at Prayer".' By the 1980s the Episcopalians had become a broad Church, encompassing both high Anglicanism and 'born again' fundamentalism. Reagan administration officials such as Robert McFarlane, John Poindexter, Oliver North and the then Vice-President, George Bush, all worshipped within its congregations.

One of Terry Waite's close friends was Director of the Episcopal Church's fund for disaster relief. Canon Samir Habiby was a Palestinian who had come to the United States as a student and stayed on. Some of his family continued to live in Jerusalem, while other relatives were part of the Palestinian diaspora and held influential positions in Jordan,

Syria and Saudi Arabia. Through his contacts he had been helpful in getting Terry Waite an appointment with Colonel Qadaffi. Waite now turned to him to arrange a Washington briefing on the American hostages. Habiby, using the Church's contacts with the administration, fixed an appointment with George Bush's office. The Vice President was at the time heading a task force on terrorism.

On 9 May, Terry Waite, Samir Habiby and his assistant went to the Vice President's suite on the third floor of the Old Executive Office Building. They were met by Donald Gregg, National Security Adviser to the Vice President and an active Episcopalian. Gregg, who had been employed by the CIA for seventeen years, was rather bemused by the Church delegation and was uncertain what he could do for them. He suggested that another Bush aide, Lieutenant Colonel Douglas Menarchik join them. The two officials discussed US policy towards the hostages in general terms – it was the kind of information available in most news-cuttings libraries.

Then Terry Waite raised an idea which he and Samir Habiby had been working on in New York. Under Islamic law, there is provision for a criminal to be released from prison if the families of those whom he has harmed forgive him; it might involve those who have suffered receiving some kind of compensation, or 'blood money' as the Moslems call it. It would therefore be theoretically possible for the Kuwaiti government to release the seventeen men convicted of carrying out bombings in their capital if the relatives of those who had been killed and injured were prepared to forgive them. It was not the concept of ransom, Waite assured the officials, but of sacrifice, of expiation. In Islamic societies this was accepted as a form of justice. Habiby thought the idea might enable the Emir of Kuwait to issue pardons without compromising his country's resolute stand on terrorism.

Donald Gregg appeared puzzled. 'I think to any American official, who's used to common law, a crime is a crime against the community rather than a family,' said Habiby in reflection on the meeting. 'The Islamic concept is not well understood in the West.'

The officials in the Vice President's office were sceptical.

Finding the relatives in the Middle East would be time-consuming, if not impossible. Donald Gregg doubted whether the Emir would agree to the proposal. Symbols mattered in that part of the world, and the release of the prisoners, however engineered, would be seen as a concession.

Terry Waite wanted to know what other plans there were as regards the hostages. Gregg responded with generalities, and Habiby detected a note of weariness, as if the Administration officials were going through the motions with yet another well-meaning Church delegation. Waite, who expected to be taken seriously, was becoming irritated at being held at arm's length. He asked who else they might talk with. Gregg suggested a number of people in the State Department, but in particular he thought they should see Oliver North, a colonel on the National Security Council who was liaising with the hostage families. Waite went to see various officials and came away disappointed. Oliver North would be different.

4

THE INNER CIRCLE

The following week, on 18 May, Terry Waite met Oliver North for the first time. North was picked up at La Guardia airport by Samir Habiby and taken to the Presiding Bishop's apartment in Manhattan – a penthouse suite with commanding views of the Chrysler building. Carol Weir, Fred Wilson and a State Department official joined them.

They had expected a sober official from the White House, but Oliver North arrived in a brown leather jacket. With his Marine haircut he looked more like a New York City cop than a security adviser to the President.

Carol Weir challenged him at once. They were very unhappy with the administration, she said. In her view it was doing nothing. She thought North looked harried and intense, but Habiby thought he handled the criticism gracefully.

They were right to feel angry, he told them, because they were Americans. It was one of North's beliefs that Americans cared more deeply than other nations about justice. He said the administration had done everything within the bounds of what was legitimate. 'We have a real dilemma,' he confessed. 'We can't negotiate with terrorists.' Then, rather surprisingly, he said that if the kidnappers wanted money, that was not an issue. Nobody in the assembled group commented on the oddity of the White House's apparent willingness to purchase the release of hostages.

Waite raised the question of whether the Church could help on the prisoners in Kuwait, which seemed to be the main concern of the captors in Beirut. North listened intently. Three of the prisoners were under sentence of death, he said, and he thought it would be useful if the Church used its influence to get the sentences commuted. Habiby said such a request wouldn't be a problem for the Church because it had a policy of opposing the death penalty.

Waite described their 'blood money' proposal. North was encouraging: he thought it worth pursuing. No idea was dismissed, and he treated the group of fellow Christians in the Bishop's apartment almost deferentially.

Before North left, he and Terry Waite spoke together. North wanted to hear about his visits to Libya; he was fascinated by his meetings with Qadaffi. 'Is he mad?' he asked. On the contrary, said Terry Waite. He had found him intelligent and willing to listen. 'You know he's public enemy No. 1,' said North with a smile. 'It's one of my tasks to keep an eye on him.' He wanted to know how Waite had got to see Qadaffi. They chatted together for some time, exchanging views about the radical regimes of the Middle East. When North said he had to return to Washington he asked Waite to keep in touch.

North left behind a good impression. Waite told Habiby that he had found him sincere – 'very American' in that he was open and direct. Waite liked his enthusiasm, his commitment. He was a man looking for solutions.

During the summer of 1985 Terry Waite and Oliver North were in contact regularly. A mutual friend spoke of an instant rapport. 'Oliver North is a very charming, engaging personality and Terry Waite is a very extrovert character in his own way.' Parker Borg, a serious-minded career diplomat from the State Department who observed some of their early meetings, said that 'Ollie North had had a good religious upbringing himself, had been an altar boy and was very accustomed to speaking in the language that was well understood by people of the Church and so they were able to communicate very easily.'

Waite was drawn to North because he shared the view that individuals and institutions like the Church should be involved in international affairs. North made Waite feel valued, whereas at the State Department he had been cold-shouldered. One official described their attitude to the Anglican envoy as 'worse than sneering'; it was only because he was 'Canterbury's man that they didn't show him the door'. But Waite was left in no doubt that many career officers in the foreign service didn't want private persons involved in foreign policy.

In Oliver North he found a human being who cared deeply about others. Tears would form in the eyes of the White House official when talking about refugees, about hostages, about those who suffered under Communism. North was a man of immensely deep feelings. At times he would be dynamic, determined and strident – and then his eyes would soften and he would become vulnerable, like a child. Terry Waite had never met anybody like him before. Ambassador Eugene Douglas explained their relationship as a meeting of two very committed people. 'Oliver North thought he was doing the right thing. He was deeply committed to his country, to his cause, to the cause of freedom and to the release of the hostages. That kind of intensity, emotional intensity, was one of Ollie North's most endearing characteristics. It is also one of Terry Waite's most pronounced characteristics.'

North's background was very different from Waite's. He had served in Vietnam where he had been wounded twice. He had been awarded a Silver Star for valour, a Bronze Star and two Purple Hearts. The war had left its residue. He felt the United States had betrayed itself, its principles, by pulling out. It wasn't a military failure, it was a failure of will. As North was later to tell a Congressional committee, 'I would also point out that we didn't lose the war in Vietnam. We lost the war right here in this city.' The war had fashioned his political outlook. The United States should stand by its friends; the United States was a force for good in the world; the United States should go on the offensive against Communism. Ronald Reagan, who had promised to make America 'walk tall' again, was his hero.

North presented himself as being at the apex of power. Waite and Habiby gained the impression that he met the President regularly, and that the two of them prayed together. When Habiby telephoned North, North would sometimes say that he had the Director of the CIA on the other line. He would spice his conversations with accounts of how he had planned the invasion of Grenada or intercepted the plane carrying the terrorists who had attacked the cruise ship *Achille Lauro*.

Terry Waite confided in Philip Turner, his old friend from Uganda, about this extraordinary official from the White House. '"He's an intriguing fellow, this old Ollie." That's the way he referred to him. He was interested in people who were painting with a large brush and involved on the grand scale, and certainly Oliver North was. North was something of an adventurer and Terry was fascinated by that.'

North was a much more complicated character than he cared to show. Commitment mingled with less attractive traits: a cowboy mentality and a penchant for manipulation. When Carol Weir and Fred Wilson had occasion to visit North in Room 392 in the Old Executive Office Building he took them aback with his opening words: 'I want you to know that I'm a born again Christian. I have accepted Jesus Christ as my lord and Saviour.'

Carol Weir was irritated. 'I am also a believer in the Lord Jesus Christ and I have dedicated my life to him, but I may disagree with you,' she replied. 'Why did he have to tell us this?' she was to ask afterwards.

North went on to say how important a part the Church played in his life. He had real concern for Ben Weir and all the hostages. Wilson thought he was trying to patronize them.

As North was talking, Weir and Wilson were disturbed at the poster hanging behind his desk at a rakish angle. White letters on a black background read: 'Khomeini eats pork.' They both thought it a strange poster for a serious official to have in his office. Fred Wilson, indeed, was offended. 'What kind of reasoning would lead a mature adult to have an expression of such absolute contempt for a revered and respected leader of his country?' Although rather bewildered by their encounter, they were nevertheless pleased that a man of North's vigour was handling the hostage crisis.

It was after the first meeting between Terry Waite and Oliver North that the Archbishop of Canterbury gave his formal approval for his envoy to act on behalf of the American hostages. It was agreed that the Episcopal Church in the United States would provide him with support and advice. The Presbyterian Church, which had originally approached

Waite, offered to pay some of his expenses. Supervision of Waite's mission, however, passed to a small 'inner circle', all of whom were committed to the Reagan administration.

First and foremost there was Canon Samir Habiby; in reality, support and advice from the Episcopal Church came down to him. Although he was running the Church's world-wide relief fund he effectively became Terry Waite's manager. Officials at Lambeth Palace, the Archbishop's office in London, had only a sketchy knowledge of Waite's activities. Samir Habiby's department in the Episcopalian Centre was able to provide flights and hotel bookings and was the conduit for access to the Administration in Washington. For the initial period he was the link man between Terry Waite and Oliver North.

Canon Habiby, whose accent still retained traces of his Middle Eastern background, was a cultivator of contacts. Like many immigrants he was determinedly patriotic. He knew influential people in American society and through his position in the Church had met Administration officials. In his office there was a picture of him with Admiral John Poindexter, who was to serve as President Reagan's National Security Adviser. Habiby was a lifelong Republican who had worked for Ronald Reagan's election in 1980. For his efforts he had received a signed photograph from the President with the inscription, 'With thanks, Ronald and Nancy'.

Habiby liked Oliver North: he was his kind of American. 'The relationship with Ollie,' he said, 'was unique. We felt close to him because, among other things, he belonged to our Church.' But his rapport with North went deeper. It was an instinctive thing, a sharing of American values.

'Ollie and I had had similar paths in previous duties,' he said. 'I had served as a chaplain, as a priest of the Church, attached to the forces in Vietnam, serving in the capacity of a clergyman. I had been in some of the areas that Colonel North had served in.' Canon Habiby had served with the Marines, winning two Bronze Stars and a Purple Heart, and he looked back on his Vietnam days with both affection and regret. Like Oliver North, he retained an intense loyalty to those with whom he had served. He attended his unit's dinners and remained a reserve naval chaplain.

As Director of the Presiding Bishop's Fund for disaster Relief, Samir Habiby had met Eugene Douglas, the administration's Ambassador at Large for Refugees. Habiby had introduced Terry Waite to Douglas in 1984. The two of them had become friends and, over the next few years, would meet between twenty and thirty times. They found themselves in Africa at the same time. Douglas had been involved in the operation to smuggle the Ethiopian Jews, the Falashas, to Israel; Waite had been engaged in relief work in the Sudan. Both men shared the view that the relief agencies should invest in indigenous institutions like the Church rather than channelling aid through central government.

Douglas was a Texan who liked the rugged individualism of Ronald Reagan, but he was no frontiersman: he was erudite, an intellectual, a man who appreciated the arts. He was both successful capitalist and philanthropist; big business, he believed, had social responsibilities. During the Vietnam War he had served in naval intelligence. Douglas had a number of friends in the Reagan administration, in particular Bill Casey, the Director of the CIA. He also knew and liked Oliver North.

For Samir Habiby, Douglas was a touchstone. When he needed 'insider' information on the administration he turned to Douglas. After Terry Waite began working on behalf of the American hostages, Habiby would frequently seek the advice of his Texan friend as to whether there were dangers for the Church in this contact or that activity. Terry Waite, too, would confide in him as his mission became more complicated and political.

There was a third member of the 'inner circle'. On 26 June, Oliver North had invited Samir Habiby and his assistant, Mrs Marion Dawson, to Washington. North had a contact who he thought might help Terry Waite establish links with the Shi'ite community in Lebanon. The man's name was 'Spiro', and North said he would ask him to get in touch.

Some time later a man telephoned Waite and came to see him at his office in Lambeth Palace. He was in his forties, with short-cropped hair, and well over six foot tall. When, later, Habiby met him he reminded him of Sean Connery. The man used the name 'Spiro' but preferred to be called something else. Waite proposed 'John Smith', and the name stuck.

'Spiro', it turned out, had been at an influential school in the Lebanon. He knew most of the religious leaders, including the leading Shi'ite families. He had direct contact with Islamic Jihad, the group behind the hostage taking, and offered to make some introductions for Terry Waite.

Who he really was remained unclear. He was sparing with details. He was a Greek who had 'business' in the Lebanon; his wife had worked as a nurse in the American University hospital. He had a house just outside Nice and another in California. He was paranoid about his security and always operated under a number of aliases; he possessed five passports in different names.

In fact, 'Spiro' worked for both British and American intelligence, although he was closer to the latter. He was described as a man who carried out 'deep covert operations'. One person who knew him said that 'he was on no intelligence register but a man without whom no agency could operate'. After the blowing up of the American embassy in Beirut and the abduction of William Buckley, the CIA Station Chief, he was regarded as one of the few resources the CIA had left in Lebanon. Later, in 1988, 'Spiro' was to play an important role in acquiring Buckley's confessions, what he had revealed under torture.

On the surface, Terry Waite's mission on behalf of the American hostages appeared similar to those he had undertaken before. In reality, it was a much more dangerous and complicated assignment. For his advice he would depend on people who were largely uncritical of the administration, whose values they shared. For some of his contacts he would rely on a man whose background would remain hidden from him – a man from the dark side of life.

5

THE IDEAS OF SUMMER

As Terry Waite began working on the hostage problem, during the summer of 1985, he was surprised how little information the Americans were able to provide him. At first he thought it was because they resented the involvement of an outsider. There was, within the State Department, a weariness with the procession of do-gooders, message carriers and hoaxers who promised to deliver the hostages. None of them could be written off, but many were consigned to the 'scumbag file', which is how David Long from the Office of Counter-terrorism described his growing pile of letters from unsavoury petitioners.

The reticence of officials, however, was largely genuine. There was considerable confusion as to who and what lay behind the hostage crisis. The kidnappers used the name Islamic Jihad, 'Islamic Holy War'. But statements, purporting to come from the captors, would appear under different headings such as the Organization of Revolutionary Justice, Islamic Jihad for the Liberation of Palestine or Cells of Armed Struggle. In time, Islamic Jihad came to be regarded less as a coherent organization and more as a convenient cover under which a variety of militant groups could operate.

There was less disagreement as to the roots of the problem. Power in the Lebanon rested with the Maronite Christians. Under the Constitution, they had been guaranteed the Presidency and the highest ranks in the Lebanese army. This had been amended in 1947 when the Christians were indisputably the majority community. But during the intervening years that majority had been whittled away, until by the seventies it was the Moslems who formed the largest grouping in Lebanon.

The Moslems felt they were second-class citizens and

demanded change. In 1976 they joined with the Palestinian refugees in openly challenging Christian rule. The savage civil war which has raged intermittently ever since radicalized the young people of West Beirut. The Palestinians, who had large camps in the city, had embraced all manner of revolutionary creeds. They were hostile to the West and, in particular, the United States for its support for Israel.

The Moslem community was divided between the Sunnis and the Shi'ites. The Sunnis were in the majority in the Arab world and had powerful backing from the autocratic emirs and kings of the Gulf. The Shi'ites, on the other hand, tended to be less well off, but what they lacked in influence they made up for in zealotry. They were to discover a champion in Iran who was to transform them into a power inside Lebanon.

In 1979, Ayatollah Khomeini had returned to Iran in triumph. The Shah's army had been defeated by the brave obstinacy of the people. The King of Kings had had to flee the country, stuffing a piece of Iranian soil in his pocket as he left. A sudden rise in the oil price had enabled him to indulge in a grand conceit, erecting monuments that compared his own rule to earlier Persian dynasties. But the flood of Western ideas, Paris fashions and consumer goods alienated the poor masses of South Tehran and the countryside. Iran's newly acquired wealth was tearing up their roots. The mullahs were quick to diagnose the problem: Iran had strayed from Islamic values. Theirs was a potent message, which pitted a yearning for the past and the anger of the poor against a glittering, decadent monarchy.

Ayatollah Khomeini promised an Islamic State, a theocracy. All things Western were to be banished: military advisers, Western clothes for women and alcohol. His followers were not content just with victory over the Shah — they saw themselves as harbingers of a new Islamic age. They seized the American embassy in Tehran and turned it into a Revolutionary shrine in front of which the masses could be mobilized to chant: 'Death to America.' The recent past was being exorcised, but the Revolution was not just an internal Iranian upheaval; it was intended for export.

They got their chance in 1982. Israel had invaded Lebanon

supposedly in retaliation for a terrorist attack in London, but the invasion's real goal was to end the Palestinian presence in Lebanon by driving them from the country. The Israeli army pounded the suburbs of West Beirut, where the PLO was at its strongest, with artillery and tank fire. The Palestinians lay low in their tunnels, watching Israel's reputation suffer. The United States became embarrassed by the nightly pictures of the Israeli army bombarding an Arab capital with American weapons. A draw was declared. Israel would lift its siege and the Palestinian fighters would withdraw from the city. The United States sent in a contingent of Marines to ensure fair play.

Although many of the Moslems in West Beirut welcomed the departure of the overweening Palestinians, and were grateful to the Americans, the Moslem community was seething with a discontent of its own. Increasingly they resented their lack of power, a grievance felt most acutely by the Shi'ite Moslems who inhabited the breeze-block slums of South Beirut and the impoverished villages of southern Lebanon. Ayatollah Khomeini became their mentor; his Revolution promised deliverance. Islam seemed to be riding an unstoppable wave, holding out the promise of liberty from oppression and the eventual liberation of one of Islam's holiest places, Jerusalem.

The Shi'ites didn't just want greater influence within Lebanon – they wanted to transform it into an Islamic State. America, with its economic and military power, seemed to stand in their way. In Iran, the United States was held responsible for sustaining the Shah and was seen as opposing Khomeini's rule. To some of the younger Shi'ite militants in Lebanon, their Islamic Revolution could not be achieved until every vestige of American influence had been removed from the country. In the early eighties they had formed a group called Hezballah, 'the Party of God'.

The Iranians had been keen to aid their Shi'ite brothers in Lebanon and the presence of Israeli troops gave them the chance. For until then Syria, which controlled access to much of Lebanon, had denied the Iranians entry. But the Israeli invasion threatened Syria's interests in Lebanon, and Damascus was prepared to welcome any group who would oppose the Israelis, particularly the fanatical fighters from Iran. So, in 1982, a contingent of Iranian Revolutionary guards set up camp in the city of Baalbek in the Bekaa valley. The impact of the guards' arrival was soon felt in Beirut.

The controller of the guards was the Iranian Ambassador to Syria, Mohammad Mohtashami-pur. Not only did the guards spread Iran's Revolutionary message, but Iran provided the funds for transforming Hezballah into a militia. It was never a highly structured organization but rather a variety of families and groups which shared the same religious tendency. What central control existed was exercized from the Iranian embassy in Damascus. Some of Hezballah's principal leaders belonged to the so-called Council for Lebanon which was chaired by the Iranian Ambassador. This loose structure and the use of the cover name 'Islamic Jihad' made the group exceedingly difficult to define and consequently rendered it almost immune from retaliation. In time, Hezballah grew into one of the dominant armed factions in Beirut. What made it different from the other militias was its fanaticism; members of Hezballah were willing to sacrifice their own lives in carrying out suicide attacks against Israeli forces. They were able to claim much of the credit for Israel's withdrawal from Lebanon with a casualty list of over 600 dead. Having helped drive out the Israelis, Hezballah wanted to rid the country of the Americans. From 1983 onwards Hezballah would be involved in suicide attacks against both US forces and their embassy buildings. As part of the same policy they began kidnapping foreigners.

The reason for seizing hostages was not just hatred of the United States; they had specific demands as well. In June 1984, a month after Benjamin Weir had been seized, his captors forced him to write a letter addressed to 'His Eminence, the Prince of Kuwait'. In it, Weir said that his freedom was dependent on the release of the seventeen prisoners convicted of bombing the American and French embassies in Kuwait.

One of those prisoners was a Lebanese by the name of Mustafa Badreddin, the brother-in-law and cousin of Imad Mugniyah, a militia leader with a growing reputation among the armed gangs of West Beirut. Mugniyah came to be regarded by the Americans as 'the most dangerous terrorist acting against Western interests in the Middle East'. Among his many exploits, he helped plan the bombing of the US Marine barracks in Beirut. He was also involved in the kidnapping of William Buckley, the CIA Station Chief.

Mugniyah, a bearded, handsome man in his mid-thirties, was a typical product of Lebanon's turmoil. He had grown up in a poor village in the south of the country and had been attracted to the radical creed of the Palestinians. They gave him military training and he joined Force 17, an élite unit set up to carry out special operations against Israel. Later he became Chief of Security to Sheikh Fadlallah, Hezballah's spiritual leader.

There were several reasons why he was determined to get Badreddin freed; foremost among them was pride. Mugniyah had built up his own militia, an offshoot from Hezballah, drawn largely from members of his family. Failure to bring his brother-in-law home would involve a loss of face among Beirut's competing gangs. Secondly, Mugniyah's wife had made it into a point of honour. There was a story that she was denying him sex until her brother returned. Thirdly, and probably more importantly, Badreddin and Mugniyah were former partners who had worked together on a number of operations. Friendship, as much as anything, drove Mugniyah to seize hostages to barter for Badreddin's freedom.

Mugniyah had also grown close to the Iranian Revolutionary guards stationed in the Bekaa valley in Lebanon. With the help of their masters in Iran they became his sponsors, providing him with finance, protection and training for his men. Several times Mugniyah visited Iran, where he developed his own contacts in the Iranian leadership. His demand for the release of his brother-in-law became entangled with wider Iranian goals. What was most difficult to gauge, for those working for the release of the hostages, was the degree of control that Iran exercised over Mugniyah.

For Terry Waite, in the early summer of 1985, it was difficult to know where to begin. He wanted to deal with the captors directly, while at the same time exploring humanitarian solutions to the problem of the Kuwaiti prisoners. In June,

he began pursuing the 'blood money' proposal he had outlined to Oliver North. It proved a difficult task. Kuwait didn't
have all the names of those killed or injured in the bombings.
Some of them had been immigrant workers from Pakistan,
who had since returned home. Through his personal contacts, Samir Habiby even got *Time* magazine working on
tracing the names. Habiby's brother, Armand, who had
excellent connections in the Persian Gulf, and who had suggested the idea in the first place, met Oliver North to see if
the United States government, with all its resources, could
help.

By July, Terry Waite and Samir Habiby realized they had
made little headway. But, ever inventive, they had come up
with a new idea which they thought would make it easier for
Kuwait to pardon the seventeen prisoners. They were both
in London at the time and called Oliver North; to their
surprise, he said he would see them the next morning. Habiby
booked a room at the Sheraton Hotel, near Heathrow airport. North caught the overnight flight from Washington;
when he arrived, despite having had only a catnap, he was
as vivacious as ever. While Habiby ordered coffee, North
showered and shaved. By now he was relaxed with the two
churchmen. As he was drying himself he spoke about his
family. Eighteen-hour days at the White House were hard on
his wife and children, he told them. Terry Waite said he
understood the problem: he had put his own family under
strain during the long negotiations in Libya.

The conversation turned to the hostages. Waite said there
were difficulties with the 'blood money' idea. Although some
of the relatives of those killed in the Kuwaiti bombings would
be prepared to endorse an appeal for clemency to the Emir
of Kuwait, he doubted whether it would be sufficient. North
wasn't so sure. He thought it might be possible to persuade
the captors in Beirut that such a deal was possible, and that
it would help if they made the first gesture by releasing some
of the hostages.

Waite was uneasy. His information was that the Kuwaitis
were decidedly cool on the 'blood money' idea.

North said it was his understanding from his own contacts
that the Emir could be persuaded. Waite didn't like what he

was hearing. 'If your contacts are lying,' he said to North, 'the hostages will end up dead.'

North was seemingly unflustered by Waite's sharp remark, but the exchange had disturbed Terry Waite and he was to mention it to Fred Wilson of the Presbyterian Church. It was a moment of insight into the way North made deals, but it passed, and whatever doubts might have been sown about the energetic official from the White House were never developed.

Habiby then spoke about their other plan. The seventeen men held in Kuwait weren't the only group of Shi'ite prisoners. Israel's ally in Lebanon, the South Lebanon Army, was detaining a large number of young Shi'ites. Habiby thought it might be possible for the leader of the SLA, General Lahad, to free some of them. This would enable the captors to claim they had achieved something and so release some of the hostages. It might also make it easier for Kuwait to pardon the seventeen. North thought it an excellent idea, and began drawing up a plan on paper. He thought Waite should go and see General Lahad. North flew back to Washington that day, while Habiby went to the Vatican to enlist its help in getting Waite to see General Lahad, who was a Greek Catholic.

Unknown to Waite or Habiby, North was working on a variety of more controversial solutions to the hostage crisis. One plan involved using private funds to ransom a hostage for $2 million. But his contacts were hoaxers and the scheme came to nothing. According to David Martin and John Walcott in their book *Best Laid Plans*, Oliver North also suggested that the United States might try to spring the prisoners out of their Kuwaiti jail and trade them for the hostages. It might be possible, North even thought, to 'trick Mugniyah into releasing the Americans while it was still possible to retrieve the Kuwaiti prisoners and send them back to jail'. Within the administration, no one, reportedly, took the idea seriously.

During the summer months of 1985 the Archbishop of Canterbury, Dr Runcie, also became involved. In July, he contacted the Syrian Ambassador in London. He wanted him to arrange an appointment for Terry Waite with the Syrian

President, Hafez Assad. Although the captors were closer to Iran, Syria was the more influential power in Lebanon; and even though it couldn't always get its way in the country, it could scupper the plans of others if it was ignored. The Ambassador promised to help. Syria, he assured the Archbishop, was doing all it could to end the hostage problem in Lebanon. But the weeks passed, and there was no reply from Damascus; so Dr Runcie wrote to the Pope, to see if the Catholic Church had any greater influence in getting Waite in to see to the Syrian President.

Eventually a letter was sent direct to President Assad from the Presiding Bishop of the Episcopal Church. In it he expressed concern that Benjamin Weir, a clergyman, was being held hostage. He asked Syria to use its influence to end what was clearly an unjust situation which did great disservice to Islam. What the Church was trying to do was to draw a distinction between those like William Buckley, who were clearly being held for political reasons, and men like Benjamin Weir, who were religious figures. If the appeal from the Christian Churches was to succeed, it was essential that it should remain separate from the efforts of government, particularly the American administration.

This activity by the Anglican Church on behalf of American hostages was surprising. Considerable energy and resources were being expended on a problem not directly related to either the Anglican Church or the United Kingdom. The Church was straying into the minefield of Middle Eastern politics. It was an indication of how Terry Waite's earlier successes in Iran and Libya had encouraged the Archbishop to believe that the Anglican Church, like the Vatican, could have a role in international affairs.

Even though Waite, Samir Habiby and the Archbishop strove hard during that summer, they saw little reward for their work. The Syrians didn't want to meet Waite; the 'blood money' idea progressed no further; neither did the idea involving the other Shi'ite prisoners. During the next eighteen months the Archbishop would not become so involved again with the American hostages. That would be left to Terry Waite and his small group of advisers.

While Waite pursued his own ideas for solving the hostage

problem, the American administration was exploring one of its more dubious schemes. Early in 1985, at a series of meetings, various arms dealers and Iranian middlemen made passing reference to trading arms for the American hostages. None of these conversations involved administration officials, but they coincided with a growing desire in Washington to renew a dialogue with Iran.

Iran was the key to the Persian Gulf. That was the conventional wisdom in Washington's foreign policy establishments. The great fear for the United States was that, because of its support for the Shah, it had become an outsider in one of the crucial regions of the world. In due course, when Iran's spiritual leader, Ayatollah Khomeini, died, it was expected that there would be a scramble for power among the various leading clerics. The United States was concerned that it had no influence with either the leading contenders or the prominent factions, whereas the Soviet Union had kept the door open through a judicious use of trade.

The CIA, in particular, was obsessed with the possibility of a Communist takeover after Khomeini's death. In May, Graham Fuller, the CIA's National Intelligence Director for the Middle East and South Asia, sent a five-page memorandum to William Casey, the Director. Fuller was pessimistic: 'The US faces a grim situation in developing a new policy towards Iran. Events are moving largely against our interests and we have few palatable alternatives. In bluntest form, the Khomeini regime is faltering and may be moving towards a moment of truth; we will soon see a struggle for succession. The US has almost no cards to play; the USSR has many.' Fuller listed a number of options, most of which, in his view, offered little hope of success. 'The best course,' he concluded, 'is to have friendly states sell arms ... as a means of showing Tehran that it has alternatives to the Soviet Union.'

Fuller recognized that it was a risky policy, but his analysis struck a chord within the administration, in particular with the National Security Adviser, Robert McFarlane. He, too, was seeking improved relations with Iran, because he believed they could influence the hostage takers in Lebanon. In April a consultant to the National Security Council,

Michael Ledeen, had visited Israel with McFarlane's blessing. They both believed that Israel had good informal contacts with the Iranians. Ledeen asked the Israeli Prime Minister, Shimon Peres, for help in securing the release of the hostages, but Peres was uncertain what he could do. Ledeen was to learn from other contacts, however, that the situation in Iran might be more fluid than outsiders thought, and that it might be possible to strengthen the hands of 'moderates' within the Iranian leadership.

Two separate ideas were being explored at the same time. One was an opening to Iran; the other was how to help the hostages. As the summer progressed, the two ideas were to become inseparable, although the main participants were later to claim that the prime motivation had been to improve relations with Iran. Through intermediaries it quickly became apparent that the price of an 'opening' to Iran would be arms, sorely needed for its war with Iraq.

In May, Israel was to seek Washington's formal approval to ship arms to Iran. As most of Israel's weapons were of American design, strictly speaking it needed Washington's agreement to sell them to a third country. On Israel's part it was, however, a way of legitimizing what already existed. Since 1980 it had been secretly trading arms with Iran, seeing a perpetuation of the Gulf War as being in its national interest.

Israel's request was to find favour in Washington, for it seemed to offer both a solution to the impasse with Iran and a potential resolution of the hostage crisis. At this stage, in the early summer of 1985, the policy had not been approved by President Reagan; but a signal had been sent to Iran that the United States was willing to trade for its hostages. A rubicon had been crossed.

An event during the summer had reinforced the view within the administration that it was the religious leadership within Iran that exercised the greatest control over the militant Shi'ite groups in Lebanon. On 14 June, TWA flight 847 had been hijacked soon after it left Athens airport; 153 passengers were on board, 135 of whom were Americans. The hijackers directed the pilot to fly around the Middle East, making several stops in both Algiers and Beirut. Among their demands were the release of seven hundred Shi'ites held in camps in Israel and the seventeen men imprisoned in Kuwait.

The hijackers, who were Lebanese, were violent and occasionally hysterical. They held grenades with the pins removed, and a pistol without a safety catch but with the hammer cocked. Kurt Carlson, an army reservist on the flight, would later describe the atmosphere of terror: 'If anyone moved or uttered a sound they pounced, karate chopping people across the backs of their necks, striking some with the barrel of a gun. With a screaming leap three feet in the air, [one of the hijackers] kicked one elderly woman in the face, shattering her glasses.' Later they forced a member of the cabin crew to read out the names on the passports; those with Jewish-sounding names were separated from the other passengers. Six men were identified as working for the US navy. One of them, Bob Stethen, was shot, and his body thrown on to the tarmac at Beirut airport.

The hijackers had demanded that the control tower allow some of their colleagues to board the plane. After the shooting of Bob Stethen the Lebanese authorities agreed, and about a dozen militiamen from the nearby Shi'ite suburbs of West Beirut joined the hijackers. Among them was Imad Mugniyah. Ironically, some of the passengers saw Mugniyah, who spoke English, as an improvement on the capricious hijackers.

After further flights around the Middle East the hostages were taken off the plane and driven into the impoverished suburbs of West Beirut. The United States was able to persuade Nabih Berri, the leader of the more moderate Shi'ite militia, Amal, to take responsibility for the hostages' safety. After Israel agreed to release some of the Shi'ite prisoners it was holding, a breakthrough was achieved.

American officials noted the pivotal role played by both President Assad of Syria and the Iranians. Assad was anxious to be seen as the dominant player in Lebanon and ensured that the deal stuck when it was in danger of falling apart. But in exerting pressure he had turned to Ali Akhbar Rafsanjani, the Speaker of the Iranian Parliament, who was in the Syrian capital during the negotiations. Also present in Damascus were Mohammad Mohtashami-pur, the man thought to be the controller of Hezballah; Mohsen Rafiq-Doust, the Iranian minister in charge of the Revolutionary guards; and Sheikh Fadlallah, Hezballah's spiritual leader. It was assumed in Washington that the hijackers only agreed to release the passengers on the orders of the Iranian leadership.

Although the hijackers won important concessions from Israel, they failed to make any headway on the prisoners in Kuwait. The Americans had tried to have the hostages included in the final deal, but that proved impossible. Two weeks before the hijacking, another American had been added to the list of hostages. David Jacobsen, director of the American University hospital, had been snatched off the streets of West Beirut. The hostage crisis went on, but Iran was now seen as the key to any solution.

In August, while Terry Waite was still trying to get to Damascus, the Americans decided to embark on one of their more sensitive ideas. The earlier discussions involving the Israelis, American officials and Iranian intermediaries had finally produced a concrete proposal. The Iranians indicated that a delivery of weapons would be seen as an expression of a desire for a better relationship with the United States. In exchange it would persuade the captors in Lebanon to release the hostages. America's hand in the affair would be disguised in that it would be Israel which would actually be shipping the arms, while the United States would merely undertake to replenish their stocks.

On 20 August, a hundred TOW anti-tank missiles were flown from Israel to Iran. The Americans had been led to believe that four hostages would be released. In fact none was. The Iranian intermediary explained at a heated meeting in Paris that the missiles had gone to the wrong faction. After further negotiations it was agreed that a further 408 missiles would be sent to Iran and that, in exchange, one hostage would be freed. The Iranians gave Robert McFarlane the invidious choice of selecting which hostage should go free. He chose William Buckley, the CIA Station Chief. It was the one hostage the captors were unable to trade, for Buckley had died on June 3. Although American intelligence had heard rumour of Buckley's death, the Administration continued to pressure the Iranians for Buckley's release. The shipment was planned for 15 September.

The decision to allow arms to be sold to Iran was approved by President Reagan during August. It ran counter to official American policy of opposing arms sales to Iran, and undermined the administration's strong line on opposing concessions to terrorists. Only a few weeks earlier Reagan had declared to the American Bar Association, 'Let me make it plain to the assassins in Beirut and their accomplices that America will never make concessions to terrorists.' When a Congressional Committee came to investigate the affair it noted that the decision to trade arms, which violated the Administration's declared principles, 'was made so casually that it was not written down, the President did not recall it fifteen months later, and the Secretaries of State and Defense were not even told of it at the time.'

6

ECCLESIASTICAL COVER

One day in July 1985 a guard had asked Benjamin Weir if he wanted to see a television programme. The clergyman was delighted. His chains were removed and he was led through a series of passageways, blindfolded. He was ordered to sit on a mattress. 'You have a friend next to you,' said the guard. 'Take his hand.' Weir reached out and felt fingers. He was elated. After fourteen months he was touching another human being.

Later the man introduced himself as Father Martin Jenco, a Catholic priest. That night they were moved to the same room. Their captivity was transformed. 'Here was human companionship after so long,' wrote Weir. 'We joked and cried. We shared the same faith. We had had common experiences. There were concerns and fears to share. It went on and on. Our communication just kept picking up in tempo. There seemed to be no end to what we had to say. Great emotions seemed to overflow.'

The next day they learnt that Terry Anderson, the Middle East correspondent for Associated Press, and David Jacobsen, administrator of the American University hospital in Beirut, were being held in the same building. Later they were joined by Thomas Sutherland, Dean of the School of Agriculture.

Their conditions continued to improve. They were allowed to worship together and exercise together. The hostages took each other on imaginary trips. Thomas Sutherland took them back to his native Scotland by reciting the poetry of Robert Burns. Father Jenco took them to Rome, guiding them through restaurants, museums and churches. David Jacobsen took them to his apartment and cooked a meal for them. In their imaginations they escaped their captivity. Each day

Jean-Paul Kauffman, a French hostage held separately from the Americans, recited to himself the names of the sixty-one wine châteaux of Bordeaux in the year 1855. 'How often I walked the roads of the Médoc,' he later wrote. 'Fastened to my chain, though I was, I never ceased to wander through the lovely hills of the Entre-Deux-Mers. I saw in my mind the rows of plane trees leading to Château Margaux, the Tuscan-style gardens of Yquem, the towers of Cos d'Estournel, the flowers at Giscours.'

Towards the end of the first week in September the guards said they were considering releasing one of them and asked the hostages which one it should be. They wanted the person to put pressure on the United States government to get the prisoners in Kuwait released. For men enduring captivity it was a difficult choice. Father Jenco was in poor physical health but Terry Anderson, with his journalistic contacts, would be best suited to carrying the captors' message. Unable to decide, they conducted a series of ballots, with Terry Anderson finally winning.

When the guards returned they had made the decision for the hostages. 'You are the one who is going to go,' they said, pointing at Benjamin Weir. It was heartbreaking for Terry Anderson. Events moved fast. Weir's beard was trimmed and he was taken downstairs blindfolded and guided into the back of a car, where he was told to lie face down on the seat. As he recalls, a guard told him, 'There are two reasons why you're being released. One is to confirm the fact that our demand is for the release of the seventeen men held in Kuwait, and the second is to show a sign of our good intention that we want to resolve this matter and wish to do it quietly, without publicity.'

Weir listened to the car driving through the city, hardly daring to hope that he had actually been freed. After twenty minutes the driver said, 'Be ready now to get out of the car when it stops. Take off your ski mask as you step out, and don't look back. You will know where you are.' He found himself in a familiar street close to the university and went to the home of some friends, who contacted the American embassy.

Oliver North hadn't been party initially to the arms deal

with the Iranians. Although he was involved in other schemes to free the hostages, the negotiations with Israel and various Iranian middlemen had been conducted by others. One of those who served on the National Security Council at the time believes that North only learnt of the deal with Iran in late August. When, in September, Robert McFarlane was told by the Israelis that one hostage was certain to be freed, Oliver North was given the task of making the arrangements and debriefing him.

The United States had an ever-ready facility for receiving hostages at its military base at Wiesbaden in West Germany. It included a fully equipped hospital with psychiatrists trained in treating those suffering from the shock of captivity. Oliver North chose to bypass these arrangements. He wanted Benjamin Weir kept in seclusion because he thought that, if there was no publicity, other hostages could be freed. One of the extraordinary features of this affair was the gullibility of the Americans. For eighteen months they kept believing the Iranians would play fair and honour deals, without realizing that they never intended to release more than one hostage at a time, having extracted the maximum payment. The frequent promise that two or three hostages would be freed was only intended to raise the price of the deal.

While Weir was at the American embassy in Beirut he asked to call his wife but was told it wasn't possible. He was flown by helicopter to the deck of the USS *Nimitz*, where he was asked to wear a flight helmet so as to avoid recognition. On the second day after his release, he was catapulted off the carrier in a submarine hunter and flown to a US base in Sicily, where he was transferred to a cargo plane which took him to Norfolk, Virginia.

Carol Weir had been contacted by Robert McFarlane while attending church in Iowa. Her husband was already with the US navy, McFarlane told her, but it was imperative that they didn't talk to the press for three or four days. Oliver North told Benjamin Weir's son that he had organized a safe house where the family could be reunited. Carol Weir was unhappy with this arrangement. She wanted to meet her husband 'when he stepped off the plane on American soil as a free person'.

Members of the Weir family and Fred Wilson met in New York and were flown in a special plane to a deserted airstrip in Virginia. Three government station wagons were waiting for them. The drivers wore dark glasses and gave no names; neither would they show any identification. They were under instructions to take the Weir party to a safe house, but an argument ensued, with the family insisting they be taken to a hotel instead.

That evening McFarlane phoned Carol Weir again. Her husband would be arriving at a different airfield, he told her. Mrs Weir was upset. She desperately wanted to be present when her husband landed. 'That's up to you to arrange,' snapped McFarlane.

The months of tension between this hostage family and the government finally broke into the open. 'Surely,' said Mrs Weir, 'you wouldn't want me to tell the press that Robert McFarlane was keeping me from being with my husband?'

McFarlane became angry. The government had spent millions to get Benjamin Weir released, he said without explanation. He accused her of being difficult and ungrateful. 'I'm tired of you, young lady,' he shouted and slammed down the phone.

Benjamin Weir landed at a military airfield. He had expected his family to be there. Instead, a couple of men wearing civilian clothes came out to the plane. They took him to a lounge where Oliver North, some CIA officials and a nurse were waiting. North explained that he wanted him and his family to go to a safe house for a few days in the hope that other hostages might be released.

'I asked him what the attitude of my wife was,' recalled Weir, 'and North said: "Well, your family is here at a hotel in Norfolk. We would like you to go into seclusion, but your family prefers to stay in the hotel." My conclusion was that I wanted to meet with my family before making that kind of decision.' Weir found North 'patient, understanding but very persistent'. The freed hostage was equally stubborn. Eventually North agreed to take him to the hotel, where he was reunited with his family at 2.30 in the morning.

The relationship between the Weirs and the government was to be further soured. Fred Wilson, who had been at the hotel when Benjamin Weir arrived, had been contacted by intelligence officials who wanted a debriefing session with Weir. Later that day he spoke with them for five hours. The following week North was to phone Wilson to say that Weir would be needed for further questioning. When Wilson mentioned this to Weir he was adamant: 'I have told them all I have to tell them and we had an agreement to finish the debriefings last week. I have other people to see and other things to do.'

Fred Wilson relayed that message to Oliver North. 'He was quite irritated,' said Wilson, 'and in a very ominous manner said it would be quite unfortunate if the body of Bill Buckley was found in the streets of Beirut and word got around that he might not have died if Ben Weir had been cooperative.' Wilson was livid. 'You bastard,' he told North, 'you must have a very short memory.' A few weeks earlier North had told him that he was personally certain Buckley was dead and had given his reasons. Wilson was chilled by the exchange. He felt the government was as duplicitous as the captors. Whatever North might have said to Wilson he continued to hope that Buckley might be saved. He had penned a speech to welcome the hostages back to the United States 'in the name of the President'. Among the hostages' names he had written Buckley.

Weir had his own reasons for not wanting to talk further to the intelligence community. From his initial debriefing he was convinced that the CIA was planning a rescue mission. He was opposed to any such idea, not only because he thought it would fail but because it would endanger the lives of his fellow hostages. But not all the hostages were to prove grateful. David Jacobsen was to write after his release, 'Ben Weir had no right to decide whether or not the US leaders should launch a raid to rescue us. He lacked the knowledge or expertise to determine the riskiness of such an attack. Furthermore, it was our freedom and our lives that were at stake. When I learned upon my debriefing in Wiesbaden, West Germany immediately after my release that Ben had refused to supply the intelligence necessary for a strike on our behalf, I was furious.' David Jacobsen's anger subsided, but government officials who had worked for Weir's release were angered by his attitude.

A few days after Weir's release, Michael Ledeen, who was advising the National Security Council on the deal with Iran, had phoned one of the Iranian middlemen who had helped set up the deal and asked him if it were possible for the Iranians 'to take Weir back, and send us a patriotic American instead'. North said that Weir was so 'hostile' and 'unco-operative' after his release that among the officials debriefing him, he was referred to as 'the Reverend Weird'. When Fred Wilson heard some of these comments he was stunned at what he called 'this venom'. Neither party understood the other. The Weirs, humbled by the joy of freedom, spoke of forgiveness and understanding. The government officials, with their questions and their subterfuge, seemed to belong back in the dark world of captivity. Weir, unrealistically, was disappointed with their values; it was a disappointment that was later to be shared by a wider audience.

Over a week after Weir's release, Terry Waite unexpectedly flew to New York and held a joint press conference with the freed hostage. Up until this moment there had been no mention of Waite's involvement in the release. At his first meeting with the press, Weir had not referred to the Anglican envoy.

There is some confusion as to whose idea it was to identify Terry Waite with Weir's release. Fred Wilson thinks he might have phoned Waite and invited him to New York. Others say that he came on Oliver North's suggestion. Eugene Douglas said that North supported Waite's coming to the United States. He believed the publicity would 'strengthen his [Waite's] role as a mediator'. The press drew another conclusion. A London paper wrote, 'The Archbishop of Canterbury's Special Envoy was revealed yesterday as the secret negotiator behind the release of an American hostage in the Lebanon.' It was a conclusion that suited the US Administration's purpose, having just authorized an arms shipment to Iran.

Even when it was revealed that arms had been traded for Benjamin Weir's freedom, Samir Habiby was to insist that Terry Waite's efforts had made a contribution. Nothing happens in Lebanon, he said, without Syrian involvement, and the Church had put great effort into persuading President

Assad that Weir was purely a Christian missionary. Furthermore, Habiby argued, Waite's public involvement might have encouraged the captors to believe that their grievances would be given a hearing.

Michael Ledeen, with his first hand knowledge of the deal with Iran, had no doubt what Waite's role was intended to be. 'I don't think that Terry Waite had any substantive role in the release of Weir. I think that Weir was released by the government of Iran as a result of the agreement it had reached with the government of the United States pure and simple. I think that North encouraged Waite to receive Benjamin Weir when he came out and I think that North may well have convinced Waite at that time that he was at least partially responsible for the release of Weir, but I don't think he was.'

North quickly recognized Waite's potential and spoke to colleagues on the National Security Council about him. Howard Teicher recalls North telling him how Waite would be an ideal 'magnet' for the press. North also bragged that he was effectively 'managing Terry Waite'. Another of those working on the NSC said that North genuinely admired Waite's courage but could be quite cynical, at the same time, in his attitude towards the Anglican envoy. 'I understood,' said this official, 'that right from the very beginning Waite was to be a cover.' During the summer North had asked him what he knew about Terry Waite and his role in Libya. Waite was unwittingly being sized up to play 'ecclesiastical cover'. North, he said, was shameless about using the Church envoy. 'Terry Waite would be a hero; the Church would be a hero.' To Oliver North it seemed almost a perfect arrangement.

Benjamin Weir found Waite 'warm and thoughtful'. He wanted to understand the minds of the captors and their likely reaction to his attempts at mediation. Weir was impressed. 'I felt Waite was ready to make great effort, even considerable personal sacrifice in order to work for the release of the men that were being held.' He found the Anglican envoy rather reluctant to identify himself with the release. At the press conference, at the Inter Church Centre in Manhattan, Waite said that he had decided to go public in the hope that a new breakthrough might be achieved. 'I ask [the kidnappers],' he said, 'to let me meet with them face to face and hear clearly their requests for myself.' It was what he had been trying to achieve during the summer and, in his eyes, was reason enough for talking to the press.

When he was questioned about his precise role in Weir's release he was careful not to claim credit, but he did say that 'I have established through an intermediary a contact with the kidnappers in Beirut and I have been in communication with them on a regular basis for the past months.' According to Samir Habiby, that intermediary was none other than 'Spiro', the man indirectly introduced to them by Oliver North.

Terry Waite was caught in an invisible web, without his knowing. The man who was one of his principal links to the captors in Beirut was also assisting American intelligence. He had brought out of Lebanon one of the pictures of the CIA Station Chief in captivity. 'Spiro's' contacts in West Beirut were excellent, and would soon be put to use in helping Waite visit the city, but his and Terry Waite's interests were not necessarily the same.

If there were hidden dangers in dealing with his intermediary, there were also new risks in working with Oliver North. The United States now had a dark secret which it was imperative remained hidden. Against all its declared beliefs it had ransomed a hostage with weapons. In Terry Waite, the well-meaning and plausible Anglican envoy, the administration had the perfect cover for acts they wished to deny. Officials noted how, at press conferences, he would appear open and candid when there was nothing he could say. Parker Borg described it as 'a great public relations ability even when there wasn't much to relate'. It was a gift that would make him indispensable to any future deals.

While he was in the United States, Fred Wilson had sought out Waite. Despite his pleasure at seeing Weir reunited with his family, the episode had been disillusioning for Wilson. The telephone conversation with North and the implied threat had particularly disturbed him. Observing Waite's growing involvement with North, he decided to tell him about the phone call. 'Terry was remarkably matter of fact, reminding me that in this kind of business one deals with the persons one has to deal with . . . one does not choose one's contacts.' Fred Wilson felt that Waite recognized that a White House official might operate with a different morality, a different frame of reference but his commitment to the hostage families over-rode all other considerations.'

By the end of September, Oliver North had assumed control of the various efforts to free the hostages, including the negotiations with the Iranian intermediaries. According to North's notes, before Terry Waite returned to London, the two of them spoke again. North was upbeat; he thought that Waite's efforts were paying off. Although Waite was being used as a cover for the arms deal, North believed the Anglican envoy did have a real as well as a cosmetic role to play. For in all the excitement over the release of a hostage, it had not gone unnoticed that the central demand of the captors hadn't been addressed – namely the freedom of the prisoners in Kuwait. North and his colleagues on the National Security Council staff realized that at some stage the captors might defy Tehran unless there was progress on the Kuwaiti prisoners. So a dual-track policy began to emerge. While North began exploring a second arms deal with the Iranians, Waite would be encouraged to work on the captors' demands. It was to prove a dangerous task.

7

MEETING THE CAPTORS

In early November 1985 the Archbishop of Canterbury, Dr
Runcie, received a letter from four of the American hostages.
Delivered to the Associated Press office in Beirut and for-
warded to London, it was handwritten and marked 'Confidential, not for publication'. Terry Waite was discreet in his
comments. 'It contains a statement I consider to be helpful,'
he said, 'and it also contains a threat.'

The hopeful sign was that, according to the hostages, the
captors wanted to talk. The letter suggested a possible
compromise. The captors might be prepared to hand over
the hostages to the Red Cross if the Kuwaitis did the same
with their seventeen prisoners. But the hostages warned that
the captors were losing patience and were threatening to seize
and kill more Americans.

The hostages had also written to President Reagan, warning him that they would die if there were a rescue attempt.
They asked him to negotiate instead. In scrawling handwrit-
ing, the letter pleaded with the President. 'Mr Reagan, we
thank you for the efforts you have made through these long
months, but your quiet diplomacy is not working. We know
of your distaste for bargaining with terrorists. Do you know
the consequences your continued refusal will have for us? It
is in your power to have us home for Christmas. Will you
not have mercy on us and our families and do so?'

The White House rejected the plea out of hand. 'We do
not negotiate concessions with terrorists,' said a spokesman,
'nor do we give in to ransom or threats of blackmail.' While
the administration in Washington was reaffirming its hard
line on refusing to deal with terrorists, some of its officials
were in Europe meeting arms dealers and Iranian middlemen.

Dr Runcie had no problem in responding to the letter from

the hostages. He asked the captors to meet his envoy 'as a matter of urgency'. As Terry Waite began preparing for his first mission to Lebanon, he spoke to Benjamin Weir about the minds of the captors. They were wary, unpredictable and given to lying, the former hostage told him. Their understanding of the West was rudimentary. The mere fact that he had once gone to the American embassy in Beirut, albeit to renew his passport, was enough to raise their suspicions. They would find it difficult to understand that the Church of England was not a branch of the British government.

In the days prior to his departure Waite also spoke to 'Spiro' about his security and travel arrangements in the Lebanese capital. He talked on the telephone to Oliver North, but he was a man living with a string of inconsistencies. In a private note to himself, North mused on the value of holding a high-level administration meeting with the families of the hostages. He believed this would send a symbol to the captors that the United States would not 'change its position', and would not 'concede to terrorist demands'. Yet even while he was contemplating restating official American policy he was working on the final details of another arms deal with Iran. In his notebook, he summed it with a simple equation:

'What's required to get hostages out:
- blanket order: 150 Hawk (missiles), 250 S/W (sidewinder) missiles, 30–50 Phoenix (missiles)
- 1,3,5 – ship hostages.
- 2,4 – ship weapons.'

Ever inventive, North was also investigating, in October 1985, another deal whereby the Lebanese Christian Phalange would be paid to release 120 Shia prisoners in exchange for the hostages. The Phalange had agreed; the only question was the price.

Terry Waite, unaware of these deals, was entering a zone of ambiguity. North was to tell him that the United States would not compromise over the prisoners in Kuwait whilst declaring that he thought it would be helpful if the Anglican Church took up their cases.

Terry Waite's trip was attended by great publicity. Sections of the British press described it as if it were a Lebanese *High Noon*, featuring an unarmed Anglican sheriff going to parley

with outlaws. 'To the rescue', was the headline of one editorial. 'Who is riding to the rescue of six Americans held
hostage in Beirut,' it continued, but 'our own Terry Waite,
the Anglican trouble-shooter and the man who made even
Libya's Colonel Qadaffi behave sensibly and release four
Britons. What a blessing Terry is to his Church.'

Expectations had been aroused. Journalists accompanied
him on the flight, and camera crews gathered in Beirut. The
press had become part of his hostage kit. Terry Waite had
used them in the past, finding that a cluster of reporters
served as trumpeters announcing his arrival. By turning his
visit into an event he hoped the captors would see an opportunity to publicize their demands by negotiating with him.
Waite added to the drama by admitting that he could be
taking a risk in going to meet the captors. 'I might be a prize
if I was kept in the Middle East,' he said, 'but it's a risk
worth taking because it may get us through a situation that
has become locked and jammed.'

He was in a jovial mood as he sat down in the first-class
compartment, appearing to relish the mission. Lebanese passengers came up and shook him by the hand. No one seemed
to mind that the flight had been delayed by his meeting with
Oliver North on the tarmac. To the journalists on board, the
delay was a further sign that something was happening.

He had brought with him the *Shorter Pepys Diary* and
Rupert Bear's Birthday Book. 'I thought I'd get on with a
little reading while dodging the bombs,' he joked. He showed
the journalists an inscription written by an old friend in the
front of the Pepys book. 'Conviviality was not second but
first nature to Pepys,' it read, 'and to Waite too.' He disclosed
during the flight that he had left behind a note giving instructions in the event of his being taken hostage. 'I wrote,' he
said, 'that no one must come after me at all. There must be
no ransom paid for me if I am kidnapped. There must be no
deal over me. I come here fully expecting to leave freely.'

At Beirut airport he was engulfed by that city's peculiar
anarchy. He was met by gunmen from two militias, both
of whom thought they were protecting him, and scores of
reporters who had flocked to the Lebanese capital to cover
his visit. The militiamen, who seemed hesitant as to how

to handle the mob besieging the Anglican envoy, suddenly charged at the cameras and journalists, thrusting them out of Waite's path. He thanked the guards for their 'enthusiasm' and shouted to reporters that he was optimistic about the visit. 'I believe,' he said, 'there is a real opportunity for a breakthrough.' Waite knew before leaving London that the captors wanted to see him. In response to an interview he had given to the BBC World Service he had received a message telling him whom to contact.

Dramatically, soon after his arrival he asked the journalists to leave him alone, to give him breathing space so that he could accomplish his 'very difficult and dangerous mission'. It was the start of a special relationship that he was to develop with the Beirut press corps. With one of their colleagues a hostage they were, on the whole, to respect his wishes. In turn, he would feed them with a regular diet of quotes and anecdotes.

The militiamen put Terry Waite in the back of a BMW sandwiched between two gunmen, with a third pointing his Kalashnikov out of the window. They sped off along the airport road, a favourite hunting ground for kidnappers, and disappeared into the sprawling Shi'ite slums of West Beirut. But he had, in fact, left with the wrong group of militiamen. The arrangement in London had been that the Druze would protect him. The gunmen he left the airport with were from the Shi'ite militia, Amal. They took him to a West Beirut hotel. There followed a heated argument between the two militias, which was only resolved when Amal agreed that the Druze could take Waite to the Sleit building, to the apartment of the American hostage Terry Anderson where he was staying. It was an early lesson for him in the realities of life in Beirut, a city that had been carved up by rival militias, jealous of their turf. Ironically, his mission, which was intended to save lives, could very easily have led to an armed clash before it had even started.

The next day Waite strolled into the Commodore Hotel, where most of the press was staying, and held an impromptu news conference. Although he hadn't met the captors he was in touch with them, he said. One of the preconditions that Waite had established at the outset was that he should deal with the captors face to face. He understood why they might be cautious. One of the reasons the captors had been able to survive was their refusal to meet any intermediary. 'I want to protect them as much as I want to protect myself,' he said. 'Protecting the lives of the captors is something I just have to do. They are taking risks in meeting me, just as much as I am taking a risk meeting them.'

He also repeated his demand to be left alone. He had been angered by some television crews, who had literally camped outside the apartment where he was staying and had tried to follow him. 'One wrong move at this moment and people could lose their lives, including me,' he told the journalists. He knew from Benjamin Weir how suspicious the captors were and how fearful they were of being identified. If he was followed to a rendezvous it could be very dangerous.

The following day Waite had still not met the captors, but he had spoken on the phone with a man who claimed to be acting on their behalf and who invited him to a meeting in the dangerous suburbs of West Beirut. Waite was cautious. The Lebanese capital was rife with people offering to trade information; there was even a ghoulish market in hostage memorabilia. Waite set the man a test. He asked him to find out the nationality of the girlfriend of the Middle East correspondent of the London *Times*. Waite knew that one of the hostages, Terry Anderson, was a close friend of the correspondent and would know the answer. Some time later the man returned with the information that the woman in question was Scandinavian, and asked Terry Waite to attend a meeting.

He went to Avenue John F Kennedy to the clinic of Dr Adnam Mroueh, a gynaecologist who had treated the wives of several prominent Shi'ites, including Sheikh Fadlallah's. Several men appeared but before Waite would agree to attend any rendezvous, he wanted further proof that these individuals actually held the hostages. He had brought with him a Polaroid camera and a recent edition of the London *Times*. He told them to go away and photograph the American hostages holding the paper.

Father Jenco, one of the hostages at the time, remembers the occasion. 'The first time that I knew that Terry was in the country was when they [the captors] rushed up one night to take a picture with us, each one individually. Terry Waite had written across a London *Times* his name, which also indicated the date. So we all stood and took a picture holding the newspaper. And we hoped that we were going home for Christmas.'

The men returned with the pictures within half an hour and asked Waite to go with them. Later he described his Beirut meetings. 'I'm taken in a car to a deserted building, usually in the night. I walk into the building alone. I'm collected by someone and blindfolded, then I'm taken to another location and I have to conduct discussions while someone has a gun in my back.'

His first meeting was frightening. He was blindfolded, neither knowing where he was taken or with whom he was talking. The conversation was in English, and American officials are convinced that he was dealing directly with Imad Mugniyah whose English is passable. Waite began his meeting by exploring what the captors really wanted. He inquired whether they were after money. Mugniyah appeared insulted and protested that he and his people were misunderstood by the West. He wanted Terry Waite to understand they were not bandits, but devout Moslems. He repeated again that the hostages would be released if the prisoners in Kuwait were freed.

They discussed the idea raised in the hostages' letter that both the hostages and the prisoners in Kuwait should be handed over to a neutral third party, like the International Red Cross. Terry Waite had discussed this with Oliver North, who had told him the Kuwaitis were unlikely to agree to such a proposal. Waite raised the 'blood money' idea that he had worked on during the summer. The captors were interested; it appealed to them as Moslems that the matter could be settled under Islamic law. Waite promised to continue working on the idea and said he would look into the cases of their relatives. The captors told him they received little or no news from Kuwait. Waite said he would try and improve communications. Before he left they told him that time was short. They gave the impression they were under military pressure from other militias and that this could endanger the hostages.

It was the first meeting between a Western emissary and the shadowy figures of Islamic Jihad. 'There is absolutely no doubt at all,' said Terry Waite the next day, 'that I have got through to the right people and that a measure of trust has been established.' Waite was tight-lipped about what had been discussed. 'I will not say at all where I met, with whom I met or what passed between us. Speculation about any of those points could cost lives.' He thought the fact that the captors had met him was a breakthrough in itself. By ending their isolation they had begun a dialogue.

On the return flight to London, Waite munched smoked salmon sandwiches and chatted with reporters and other passengers. Although clearly exhausted, he was in excellent spirits. 'I'd like to say to the families of the hostages that I am hopeful.'

He was only intending to stop briefly in London before travelling to the United States to talk with American officials. But at Heathrow airport he was given a message that Oliver North was waiting at the nearby Penta Hotel. The arrangement was that they would meet each other in the lobby. When Waite got there he couldn't find anyone and had to scour the hotel, much to the curiosity of the management who wondered what the Anglican envoy was doing. Eventually he found North. A room had been booked in the name of Parker Borg, the State Department official whom Waite had met on the tarmac before his visit to Beirut. Other men were present, among them a senior diplomat at the American embassy in London, and a political officer from the US embassy in Beirut; a man fluent in Arabic and well versed in the ways of the Moslem militias.

When North saw Waite, he was effusive. 'I can't tell you how much the President appreciates what you're doing,' he said. Everyone congratulated him. Waite was buoyant. His meeting with the captors, which no one had achieved before, had clearly enhanced his standing with the Americans. North was impatient for details. As he listened to Waite's account his excitement grew. Although he was curious as to what the captors had demanded he was more interested in the

circumstances surrounding Waite's meetings. The fact that
the captors had only taken thirty minutes to return with the
Polaroid pictures of the hostages was the first positive proof
that they were being held in the Lebanese capital. In the
weeks prior to Waite's visit, intelligence officials had been
convinced that the hostages were being held in the Sheikh
Abdallah barracks in the Bekaa valley. That was an hour from
Beirut. In early October they ordered aerial surveillance of the
barracks and by October 23 North was receiving quality
photographs. By early November, Washington believed that
five out of the six American hostages were held there. Despite
frosty relations with Damascus, a plan was discussed with the
Syrians which would have involved Syrian special forces
storming the building. Administration officials were sceptical
as to the seriousness of Syria's intentions. Some favoured
exerting more pressure on Damascus while others thought the
operation was foolish. Terry Waite's information suggested
that either the hostages had been moved or that the original
intelligence was inaccurate.

The location of the hostages was a vital piece of intelligence for the Americans. Ever since William Buckley, the
CIA Station Chief, had been kidnapped they had been planning a rescue attempt. The obstacles were formidable. Any
operation would involve deploying special forces in the
heavily fortified suburbs of West Beirut. Surprise would be
essential, and so would be the ability to extract the hostages
and the troops quickly. But before any operation could be
planned it was essential to know where the hostages were
being held.

Waite's information that the captors had returned within
half an hour intrigued North. There were several buildings
within a fifteen-minute radius of Dr Mroueh's clinic which
could be used to hide the hostages. In the discussion which
followed, someone said the captors might have used a motorbike and that they should examine a wider area. North disagreed: with so many roadblocks to pass through he didn't
think a motorbike would make much difference. He then
produced maps of the city and high-definition photographs.
They were of better quality than satellite pictures, and had
been taken from either a high building or a low-flying air-

craft. North laid them out on the floor and the bed. He, Waite and the officials studied them. They peppered Waite with questions. Had he gone round any roundabouts on his journey to meet the captors? North wanted to know. Waite wasn't certain.

It was a measure of how little American officials knew about the whereabouts of the hostages that Terry Waite's snippet of information should be greeted with such interest. With the aid of satellite pictures, intelligence officials in Washington immediately began a photo-analysis of selected buildings within a fifteen-minute radius of the clinic. 'It was rather embarrassing really,' said one official. 'There was fevered excitement. I remember someone suggesting we build scale models of likely locations in West Beirut.'

North then asked Waite whether on future missions he would wear a tracking device. He said it was for his own protection. If he went missing, North went on, they would always know where he was. North produced from a bag a belt with a locating bug hidden in the buckle. One of those present described it as 'ostentatious and unconvincing; like something out of Star Wars.' He thought it very dangerous and warned it could easily backfire.

As North explained how it worked, how his movements could be monitored, Waite became interested. Although he had been exhilarated by his meeting with the captors, the blindfolded encounter had been a frightening experience. It would be all too easy to disappear into the labyrinthine streets of Beirut's southern suburbs. There was comfort in knowing someone was tracking him.

What North did not say was that the device could also help in locating the hostages; adding to the intelligence profile that was essential for a rescue mission. Unknown to Waite the planning for such a mission was well under way although the Administration was pinning its hopes on the arms sales.

North also did not mention that the belt had been made up by the CIA under the instruction of Bill Casey, the CIA Director. The Agency is forbidden from using Church officials; Terry Waite, a British subject, was seen, curiously, as being exempt from that restriction.

Eugene Douglas, to whom both Waite and Habiby looked

to protect them from being compromised, defended North's action. 'The danger in the Middle East had risen so alarmingly,' he said,

> that the concern for his safety and the anxiety that there might be yet another hostage led North, I understand, to propose that Terry Waite take with him some means of being located. You put them on children if they're going into Harrods for the Christmas period so that if you lose your child you can find him by electronic device. And there was a hope that if Terry were somehow in danger and went off the track, there might be some way of knowing where he would be.

Later it was put to Ambassador Douglas, in a television interview, that the wearing of the device would also have helped intelligence officers locate the hostages.

> *Douglas*: Assuming that he was with the hostages, it would have. But in that world, in that transitional world between overt and covert, you always weigh the risks.
> *Interviewer*: But that was one of the motives, wasn't it, on behalf of some people?
> *Douglas*: Well, it is reasonable to assume it was one of the peripheral or marginal [reasons]. That's also a good result if we know where Terry is, and if he gets to the hostages, we might have some idea of where they are too.

Others, however, remain convinced that the main purpose of the idea was to gather intelligence.

Far from protecting him, fitting Terry Waite with a tracking device could have undermined his status as an envoy and, more seriously, risked his being taken for an agent of the CIA. The idea took no account of the paranoia of the captors. David Jacobsen, one of the hostages, said the captors 'think there's a CIA agent behind every bush. They think Delta Force [America's anti-terrorist special forces] is only fifteen minutes away by helicopter.' The captors had the instincts of street fighters – men who had survived in a sea of warring militias. At the moment North was proposing 'wiring' Waite, another of the hostages, Father Jenco, was suffering from their obsession with security.

Father Jenco was a quiet-spoken Catholic priest who had been taken hostage earlier in 1985. He had been living in a clothes closet for about a month and a half when one day his captors opened the door.

'Open your mouth,' they told him. Father Jenco was blindfolded and didn't know what was happening, but he did as he was told.

'What are those?' he was asked. The captors were poking inside his mouth.

'My teeth,' Jenco replied, bewildered.

'No the black pieces.'

He told them they were fillings.

'No, they're not,' said the captors. 'They're some kind of communication device to contact your government.'

Father Jenco protested. 'You can't be serious – they're fillings.'

The men didn't believe him and said, 'We'll give you half an hour to take them out.'

Father Jenco was terrified. He didn't know whether they really were going to come back and take the fillings out for him. 'You sit in utter darkness for hours waiting for that,' he said. When, at a later date, they did pull a tooth he passed out.

Oliver North had repeatedly promised Habiby and Douglas that the Church would not get hurt. But in his zeal to free the hostages he was willing to adopt schemes which might have endangered the life of the Anglican envoy. Waite was, however, becoming caught up in the Administration's increasingly frantic search for solutions to the hostage crisis.

Despite North's interest in the location of the hostages, he was actually pinning his hopes on another arms deal with the Iranians, which was near completion. Before the meeting in the Penta Hotel ended he told Waite there were strong indications that a hostage was about to be released. 'There are positive omens,' he said. He urged Terry Waite to return to Beirut at once. Waite wondered whether, as a result of his meeting with the captors, they had decided to make a gesture in order to help him with the Kuwaitis. North made no comment.

Terry Waite didn't really have anything new to tell the captors, but agreed to return to Beirut that day. At his first meeting with them, a few days earlier, he had told them that he would try and visit the prisoners in Kuwait. North suggested that he could now report that he had got American backing for a mission to Kuwait. 'We said we'd do what we could to help get him in Kuwait,' said Parker Borg. North promised to cable the Gulf state that day.

Unknown to Waite, a second shipment of missiles was due to be delivered to Iran, which was why North expected a hostage to be freed. This time the United States was more directly involved in the transaction, with the CIA providing a plane to pick up the shipment. Secretary of State George Shultz, who was in Geneva at the time, was told by Robert McFarlane that some hostages would be released on 21 November.

What Terry Waite also didn't know was that the Americans were planning to use his return mission to Beirut as the explanation for the sudden release of the hostages. The timing was perfect. No one would suspect that arms had been traded. As one senior administration official put it, 'All eyes would be on Terry.' Officials even began preparing the ground for a hostage release in their briefings. 'The fate of the American hostages may be decided in the next few days,' it was announced. They actually cited Terry Waite's mission as one of the reasons for their optimism. In fact, so vital was Waite to the operation that there was some anxiety when they heard he had left Beirut. North's diaries for 17 November contain a reference to a call from McFarlane; among the items discussed is 'Waite back to Beirut urgent.'

On the afternoon of 18 November, Waite met 'Spiro', who had already spoken to North. 'Spiro' had helped set up Waite's security on the first visit to Beirut, and agreed to make the arrangements for his immediate return to the Lebanese capital. Terry Waite thought he was continuing his humanitarian work, but his mission had become inextricably tied into American plans.

Later the same day, Waite left London for Beirut. His

sudden return was seen by the press as 'unexpected', and speculation grew that a hostage release was imminent. Waite did nothing to dampen hopes. 'I believe,' he said, 'that last time was a good step forward. I think now it's possible to take another step forward.'

En route he stopped overnight in Paris, where he met a French government official. Islamic Jihad, the group holding the Americans, also had four French hostages including two diplomats. It had been learnt twenty-four hours earlier that one of the French hostages was seriously ill, and now the French government was planning to send a senior diplomat and a heart specialist to Beirut. The official asked Terry Waite not only to mention the Frenchman in his talks but also to raise his case publicly. On arrival in Beirut, Waite appealed for his immediate release. 'If a man is sick . . . it is simply the humane and right thing to do to immediately return him to his family.'

In Beirut, militiamen took Waite once again to the apartment of Terry Anderson, one of the American hostages, where he stayed. North had arranged for him to have a two-way radio linking him with the American embassy. For if a hostage was released, as a result of the arms deal, it was essential that Waite be informed at once. Although he wasn't aware of it, the Americans were already choreographing his activities in order to cover up their other operations.

His mission was extremely delicate. He had very little to tell the captors, yet he had been led to believe that they were thinking of releasing a hostage. If they were about to make a concession he had to encourage them. At his first press conference he said, 'I have very important things to tell the kidnappers.' It is not clear whether on this, his second mission, he actually met the captors or just intermediaries. In his conversations Waite said that, having consulted in London, he had secured American support for a visit to Kuwait and was hopeful of visiting the seventeen prisoners. He was also working on improving contact between them and their families in Lebanon. The captors were encouraged by these undertakings and entrusted Terry Waite with three letters for the prisoners.

While he was in Beirut, the plan to send more missiles to

Iran ran into trouble. By the third week in November, Oliver North believed an agreement had been reached with the Iranian intermediary, Manucher Ghorbanifar, that would result in the release of all the hostages by the end of the month. According to the Congressional committee which investigated the affair, 'The plan was, in essence, a straight swap: US-made missiles in Israeli stocks would be sold to Iran in exchange for American hostages.'

North's plan was that eighty Hawk missiles would be moved from Israeli stocks on Friday, 22 November. They would be divided into three consignments and placed in three separate aircraft. After the first plane was launched, but before it landed in Iran, two American hostages would be freed. Three hostages were to be released after a second shipment, until all five American hostages and the sick French diplomat were freed. Robert McFarlane, the National Security Adviser, had instructed Oliver North that 'not one single item' of armaments should be shipped to Iran without the release of 'live Americans'.

The plan involved the planes stopping in a third country, Portugal, where the missiles would be transferred to other aircraft. The purpose of the circuitous route was to disguise the fact that Israel was doing business with Iran, something both countries were anxious to hide. But, at the last moment, Portugal denied the Israelis landing rights. They insisted on the United States providing them with a diplomatic note setting forth the nature of the cargo, and the shipping route, and stating that the release of the American hostages was the purpose of the shipment. The Portuguese government wanted a piece of paper because it recognized that the operation clearly violated United States policy.

But the Israelis and the Americans wanted the operation kept secret. The storyline they adopted was that the cargo was oil-drilling equipment. As the operation began to founder, North turned to the CIA. He not only wanted the Station Chief in Lisbon to put pressure on the Portuguese government, but for the Agency to provide alternative aircraft. Even with the CIA, North wasn't straight. As he later testified, 'I lied to the CIA because that was the convention that we had worked out with the Israelis, that no one else was to know.'

With Portugal refusing to cooperate, the operation began to fall apart. Aircraft which had been available had to be returned to their airlines; Turkey denied them overflight clearance; Cypriot officials insisted on inspecting the cargo. Eventually on 24 November a CIA plane, with St Lucia Airways markings, landed in Tehran with eighteen Hawk missiles. Iranian officials were not pleased: the wrong models had been delivered.

The Iranian middleman who had arranged the deal, Manucher Ghorbanifar, called the National Security Council. He was 'on the edge of hysteria'. The most horrible thing had happened, he said; the missiles had arrived and they were the wrong missiles. Ghorbanifar's emotional call also contained a threat. He passed on a message from the Prime Minister of Iran: 'We have done everything we said we were going to do, and you are now cheating us, and you must act quickly to remedy this situation.'

Not only was no hostage freed, but missiles had been shipped to Iran before any of the captive Americans had been freed, which McFarlane had expressly forbidden. 'This precedent,' argued the Congressional enquiry, 'gave the Iranians reason to believe that the United States would retreat in the future from its demand for the release of hostages prior to any weapons shipment.'

Within four days of his returning to Beirut, Terry Waite was informed by the Americans that there had been a hitch and that no immediate release of the hostages was expected. Before he could leave the city a fierce battle broke out between rival militias over the flying of flags on the country's Independence Day. Over fifty people were killed and more than a hundred injured.

Waite was trapped in the fourth-floor office of the Associated Press building. Outside, gunmen fought in the streets with automatic weapons and rocket launchers. An armour-piercing round smashed into the wall less than twelve feet from where Waite was standing, showering the room with dust and plaster. The fighting was so close that reporters noticed the changes in air temperature as the rockets and mortar shells exploded. In the midst of the battle, when conversation was impossible, Terry Waite went off to take a shower. 'If you can't do anything else,' he explained, 'you might as well make use of the time.'

An American reporter remarked that he had finally witnessed the imperturbable Englishman he had read so much about. In a lull in the fighting Terry Waite emerged to say that he had been catching up on his sleep and listening to some Schumann. On another occasion he was seen sitting on the floor sipping a glass of chilled wine, enjoying the camaraderie of the journalists around him.

When a middle-aged man was killed, almost carelessly, in the street outside the hotel, Terry Waite's stoical mood turned to weariness. 'You feel the absolute senseless futility of war,' he said with exasperation. 'It's part of the tragedy of the country.' For three days he was trapped in the fighting. To get to the airport his bodyguards took him on a dangerous route through one of the battlegrounds, which only the day before had been impassable. Waite called his journey 'an invigorating experience'. As regards the success of his trip, he was ambivalent. When asked whether he had achieved the major move towards freeing the Americans that he had hoped for on his arrival he replied 'Yes.' But he also said that 'Very grave difficulties remain.'

He said he expected to return soon, possibly by the end of the week. It would have been surprising if he had been able to make progress on the cases of the Kuwaiti prisoners by then. But North, ever optimistic, still thought he might be able to rescue the arms deal, and wanted the door left open for Terry Waite to return suddenly in the event of a hostage release.

8

THE KUWAITIS

Terry Waite was exhausted after his nights in Beirut, interrupted by the crashes and whines of street battles. But Oliver North was anxious to see him and so he flew directly to New York, having caught a connecting flight in Athens. At Kennedy airport, Samir Habiby had arranged with TWA to meet Waite at the steps of the plane rather than at the gate. He took him through a special customs area. North was flabbergasted when Habiby proudly told him what he had done. 'We can't even do that for our own people,' he said. Habiby drove Waite to the Presiding Bishop's apartment in Manhattan.

It was very different from when Waite had last been in the United States a few weeks earlier. Then he was still a little-known intermediary; now camera crews were waiting in the lobby of the Episcopal Centre. His two trips to Beirut had received extensive coverage in the United States, and almost overnight he had become a public figure.

When Waite and his bodyguards had used a lull in the fighting to race to Beirut airport, he had left behind all his clothes. While he was showering at the Bishop's apartment, Samir Habiby went out and bought a suit for him. According to Habiby, camera crews even pursued him round the clothing stores of Manhattan.

Oliver North and Parker Borg flew up from Washington. They had to be guided through a back entrance to avoid the press. By the time they sat down together it was seven in the evening in Manhattan and the middle of the night in Beirut. North thrived on eighteen-hour days: there was almost a pride in weariness, as if the very act of pushing oneself confirmed the importance of the activity. He was becoming impossibly busy. By now he was overseeing the arms deals with the Iranians; directing multifarious schemes to get the hostages out of Lebanon; and coordinating arrangements to ship privately purchased arms to the rebels in Nicaragua. But he felt an exhilaration at being at the centre of events, and it was an excitement that Waite shared. There was no reason for the meeting to be held that day rather than the next, but some of the drama would have evaporated.

The conversation was relaxed. North asked Waite how he had enjoyed the war. The Anglican envoy joked about his narrow escapes: the bullet-proof vest had come in useful. North wanted to know whether he would do it again. 'Why,' said Waite, 'you're not wanting me to go back tomorrow?' They all laughed. He didn't mind returning to Beirut, he said, although he would prefer not to make a habit of going there. North suggested he start learning Arabic just in case.

North was sorry that things had not worked out. Certainly, from his information, the captors had considered releasing a hostage. It wasn't clear whether Waite had actually met with the captors during his second visit or only with an intermediary but he had been passed three letters for the prisoners in Kuwait. North sat up: they might reveal what the captors were thinking.

The letters were unsealed and in Arabic, a language that Samir Habiby understood. Seated in the Bishop's apartment, he began reading them aloud. North sat with his head in his hands, concentrating intently. Occasionally he would interrupt and ask Habiby whether there was a different meaning to a sentence; he wondered whether the captors were trying to send a message in code. But the letters were what they purported to be: a communication between relatives concerned with the mundane details of family life. There was nothing of substance in them and no mention of the hostages. None of those present in the apartment thought it strange for a priest to be reading someone else's letters to an American government official.

The Bishop's wife brought them a buffet meal and Bishop John Allen said grace. North stood up. He was very courteous. 'Ollie was deferential to all Church authority,' said a former colleague. 'He was like an altar boy preparing for confirmation.' He was particularly respectful towards Canon Habiby, who came to regard himself as a quasi chaplain to North.

When the conversation resumed, Waite said that it was imperative for him to go to Kuwait. He had given an under-taking that he would try and talk to the Kuwaiti government and visit the prisoners. It was dangerous, he thought, to disappoint the captors. North, however, had made enquiries with the Kuwaitis and he wasn't hopeful that they would agree to see the Anglican envoy. The Emir was not prepared to acknowledge any link between the hostages and convicted prisoners in his country. It was a stand that the United States publicly supported.

Waite and North realized their dilemma. If they weren't careful they could end up harming the hostages by letting down the captors. As they talked, an idea formed. If Terry Waite was to meet with people at the highest level of the American government, it would demonstrate to the captors that their demands were receiving serious consideration; but, just as importantly, it would signal to the Kuwaitis that Waite was an envoy who had the stamp of approval of the United States.

'Terry wanted to see Reagan,' said Habiby. North was certain the President would have been happy to meet him, but he was out of town. He thought the Vice President might be available. North phoned the Vice President's office and a meeting was scheduled for the following afternoon. But George Bush's aides were insistent that the meeting be seen as taking place at the request of the Church – otherwise it might appear as if Terry Waite was working for the US government. North rejoined the others and said it would be helpful if the Bishop could make a formal approach. Bishop Allen, it turned out, was a personal friend of George Bush, and he agreed to call Washington. It enabled him later to assert confidently: 'I arranged the visit.'

The next day, 26 November, Terry Waite met Vice President Bush at the White House. They were joined by senior administration officials and his closest aides. John Poindexter, Oliver North, Parker Borg, Don Gregg and Craig Fuller all attended. Waite brought with him Samir Habiby,

Bishop Allen and Marion Dawson, Habiby's assistant.

Up until this time the administration had wanted to keep their contacts with Waite as low-key as possible, but the purpose of this meeting was quite the opposite. 'We wanted to give Terry Waite a high profile,' said one of those who was in the Vice President's office. 'We wanted to demonstrate he was taken seriously.' Parker Borg said it provided 'a little publicity for him so that when he returned to Beirut, the people with whom he was talking would recognize that this man had the ear of high officials in the US government.'

Terry Waite briefed the Vice President on his meetings in Beirut. Although he did not ask for the US administration to put any pressure on Kuwait, he said that the prisoners in Kuwait remained central to solving the problem. He thought it would help if he could visit the Gulf state. George Bush praised him for his courage and concern, but reaffirmed that it was US policy not to ask its allies to compromise on terrorism.

After the meeting, which lasted for about forty-five minutes, Waite was interviewed on the White House lawn. The meeting had served its purpose. He was able to say that he had relayed the captors' demands to the administration. More importantly, he was able to use the setting of the White House to appeal to the Kuwaitis to receive him. There were matters, he said, which could be discussed without compromising their stand on terrorism. It was a diplomatic argument of the finest delicacy. 'I support the position of the American Administration,' he went on, 'in not putting pressure on the Kuwaiti government. I would not wish to see any principle of law and justice breached in any way ... Having said that, I would wish to have a meeting with the Kuwaiti authorities ...' What Waite and North were hoping was that by signalling in advance that they were not intending to get the Kuwaitis to soften their position, the Gulf State might agree to a humanitarian visit from a Church envoy. It could be presented to the captors in Beirut as a sign of progress.

The occasion was spiced with ironies. There was Terry Waite, outside the White House, supporting the American policy of refusing to negotiate with terrorists, while their officials were happily selling arms to the terrorists' pay-masters. The next day the *Washington Post* reported, on the basis of a briefing, that officials were 'known to feel that Terry Waite's mission could be damaged seriously if the captors . . . came to regard him as a US agent rather than an independent negotiator'. Terry Waite and Oliver North were now working closer together than ever.

Later, when George Bush was running for President, his office was curiously reluctant to acknowledge the meeting with Terry Waite. It was at first suggested that no such occasion had taken place. Later, that statement was modified to say that President Reagan, Vice President Bush and Waite had 'probably' met at a 'gathering' with the hostage families. The enquiry was referred to the President's office, which correctly claimed that Ronald Reagan had never met Terry Waite.

On 29 November 1985, Waite returned to London, and on his arrival he spoke very directly. He wanted to discuss the hostages in Lebanon with the Kuwaiti government and was waiting for an answer. He calculated correctly that after he had made such a public appeal the Kuwaitis would be forced to reply. The following week he was rebuffed: the Kuwaitis refused to issue him with a visa. In their view, receiving the Anglican envoy would establish a link between the hostages and the prisoners. Later, a Kuwaiti official was to say impishly, 'Mr Waite would be welcomed here as a tourist, but this is not a tourist country.' The United States could only applaud Kuwait's firm stand.

North and Waite were very concerned about the impact this would have on the captors. Waite put the best face on the Kuwaiti rejection. He remained, he said, 'cautiously optimistic'. Through a secret channel a message was sent to an influential Shi'ite in Beirut that, despite Kuwait's public position, Waite's mission was continuing.

There followed intense behind-the-scenes efforts to get the Kuwaitis to soften their position. Private appeals were made by administration officials. 'Spiro', had been at school with members of the Kuwaiti Royal Family and used his influence. Samir Habiby had one of his relatives petition aides to the Emir. But the Kuwaitis would not consider going back on their decision. In the Middle East, wavering is regarded as a prelude to capitulation. They were, however, prepared to hear what Terry Waite had to say on the condition that they could deny that any meeting had taken place. An elaborate formula was found.

On 18 December 1985, Waite flew to Geneva. Samir Habiby had preceded him and had set up a meeting with the Kuwaiti Ambassador to Switzerland. The Kuwaitis had insisted on the utmost discretion. Terry Waite was not, however, easily disguised. The agency reporters who stake out most international airports did not fail to recognize the towering, bearded figure whose face had recently been pictured in most of the international news magazines. They soon discovered that he was staying at the InterContinental Hotel.

Habiby did not like the presence of reporters, but he was even more concerned when he learnt that Waite had revealed his whereabouts to a British television reporter whom he liked and trusted. When the reporter telephoned, Habiby insisted that Waite change rooms and take no further calls. When another reporter did manage to reach Waite he was unusually flustered. 'I don't want to speak. I'm not here,' he was quoted as saying. His reaction only intrigued other Swiss journalists. After calling several embassies they found a diplomat who said that Terry Waite was seeing officials from the International Red Cross, whom he had met on a previous visit. It was true, but a small group of reporters gathered in the hotel foyer.

Waite and Habiby sat in their rooms like fugitives. Far from this being a secret trip, their every move was being watched. Habiby approached the hotel manager, who agreed to help. He was used to sensitive guests, he assured them. Yasser Arafat, the PLO Chairman, always stayed there when visiting Geneva. It was a matter of pride with the hotel that guests could come and go without being observed by reporters. He arranged for a car to be parked at the back entrance of the hotel where the deliveries were made and the rubbish collected. Waite and Habiby took the service elevator to the basement and then walked up some steps to the loading bay, which was conveniently shielded from the street by a brick wall.

Although the Kuwaiti embassy was only a street away, they drove to the residence of the Kuwaiti ambassador on a hill outside the city, almost in France. The occasion was arranged like this so that the Ambassador could deny that he had had a meeting with Waite. He was officially meeting Canon Habiby, an accreditied Church representative of the United Nations Economic and Social Council. 'Terry was with me in Geneva,' said Samir Habiby, 'as my guest. The ambassador obviously met with me and was gracious enough to say that whoever came with me would be welcome. In the Arab tradition your friends are received with you, but you don't necessarily have to say, "Well, so and so was with me at this point." '

The ruse seemed unlikely to convince anyone, but such was the Ambassador's sensitivity that some of the conversation was conducted in Arabic with Waite sitting in the background. Habiby told the Ambassador that their concern was humanitarian. They wanted to visit the seventeen prisoners held in Kuwait. The Ambassador said the Kuwaitis were not prepared to link the health or conditions of their prisoners with another group in another country. The two churchmen stressed that they were only seeking to improve human contact between individuals as lives were at stake. They discussed whether it would be possible to exchange letters or videos. Terry Waite asked whether the letters from the captors' families, which he had brought with him from Beirut, could be handed over to the prisoners.

The Ambassador was reluctant. It would be asked how these letters had arrived. Kuwait preferred them to be delivered by an international agency rather than by Terry Waite. In fact one set of letters had already been exchanged through the International Committee of the Red Cross as Waite had told North on December 3. The Ambassador questioned why these prisoners merited special treatment. If there were other letters, could not the relatives use the postal service?

Waite and Habiby began to realize the strength of the Kuwaitis' determination not to make the slightest concession to terrorists or hostage takers. It was proving to be a difficult encounter. 'We tried to explain to the Kuwaitis,' said Habiby,

'that the families were not satisfied with the current opportunities [for contact]. There was a great deal of fear on the
kidnappers' part that they could become targets for possible
action. They did not want to be in a position whereby they
could be identified through using the mail.'

The Ambassador was not prepared to take the letters without consultation. A second meeting had to be arranged. He
reported back that the Kuwaiti government would on this
occasion deliver them, but that in future they would have to
come through either the Red Cross or the postal system. The
Ambassador said Kuwait would happily demonstrate that
the prisoners were being well looked after, but that could
not involve a visit by Terry Waite.

Ironically, despite all the precautions, news of the meeting
leaked. *Al-Khaleej*, a newspaper in the United Arab Emirates,
reported that Mr Waite had held secret talks with a senior
Kuwaiti envoy in Geneva.

Terry Waite had discovered that the Kuwaitis, unlike the
Americans, meant what they said. The United States talked
tough, but their words sounded hollow when compared with
the resolution of a tiny Gulf kingdom. He knew that it was
time to report back to the captors, even though the offerings
he would be bringing were meagre. But Waite always looked
on the optimistic side. He gave North an upbeat account of
the meeting in Geneva. In his diaries, North wrote,
'December 19th. Waite called. Reports friendly meeting with
Kuwaitis.'

Waite left for Beirut immediately, infusing his third visit
with optimism and expectation. Twice before, in Iran and
Libya, he had negotiated at Christmas, and both times he
had returned with good news. In the absence of a strong
hand he appealed to the captors' religious values. 'It would
be marvellous,' he said before leaving London, 'if we could
see peaceable gestures coming from the Lebanon rather than
all those pictures of violence and war.'

On 20 December Terry Waite arrived in the Lebanese capital. Inexplicably, airport officials refused to allow reporters
to meet him. He was collected by Druze bodyguards, who
drove him to the Summerland Hotel for a press conference.
The gunmen, who seemed unaware of the purpose of the

event, began screaming at the journalists to clear the lobby. Waite calmed his bodyguards down by publicly thanking them for bringing him from the airport with their 'usual charm and efficiency'.

Invoking the spirit of Christmas, he appealed for the hostages to be released. He was bringing with him, he said, 'just and fair proposals'. It is not clear whether he did have some new initiative or whether this was purely a way of enticing the captors to meet him.

For five days he remained in hiding. American officials doubt whether he ever saw the captors. There was a conversation with an intermediary, but it didn't go well. The Shi'ite gunmen holding the hostages were hard individuals unlikely to be persuaded by emotional appeals or the promise of improved contact with their relatives in Kuwait. They gave Waite twenty-four hours to leave the country, and told him not to return until he had better news. 'When we spoke with him following his visit,' said Parker Borg, 'he indicated that they were upset that he had not come back with something more concrete. And he was forced to leave rather quickly. I believe he was afraid there might have been a threat against his life.'

He was right to be concerned. One of the hostages, David Jacobsen, remembered the Christmas visit. 'The guards once told us that they had considered taking Terry and keeping him in December 1985 because he had come to Beirut without the signed agreement or with the deal to get the seventeen out of the Kuwaiti jails.'

Waite acknowledged that the visit had been a setback. 'One has to recognize,' he said, 'that in Beirut the waters are very turbulent and very deep.' In fact he was downcast and, according to friends, began to question whether his mission on behalf of the American hostages had a future. One of the people he spoke to was Marion Dawson, personal assistant to Samir Habiby. 'I remember receiving a phone call from him on Christmas Eve in 1985 when he was really a bit down. He called to wish me a Merry Christmas, but it was clear that he was discouraged.' From Marion Dawson's conversation it appears that he had put great store on it being Christmas and had persuaded himself that the captors might make a concession. At heart Terry Waite was an optimist who believed in the essential goodness of those he met. 'I think probably,' said Marion Dawson, 'that he had had a great deal of hope and expectation about that Christmas visit because it had been at Christmas time the year before, in the famous meeting in the tent, that he had had such success with Colonel Qadaffi.' Listening to him, she felt that he was looking for encouragement, for reassurance that what he had done so far had been important and significant.

The failure in Beirut wasn't felt only by Terry Waite – it was mourned by the hostages themselves. During Christmas 1985 the five Americans were held together. Sharing their captivity made the long days bearable: they could escape into each other's memories and fantasies. They would take it in turns to conduct a service inside the cell which they had dubbed the Church of the Locked Door. They were not permitted to see their captors, and were instructed to put on blindfolds whenever they entered the room.

Yet occasionally they would pick up snippets of news about outside efforts to help them, overhearing the radio before the guards could turn it down. Father Jenco once heard his nephew appealing for his release on the 'Voice of America'. One night, David Jacobsen remembered hearing the former Secretary of State, Henry Kissinger, talking about how he would advise the President on the hostage crisis. 'In the last resort,' he was heard to say, 'they [the hostages] are going to have to use their own resources to get out.'

Jacobsen was nonplussed. 'I was sitting in my underwear on a pad,' he later wrote. 'The room had no windows. There was a double lock on the door. An armed guard was outside the door and another armed guard was watching down the hall. I said, "My God, Henry, what resources do I have? What resources do you think I have?" '

The hostages had learnt of Terry Waite's mission and would question the guards as to how it was going. It was a source of hope and encouragement. Could it be, they asked each other, that they would be celebrating Christmas with their families? Then Father Jenco heard on the BBC World Service that Terry Waite's negotiations had failed. It was a bitter disappointment. 'It was Christmas Eve,' recalls Father Jenco,

> and so I celebrated midnight mass. We sang Christmas carols, and you could hear voices that weren't sharp any more. There was an emotion in the room. I'm sure if one guy started to cry they all would have cried. The following day, however, the young captors, knowing that we were so depressed, came in and brought a lovely birthday cake with 'Happy Birthday, Jesus' written on it. They gave us ice cream, Pepsi and a chicken, and they came in and sang 'Happy Birthday' to Jesus.

Soon afterwards the captors' mood changed and the radio was removed; the hostages felt isolated and forgotten. When they complained they were told, 'You're just asking too many questions and you know more than we do.' David Jacobsen believes that the real reason for the guards' behaviour was that they did not want Terry Anderson to learn that his father had died that month and that his brother, Rich, who had only recently made a dramatic appeal on his behalf, was dying of cancer. During his brief visit to Beirut, Waite had brought letters for the hostages from their families. The captors chose not to deliver them for two months.

After December, said Father Jenco, they really didn't hear much about Waite. 'So we would ask the guards whether Waite was still holding talks and they would never give us any information whether he was or not.' But Father Jenco also detected that the captors had changed their opinions on Terry Waite. 'There was a certain feeling, which I think we all picked up from them, that they'd moved back from Terry, and they didn't trust Terry.'

Waite spent what remained of Christmas with his family at Blackheath in London. He was convinced that he could take the matter of the Kuwaiti prisoners no further. North knew that it was one of the levers that could free the hostages, and was reluctant to give it up. In his diaries he reminded himself 'to put more pressure on the Kuwaitis'. During December he had been engaged in a bitter dispute in Washington over the future of the arms-to-Iran policy. He would quote Terry Waite in his support as he battled with the more cautious members of the Reagan administration. In a memorandum to Poindexter and McFarlane, North had written: 'Waite shares our belief that the hostages are increasingly endangered and that one or more of them could well be executed by the end of the week.'

While Waite's efforts were floundering in the face of Kuwaiti resolve, the administration was having a moment of doubt. The failure of the shipment of Hawk missiles in November had sobered everyone except North. The stark facts were that three consignments of missiles had been sent to Iran and only one hostage had been freed. Secretary of State George Shultz saw the general mood of disillusionment as an opportunity to kill off the trading of arms for hostages once and for all. From the start he believed it had been a bad idea, and had told President Reagan that 'we were just falling into the arms-for-hostages business and we shouldn't do it.'

On 6 December a White House meeting on the Iranian arms sales was convened. In a telephone call to Admiral John Poindexter, the new National Security Adviser, George Shultz had signalled his opposition to any future deals. The operation, he said, should be stopped. 'We are signalling to Iran that they can kidnap people for profit.' It was a view supported by the Secretary of Defense, Caspar Weinberger. The whole policy, he thought, would expose the United States to 'blackmail of the most elementary kind'.

Oliver North, undeterred by the policy's meagre returns, was already planning another deal. It was much grander than before: 3300 TOW missiles and 50 Hawks would be traded for all the hostages. Far from being concerned about blackmail, North used it to support his case. The United States, in his view, couldn't pull out now without risking the lives of the hostages. His argument was powerful and emotional. 'Based on what we can conclude from intelligence in Beirut,' he wrote to Admiral Poindexter, 'we believe that they are very concerned that the hostages . . . may be killed . . . in the near future. Waite's contacts with the captors seem to corroborate this assessment.'

North would use any argument to achieve his goal: the freedom of Americans held captive. Having been assigned that mission, he was obsessively single-minded. It was a form of blindness; contradictions went unseen. If his ideas trampled on other values that he held, it appeared not to disturb him. At other moments in his life the brazen threat of kidnappers would have stirred in him the fiercest resistance, but now he was the exponent of their cause. 'We are so far down the road,' he wrote in one of his memos, 'that stopping what has been started could have even more serious repercussions. If we do not at least make one more try at this point, we stand a good chance of condemning some or all of the hostages to death and a renewed wave of Islamic Jihad terrorism.'

After the White House 'crisis' meeting, George Shultz was under the impression that his arguments had prevailed. One of his allies thought they had 'strangled the baby in the cradle' – that the President had agreed to halt the arms sales. Others formed a different view, that there had been neither a consensus nor a decision. The President would later testify that there had been a stalemate.

President Reagan's meetings were often imprecise – it was his style. Questions would be asked, comments dropped and asides made, but decisions could evaporate in the air of conviviality. Afterwards it would be up to the Chief of Staff to interpret the President's mind. His management style, ironically, mirrored that of Ayatollah Khomeini, his *bête noire*. The Iranian leader governed his country through facial expressions, the movements of his hand and cryptic religious references; the mullahs squabbled over their meanings. If the policy subsequently ended in failure, then Ayatollah Khomeini was conveniently immune from responsibility.

During December, Robert McFarlane, believing he was carrying out the President's instructions, went so far as to tell the Iranians that there could and would not be any further trading of arms for hostages. Oliver North, however, interpreted the President's wishes differently. He thought a missile deal remained an official option. In this he was supported by William Casey, the Director of the CIA, who was convinced the President had not completely given up on the idea of trading with the Iranians.

This confusion was tailor-made for an activist like North, and his meetings with Israeli officials and Iranian middlemen resumed. Working in his favour was President Reagan's personal agony over his failure to secure the release of the hostages. Reagan told his Chief of Staff that it would be another Christmas with hostages still in Beirut. He was troubled at looking powerless and inept. During the festive season he held a series of emotional meetings with the families of the hostages: the President was visibly disturbed by their suffering. Afterwards, he ordered his staff to redouble their efforts to bring the hostages home.

It was a green light to Oliver North. Only one policy had so far succeeded, and that had been trading weapons. As the year ended he worked tirelessly on a variety of schemes, confident that his passion was shared by the President. Almost any plan, if it stood a chance of freeing the hostages, could expect Presidential backing. Terry Waite would remain indispensable to many of the operations North was working on. Even though his third mission to Beirut had ended in failure, North encouraged the Anglican envoy by saying that things were still moving and that they should meet.

9

OPERATION RECOVERY

The wind whipped off the Hudson River and tore down Manhattan's long avenues. The people stiffened before crossing the city's icy corridors, their clothes flapping about them like pieces of bunting. Terry Waite looked down on the bleak streets of New York in January. The apartment seemed unconnected to the scene below; its elegance was mature, nineteenth century, borrowed from France. With its glimpses of Central Park it would have fetched several million dollars – it was the home of the Havemeyers, one of New York's prominent families. They were Episcopalians and had invited Waite to stay, since the Bishop's penthouse was unavailable. On 8 January 1986 they had invited Oliver North to join them for dinner.

The Havemeyers had made their wealth from the refining of sugar and had spent it on paintings: over the years they had acquired one of the largest collections ever owned by an American family. Most of the works had gone to the Metropolitan Museum of Art in the twenties, but they had held on to many of their Impressionist paintings. Then, in 1983, they had decided to sell. One of the pictures, Degas' *L'Attente*, had fetched $3.4 million, which at the time was the highest auction price paid for an Impressionist work. 'I'm sure the Internal Revenue Service will be happy,' quipped Horace Havemeyer afterwards.

Although the Monets and the Cézannes had been disposed of, other paintings remained. Samir Habiby left Terry Waite to browse as he went to the airport to collect Oliver North. Among its dwindling congregations the Church of England could count certain members of the British aristocracy, but there was no equivalent of these New England Episcopalian families. Their wealth was old, frequently understated. They were conservative and Protestant, yet they were also the benefactors of multiple social causes. Their children went to Ivy League Universities and moved effortlessly into business or government. Washington was a city of 'friends', most of them Anglophiles: the Havemeyers had a house in London. For Terry Waite this America was strange yet reassuringly familiar.

When North arrived they joined the Havemeyers for dinner. Habiby offered grace: he asked for guidance in handling the tragedy of the hostages and prayed for America's enemies. During the meal Terry Waite talked about his previous visits to Beirut. He described how on his first trip they had stripped and searched him. It was the most frightening experience in his life, he said. Habiby hadn't heard the story before.

Afterwards, as dinner was being cleared away, North, Waite and Habiby went and sat in front of the fire in the library. All of them felt the mission was at a crossroads. The Christmas trip had reconfirmed the importance of the Kuwaiti prisoners. Yet, despite all of North's pressure behind the scenes, the Kuwaitis were unmoved.

North raised an idea they had discussed the previous summer. If they could not deliver the Kuwaiti prisoners, then perhaps they could help free other Shi'ites. Several hundred were being held by the South Lebanon Army at a prison in Khiam; many of them had been seized during raids by Israeli forces and were regarded by the Shi'ites, in their own way, as hostages. The SLA patrolled a strip of land in southern Lebanon which ran along the border with Israel. Most people regarded the SLA as Israel's client militia: the Israeli army provided it with weapons and training, and Israeli soldiers operated freely within the zone they controlled.

The SLA was controlled by General Antoine Lahad. Lahad was a Lebanese Christian and North felt he would be susceptible to a plea from the Church, especially if that request were made in person by the envoy of the Archbishop of Canterbury. North mentioned that the Roman Catholic Cardinal of New York, John O'Connor, had offered to intercede with Lahad. Personally he thought it would be better if Waite carried a letter from the Pope. Lahad would be asked to free those prisoners who 'didn't have blood on their hands'. The problem was where to hold the meeting.

Lahad was hated by the Shi'ites, who regarded him as an Israeli puppet. If they learnt that the Anglican envoy had been meeting him, then Waite's neutrality would be compromised and the hostages could be endangered. It was therefore necessary to keep the meeting secret until it could be shown that, as a result of it, Shi'ite prisoners had been freed.

As they sat round the fire, North worked out a plan. Waite would fly to Cyprus and then on to Tel Aviv. In Israel he would be met and taken to a safe house. During the night an Israeli army helicopter would fly him into southern Lebanon to meet General Lahad. When, later, the prisoners were freed Waite could claim that the meeting had taken place on neutral ground. If his visit to Israel became public, he could claim he was seeing the Anglican Bishop of Jerusalem. Habiby, whose family's home was in East Jerusalem, would make sure he was in Israel at the time. Waite wondered whether it was necessary to meet in Lebanon or Israel – why couldn't it be in Cyprus, he asked. North was doubtful whether it could be kept secret and he thought Lahad would be nervous about his security.

Habiby and Waite were enthusiastic about the plan. Waite thought it would enhance his credibility with the captors in Beirut if he could be shown helping to free Shi'ite prisoners.

'Do you think Lahad will go along with this?' he asked North.

'From what we know,' said North, 'Lahad may be willing to make some concession.'

North didn't know when the plan would go ahead; that depended on the Israelis. But he promised to contact Waite in London. They talked briefly about their families before Habiby drove North back to the airport.

What Terry Waite wasn't told over dinner was that his proposed meeting with General Lahad was only an item in a much larger deal involving the sale of arms to Iran. For over a month, Oliver North had been working on a plan which, he hoped, would result in the freeing of all the American hostages. It was called Operation Recovery and involved the sale of 3300 TOW anti-tank missiles to Iran. In North's mind this was to be the deal which ended the hostage crisis.

Over Christmas, President Reagan's frustration over the hostage issue had grown. No one in the administration seemed to have any fresh ideas on how to solve the crisis. North had come up with a memo outlining Operation Recovery. The arguments were the same as the previous summer: the weapons would be going to 'moderates' in Tehran, and the deal would herald a new relationship between Iran and the United States. Cleverly, North added a clause which appeared to protect the administration from being cheated. 'If all the hostages are not released after the first shipment of a thousand weapons, further transfers will cease.'

On 6 January, President Reagan initialled North's memo, although there is some doubt as to whether he intended to give his authorization. But ten days later, at the end of a meeting in the Oval Office, the President signed a document which made his approval official. Admiral Poindexter, who collected the signature, later said that Reagan remarked, 'Well, if we get all the hostages out we'll be heroes. If we don't we'll have a problem.'

Oliver North had been given a blank cheque. His partner in Operation Recovery was a young Israeli, Amiram Nir. They had got to know each other well during the crisis over the hijacking of the cruise ship *Achille Lauro*. Nir had been a television reporter in Israel who specialized in covering the Israeli defence forces. Rather surprisingly, as he had no expertise in the field, he was chosen to be adviser on counterterrorism to the Prime Minister, Shimon Peres. Officials in the Israeli Foreign Ministry and in Mossad, the intelligence service, disliked him, but Nir was artful and found a way of outmanoeuvring them. He began visiting Washington secretly and forging contacts with officials in the adminstration and the Pentagon. In Israel there is kudos in having an entrée in Washington, the capital of Israel's chief benefactor and its closest ally. By December 1986 Amiram Nir was orchestrating Israel's role in the arms for hostages deal.

Nir was the mirror image of North himself – energetic, determined, obsessed by goals and disdainful of 'normal channels'. Each had heroic stories from their past which no one could verify. Nir had lost an eye in a car accident. Michael Ledeen, who worked on the initial deal with the Iranians, relates that in Israel there is a story that Nir found the eye and carried it 'pressed into the bloody socket, as he drove at top speed to the Hadassah hospital in Jerusalem'. In December 1988 he was to die in a plane crash in Mexico.

Some members of the National Security Council were scornful of the Israeli. 'Nir saw himself as a master spy,' said one, 'but he didn't know shit about the real world.' At this time the BBC's programme *Panorama* interviewed him in his office in Tel Aviv: he gave a lengthy exposition on Palestinian terrorism. Two hours after the interview he sent officials to Jerusalem to demand the tapes, claiming they would reveal his identity and endanger 'sensitive missions'. Israeli officials, who insisted the material should not be used, were themselves puzzled that he had given the interview in the first place.

While North was excluding the State Department and certain officials in the CIA, Nir was bypassing Mossad and the Foreign Ministry. The two men were drawn to each other. Both saw themselves as activists, former soldiers who could cut through the bureaucracy of government.

In December 1985 they had started drawing up Operation Recovery. Although they were convinced they could buy off Iran with missiles, they wanted to offer Islamic Jihad something as well. Nir proposed that, while the captors were freeing the hostages, the South Lebanon Army would simultaneously release twenty-five or thirty Shi'ite prisoners. Before North had dinner with Terry Waite in New York he already knew, through Nir, that Lahad would release the prisoners. Although Waite didn't realize it, he would merely have been given the credit. North and Nir wanted the captors in Beirut to believe that their Shi'ite comrades had been freed as a result of the intervention of the Church. But as North's diaries reveal, the operation had been worked out in advance.

On 6 January, North had met Nir at 14.30 and had discussed three options for obtaining the release of the hostages. North jotted down in his diaries how he thought the first of these would work:

Option 1. Terry Waite. Release based on religious grounds. Plan involves: Pope letter to Lahad; letter to Lebanese Shi'ite leaders [promising] to 'use influence to release those who'd committed no wrong.' Nir to advise Lahad on how many; Lahad tells Waite how many/when release. Nir works out contract w/ Hezballah; Waite to Beirut; Amcits [American citizens] released to Waite.

The Church would have told the Shi'ite leaders that it was doing what it could to get Shi'ite prisoners released, but Waite's proposed meeting with General Lahad would have been a charade. As North's diary makes clear, Nir would have advised Lahad beforehand on precisely how many prisoners were to be freed. Waite would have only been the public face of the operation.

In the deal with the Iranians, North saw other, more dubious opportunities. At one of his meetings with Nir, the Israeli had suggested overcharging the Iranians for the missiles and using the surplus funds to support the Contras in Nicaragua. The Contras were North's other passion. Like President Reagan, he saw them as freedom fighters resisting the spread of Communism in Central America. North visited Contra camps in Honduras, raised money for them and arranged a supply of weapons. Now there was a simple way of financing an operation that Congress opposed. Nir's suggestion may only have been encouraging an idea which was already in North's mind, for it is apparent that he had already thought of it. North was amused. 'There's something beautiful,' he told Nir, 'in getting the Ayatollah to bankroll the war against the Sandinistas.'

During January, North was juggling with a bewildering number of schemes to free the hostages. Bill Rogers, the former Defence Secretary, had been in Tripoli. He had a message from Qadaffi. The Libyan leader was willing to purchase the hostages for $10m and prohibit all further acts of terrorism. Another plan involved the American hostage, Peter Kilburn. Six months earlier, a Canadian of Armenian descent had approached American officials saying that he represented the kidnappers. He produced Kilburn's identity card as proof. The kidnappers wanted money. The price fluctuated from $500,000 to, at one stage, $12 million. North agreed to pay $3 million. But he fretted over the operation. Could the Armenian mafia be trusted? What happened if there was snow on the Beirut/Damascus highway? What would be the consequence if the deal was accidentally discovered? How would the Syrians react when they realized one of the hostages had been purchased without their knowing? North, in conjunction with the FBI and the CIA, planned a sting operation whereby the dollar bills would be chemically treated so that, after a few days, they would disintegrate. In his notes, North writes, 'Army to do treatment, money/fully treated by end of week.'

On 22 January, North flew to London and arranged to meet Terry Waite later in the day. Beforehand he went to the Churchill Hotel, where he was joined by Amiram Nir and Richard Secord, a retired air force general whose company was handling many of the transactions involved. The three of them then had a meeting with Manucher Ghorbanifar, the Iranian middleman who was arranging the deals with the leadership in Tehran. North had the meeting bugged by the CIA.

Ghorbanifar was gleeful at the prospect of the money to be made. 'I think this is now, Ollie, the best chance because we never would have found such a good time, we never get such good money out of this.' Ghorbanifar gave a conspiratorial chuckle and went on. 'We do everything. We do hostages free of charge; we do terrorists free of charge; Central America for you free of charge.' The Iranian had seen that the hostage deal would enable North to finance a variety of other activities, including the Contras.

North, who knew the meeting was bugged, was extremely uncomfortable at this revelation. 'I would like to see . . . at some point this, uh, idea, and maybe, y'know, if there is some future opportunity for Central America.' North rambled on, not wishing to acknowledge Ghorbanifar's suggestion.

That afternoon North took Nir to see Waite at Lambeth Palace. It was an incongruous moment. Here were the Assistant Deputy Director for Political–Military Affairs at the National Security Council staff and an adviser on counterterrorism to the Israelis walking through the redbrick Tudor

Tower to discuss an initiative with an aide to the Archbishop of Canterbury. With their business suits and close-cropped hair they looked like salesmen or Mormon missionaries.

Terry Waite escorted them along the Great Corridor, with its portraits of former Archbishops, into the pink drawing room, where the Archbishop sometimes receives his guests. In a way it was an appropriate venue, for Waite had by this time become the best-known figure in the Church of England. To many, he had brought the Church a measure of respect while it was weighed down with doctrinal uncertainty and bitter arguments over the ordination of women.

Waite was sensitive about the visit. When Samir Habiby, who was also present, brought the Anglican envoy's secretary into the room to meet Colonel North, Waite was horrified. North and Nir were introduced, however, to the Archbishop but they left no impression, being indistinguishable from the many other visitors his envoy received.

When, much later, Oliver North's many operations were exposed and he had achieved notoriety, Samir Habiby was embarrassed by the Lambeth meeting. When he was asked during a BBC interview who was present on that occasion, he was unusually hesitant.

Habiby: Well, there were a number of people. There were, er, significant, er, there was a significant representative of a nearby country to Lebanon that had a tremendous influence on . . .
Interviewer: I think we can be specific here. Colonel North was there, wasn't he?
Habiby: Colonel North visited Lambeth on a number of occasions. He was part of the discussions, yes, because at that time we were, we had, er, no idea that there was any other initiative taking place on behalf of the US government.

At the meeting North said that, although they still wanted Terry Waite to meet General Lahad, it would not now be possible. Amiram Nir explained that in the past few days there had been attacks on Israeli forces inside the security zone in southern Lebanon. 'We can't therefore guarantee your personal security,' he told Waite. 'The visit will have to be called off.'

The excuse was a strange one. Although there were occasional clashes close to the border, the area was firmly under the control of the South Lebanon Army and Israeli troops. In any event, another location could have been found. It was more likely that they had run up against the limits of Nir's remit. Terry Waite could not have flown in an Israeli helicopter without the knowledge and approval of the Defence Minister, Yitzhak Rabin. The Israeli government, which had its own agenda, had not approved Waite's meeting with General Lahad. It was one of the many difficulties in dealing with North and Nir that they were frequently running operations which were unknown to their own governments.

Ironically, Waite and Habiby spent time trying to convince Nir that a meeting with Lahad was still important – unaware that they were talking to the man who would give Lahad his orders. After two hours the discussion broke up. North and Nir left Lambeth Palace on foot, as anonymously as they had come.

North continued to work on a detailed timetable for the movement of missiles and the release of the hostages. In his diary for 3 February he wrote, 'Lahad responds to Papal letter that he will release 50 Hezballah prisoners in two groups of 25.' The fact that Waite would not now be seeing Lahad had clearly had no impact on the plan. North took it for granted that Lahad would agree. In a bizarre footnote to his timetable, North selected Tuesday, 11 February, the anniversary of the Iranian Revolution, as the day when 'Khomeini steps down'. It was a dangerous cocktail of optimism and outright fantasy.

The day after the Lambeth meeting Waite and Habiby flew to Rome to collect the letter from the Pope appealing to General Lahad to release some of the Shi'ite prisoners. It was an uncomfortable moment for the two men in view of the fact that the meeting had been vetoed by the Israelis. Habiby felt it necessary to fly on to Jerusalem to explain to Bishop Kafity, the senior figure in the Anglican Church in the Middle East, why Terry Waite would not now be coming. The

Bishop would have officially received Waite during his time in Israel. At one point during Habiby's visit he found Amiram Nir observing him, although the Israelis did not make contact with him. Nir was no doubt curious why Habiby was in Israel just two days after he had told him in London that the meeting with Lahad had been cancelled. The Israelis, baffled by his presence in the country, detained him at the airport on his departure. Habiby had to place a call through to Oliver North in the White House before he was allowed to leave.

The more Samir Habiby pondered over the Lambeth meeting, the more uneasy he became. The presence of Nir had unsettled him. He telephoned North and asked to see him. They met on 5 February at North's office in Washington.

Habiby told North that he was concerned about how Nir's veto of Terry Waite's trip would be interpreted. The Vatican expected the Anglican envoy to meet General Lahad. Suddenly the meeting was cancelled, said Habiby: 'What's the excuse?' If Waite were to say that the Israelis had vetoed the trip, then the Church's humanitarian mission would be seen as being dependent on the Israelis.

North was upset. There was no question of Terry Waite's role being compromised, he assured the Episcopalian minister. It was an assurance he was to repeat on many occasions. North said the Israelis had taken the decision at the highest level. He did not think this would be difficult to explain to the Vatican.

Sadly, Habiby genuinely believed the Lahad meeting was a Church initiative. He was shocked to see it so easily shelved by the Israelis. It was a measure of how little Terry Waite and Samir Habiby understood the man they were dealing with.

Later, North phoned Habiby's wife and asked her: 'Why is Samir so upset?'

'Because he feels you're not telling him everything,' she replied candidly.

Throughout February, North and Nir were uncertain as to whether the intended missile deal would free the hostages. The intermediaries were forever changing their demands. The question of whether Waite should meet with Lahad remained an option. During February, North made several notes in his diary about Waite. 'Have decided to proceed w/Waite operation' and 'Waite/Israel:Mtg, tomorrow.' There were always difficulties. The Israeli government was unwilling to allow General Lahad to release any of his Shi'ite prisoners because two Israeli soldiers were being held by Hezballah. The Israelis were not prepared to see Lahad make a concession unless there was progress towards the release of their own people.

All the same, in February, a thousand TOW missiles were shipped to Iran without any release of the Lahad prisoners. No hostages were released either. Instead of calling off the deal, as North had promised President Reagan, he continued meeting Iranian officials. His optimism was boundless. After seeing an intermediary from the Iranian Prime Minister's office, he wrote to Robert McFarlane: 'With the grace of the good Lord and a little more hard work we will very soon have 5 Amcits [American citizens] home.'

Robert McFarlane was encouraging in reply. 'Ollie. Well done. If the world only knew how many times you have kept a semblance of integrity and gumption to US policy, they would make you Secretary of State. But they can't know and they'd complain if they did – such is the state of democracy in the late twentieth century.'

North did expect that one hostage would be freed during the last week in February. Terry Waite went to Cyprus, where he would have been conveniently placed to receive any hostage coming out of Lebanon. While on the island, Waite was able to attend to Church matters relating to the Bishop of Cyprus and the Gulf. It was a pattern that would be repeated in the future, when many of his trips would be influenced by calls from Oliver North.

'Ollie would say, "Conditions look good at this time. There are some very positive things happening," ' recalls Habiby. 'Obviously we knew that he had access to information that the National Security Council had . . . I would convey that information to Terry. Now Terry maybe had arranged to go to South Africa, which he was doing on several occasions, and he would revamp those and do a trip closer to the Middle East.'

Oliver North had begun to regard Terry Waite as an invaluable member of his network, although Waite, with only limited knowledge of what was happening, continued to envisage his role as humanitarian and independent. The intelligence services, too, saw the Anglican envoy as useful and built plans around him.

10

'OUR ONLY ACCESS TO EVENTS IN LEBANON'

Ever since William Buckley had been taken hostage in March 1984, the CIA had devoted its vast resources to getting him released. Many of the Agency's intelligence secrets in the Middle East were deemed to have been compromised by his capture: in the months that followed, some of the Agency's informants were killed, and several networks of informers had to be dismantled.

The seizure of Buckley was a personal blow to William Casey, the Director of the CIA. A former undercover agent for the OSS during World War II, Casey had come to the Agency determined to revive its 'operational' role. Many Republicans believed that under President Carter the Agency had effectively demobilized. Casey was determined to get his Station Chief back. The picture of Buckley in captivity, with his harrowed face, was hung on the wall at CIA headquarters as a daily reminder of the Agency's failure.

Buckley had had a premonition of his capture. Three weeks before he was taken, he had spoken of his fears to Chip Beck, an old friend from their Vietnam days and a partner in an antiques business. Buckley had asked his friend to make sure that, if he were taken, the administration did not allow him to die slowly through bureaucratic inactivity. He knew of colleagues in Vietnam who had wasted away in captivity, and he was resolved not to suffer the same fate. When Buckley was seized, Beck was to harass the government demanding action.

The CIA tried everything. A military satellite, normally stationed over the Soviet Union, was repositioned over West Beirut. Although it wasn't able to identify faces it was able to observe certain buildings suspected of being hiding places for the hostages. Armed guards, visitors, vehicles, deliveries, even washing on the line – all were noted. Telephone calls originating from the Iranian embassies in Beirut and Damascus were monitored from a listening post in Cyprus. Syrian communications out of the Lebanese capital were intercepted. That task proved easy at first for the Syrians were using landlines, although later they switched to couriers and constantly changed their transmitters. The FBI conducted extensive surveillance of Shi'ites living in the United States, an operation which was 'surprisingly useful'.

The CIA had some success in locating Buckley. They found the building where he was being held. They even managed to position an asset in the building across the street. Contact was established with one of the guards and a picture was taken of Buckley. William Casey was in favour of mounting a rescue mission but was told by the military that the intelligence was not good enough. There are those in the CIA who still feel bitter about this and believe they badly let down a colleague in his hour of need.

There were several attempts to infiltrate Hezballah. They all failed; one of them tragically. A former CIA official said ruefully, 'We had people executed.' Even Israel failed to penetrate the clans of Hezballah and was unable to determine the fate of its captured soldiers.

Despite these failures some intelligence was gathered but it was generally of insufficient quality to base a rescue mission on it. There were two fundamental problems. First, they never achieved what the CIA calls 'real-time intelligence' – knowing the precise location of the hostages at any particular moment. The importance of having that up-to-the-minute intelligence was underlined when one of the hostages escaped. One day in February 1985 Benjamin Weir was wakened by the shouts of the guards. 'It was clear from the confusion that a hostage was not in the room,' he said. Jeremy Levin, a correspondent from the Cable News Network, had escaped. He was able to give his debriefers precise details of the building where he had been held. The intelligence community was certain they had identified it correctly from satellite pictures. Some members of the administration favoured an immediate rescue mission, but it would have been a disaster. The hostages were moved that evening.

The second problem was that the hostages had to be together. Although it was not impossible to coordinate an assault on several buildings at once, it greatly complicated the operation.

Several times the CIA came close to overcoming the difficulties. In November 1985 they thought they had located five of the six American hostages. A group within the agency began constructing models of the houses where they were being held, the nearby streets, the exits and the likely position of the guards.

Oliver North thought that for a rescue to be successful it was necessary to have support from a local force inside Beirut. As the most likely candidates he selected the Druze, an independently minded people from the Chouf mountains whose loyalty was first and foremost to their own survival. Under their leader, Walid Jumblatt, they were both friendly with the Soviets while maintaining ties with the Israelis; they had become increasingly resentful of the high-handed behaviour of the Shi'ite fundamentalists. During the first few months of 1986 North financed a forty-man Druze rescue team.

The captors, however, were expecting a rescue attempt and started deliberately false rumours about the location of the hostages. Each day the American embassy in Beirut received offers of information. Every snippet of street gossip had to be checked out. Most of the reports were either outdated or erroneous, but some were designed to mislead. Knowing what the captors were doing made the Americans even more cautious.

An indication of the mood of frustration gripping officials was an attempt by General Dick Secord to persuade the Iranians to tell him where the hostages were being held. Secord had become operations manager for Oliver North, arranging both shipments to the Contras in Nicaragua and arms sales to the Iranians. During 1986 he met a variety of Iranian intermediaries. He believed the Iranians were cynical enough to betray their allies in Hezballah, and tried to get them to tell him the buildings where the hostages were being held. The intermediaries claimed not to know. Why Secord thought that Iran would want to aid a rescue mission when the hostages were bringing them such rich rewards was never clear. It was an idea born out of desperation.

Disenchantment with the quality of intelligence coming out of Lebanon led, in December 1985, to the setting up of the Hostage Location Task Force. There had been a similar body before, but it was thought to be inefficient in drawing together the many strands of American intelligence. The task force was set up by the Operations Sub-Group, a cell within the White House which coordinated operations during crises.

The Hostage Location Task Force met weekly at CIA headquarters in Langley, Virginia. Its members were drawn from the National Security Agency, the CIA, the Pentagon, the Defence Intelligence Agency, the Drug Enforcement Administration and the FBI. The group was chaired by Charles Allen from the CIA, and each week it produced a bulletin which analysed the latest intelligence on the hostages. It reported where they were thought to be, what their health was and the mood of the captors, and it assessed the level of threat to their lives. The task force's main function was to see if there was sufficient intelligence to mount a rescue mission.

Some members of the administration were pushing for a rescue mission. They thought it would be 'good for the West if a few terrorist heads were cracked'. On at least two occasions American special forces, of battalion size, were placed on alert, although there was no forward deployment to the Middle East. Many of the personnel had been involved in planning a second rescue mission of the American hostages held in the embassy in Tehran in 1980.

Even if the necessary intelligence was to become available, opinion was divided as to the wisdom of going into Beirut. The Joint Chiefs of Staff were known to be sceptical. They had an abiding fear of hitting 'a dry place' – military jargon for finding the hostages had been moved. They were also scared of a unit becoming pinned down in the treacherous streets of West Beirut and having to extricate them under fire. Others, like General Secord, thought the circumstances for a rescue mission were 'better than average', provided the intelligence was good. The target was close to the sea, and in a city where most nights were punctuated by gunfire it would be some time before it was realized that an operation was underway.

Oliver North wasn't on the task force, although he was intimately involved in its activities and received its reports. He encouraged a major from the Defense Intelligence Agency to join it; Julius 'Chris' Christensen wrote a report every Friday, his first appearing on 3 January 1986. He examined a number of North's schemes and travelled to Europe, introducing himself to various dubious characters with the words: 'I'm the man from Mr Goode', which was North's codename. He was fairly damning of some of the characters whom North was using. He characterized two Drug Enforcement agents as 'street toughs in camelhair coats' who were 'street smart but not very knowledgeable . . . in any way, shape or form, about the Middle East'.

On 24 April 1986, Major Christensen sent North an analysis of options to secure the release of the hostages. Among them were 'doing nothing, diplomatic efforts, Waite, paying ransom, and using force, unilaterally or multilaterally'. The details of this particular 'Waite Option' remains classified, but there was a plan to use Waite as the centrepiece of a rescue mission.

After Terry Waite had succeeded in meeting the captors in November 1985, his status changed: North referred to him as 'our only access to events in Lebanon'. Having offered Waite a tracking device for his own protection, the intelligence community saw other possibilities in the humanitarian mission of the Anglican envoy. A plan began to take shape. It never achieved the status of an official option, but it was discussed by Oliver North and within the CIA.

Terry Waite would be encouraged to return to Beirut, tempting the captors to meet him by announcing he had a deal on the Kuwaiti prisoners. Before they could be released, he would tell the captors, he needed to have a face-to-face meeting with all the hostages to ensure they were in good health. Waite's movements would be monitored by a military team from Intelligence Support Activity (ISA). If it was confirmed that all the hostages were together, American special forces and the allies in the Lebanese capital would move in shortly after Waite had left his meeting. Waite unwittingly would have served as a beacon for a rescue mission.

A member of ISA said such an attack would only have taken place if there was already extensive intelligence on the location, the number of guards, their back-ups and the weapons at their disposal. The chances of the plan succeeding were not rated highly. The captors had shown they were wary of intermediaries. Terry Waite had been stripped on one occasion and forced to attend a meeting draped in a sheet. The captors were also primed for a rescue attempt. Father Jenco said that, whenever there was a noise around the building, the guards were immediately in the room with 'guns at your head'.

The plan was considered highly dangerous for Terry Waite. It is unclear what, if anything, Waite would have been told. One of those who discussed the operation said they were aware of Waite's likely objections. 'I'd have liked to think that Waite would have been informed of his role,' he said guardedly. He could not, however, be certain that Waite would have been told.

When interviewed, Ambassador Eugene Douglas denied it was ever a serious option. 'There were discussions about many, many, many things. Would it be a formal contingency plan? No.'

'But it was an option discussed by members of the administration?' he was asked.

'It was one of the five hundred topics that came on to a table during a discussion.'

In their book *Best Laid Plans*, David Martin and John Walcott say there was another plan to use Waite as a lure. In 1986, the administration was planning to bomb Libya. Oliver North wanted to ensure that Colonel Qadaffi was in his compound in Tripoli when the planes struck. The plan, as he explained it to the administration's Crisis Pre-planning Group, was for Terry Waite, who had met the Libyan leader before, to request a meeting with him to seek his help in freeing the hostages in the Lebanon. Waite would then depart, leaving him (Qadaffi) at his headquarters. The envoy would not be told that he was being used to set up Qadaffi's assassination.

Both ideas were far-fetched, but they were indicative of

how Terry Waite had come to be seen. While lip service was being paid to respecting his independence, in practice he was regarded as an asset. An NSC official said that Oliver North 'ran Terry Waite like an agent although he wasn't operational.' Even a former Director of Central Intelligence as fastidious and as opposed to illegality as Admiral Stansfield Turner recognized the potential of a figure like Waite. 'I think you use people like Terry Waite,' he said. 'You use almost anybody who has access and some reasonably good intention.'

Waite never knew of the plan to use him to locate the hostages. It may never have gone much beyond North's fertile mind and its penchant for special operations. But there were other risks, less recognizable, in keeping company with North. It put Waite in touch with the world of intelligence, where things are rarely what they seem.

Meetings, however innocent, could always be interpreted differently. In Cyprus, Terry Waite would go to see Howell Sasser, the Dean of the Anglican Cathedral, and discuss Church affairs with him. Sasser was an Episcopalian priest, but he also happened to be the American military attaché on the island, with responsibility for arranging helicopters in and out of Beirut.

Terry Waite knew he was of interest to the intelligence community but was confident he could meet with such people and yet remain sacrosanct. He understood there were dangers but he was unwilling to abandon his mission. Eugene Douglas saw the struggle going on inside; a struggle made more intense by a natural fascination as to how North's world, with its hidden layers, actually worked. 'It was not in an improper way,' said Ambassador Douglas, 'but much as millions of readers are drawn to the pages of spy novels. As an envoy Terry Waite was able to witness first hand many of the ploys and strategems of the grey world, the 'wilderness of mirrors'. It was natural he would be interested. Who wouldn't be?'

Any association with the intelligence community, however understandable, was potentially perilous for it risked eroding Terry Waite's independence, so essential to his survival. In the end the danger would come, less from his being compromised by some covert operation, but more from his being perceived as belonging in the American camp. For in the Middle East perception is often mistaken for reality.

THE SECRET TRIP

Oliver North always saw a bright tomorrow. After the delivery of missiles to Iran in February had failed to produce a hostage, many officials would have been disillusioned. Not so North, for whom every failure had a silver lining. The Iranian contact whom he had been talking to in Europe had promised that the hostages would be freed if the Americans agreed to hold a meeting in Tehran with the Iranian leadership. It was proposed that, following the arrival of the US delegation in the Iranian capital, the hostages would be released.

North and other administration officials were enthusiastic. A top-level meeting promised a new era of US–Iranian relations, the original excuse for starting the arms sales. No sooner had the details of the meeting been agreed than the Iranian official threw in the small matter that the delegation should bring with them spare parts for Hawk missiles. 'It was like dealing with rug merchants in a bazaar,' said one State Department official.

Admiral Poindexter, the National Security Adviser, reacted sharply to the change of plan. He sent North a memo: 'There are not to be any parts delivered until all the hostages are free in accordance with the plan that you laid out for me before. None of this half shipment before any are released crap. It is either all or nothing. Also you may tell them that the President is getting very annoyed at their continual stalling. He will not agree to any more changes in the plan.'

By mid-May the arrangements for the Tehran meeting had been finalized. Manucher Ghorbanifar, the intermediary, promised that they would be meeting the most powerful figures in the Iranian leadership. He named Prime Minister Musavi; the Speaker of the Iranian Parliament, Ali Akhbar

Rafsanjani; President Khamen'ei; and possibly Ayatollah Khomeini's son, Ahmed. The US plane would carry as many spare parts as it could. When the hostages were released, the remainder of the Hawk missile parts would be flown directly from Israel to Iran. The mission was set for 25 May.

The American delegation to Tehran was led by Robert McFarlane, the former National Security Adviser. He was accompanied by North; Howard Teicher from the National Security Council; George Cave, a retired CIA official; and the Israeli Amiram Nir. Some travelled using aliases: Nir posed as an American; Howard Teicher as an Irishman called Tim McGann from Dingle.

Expectations were high. Robert McFarlane compared the mission to Henry Kissinger's historic meeting with Premier Chou En-lai that paved the way for US–Chinese reconciliation. He believed that Iran and the United States could be on the verge of restoring a friendship that had been soured during the final days of the Shah. He also expected that the hostage affair would at last be settled. North, too, thought the hostages would be freed. He alerted the military hospital in Wiesbaden and put the US embassy in Beirut on standby. A press kit had been assembled at the White House and Terry Waite alerted.

As always, North was concerned that the captors in Beirut were not left out. He was fearful, with good reason, that at the last moment they would baulk at releasing their assets. Throughout the entire period of the negotiations with Iran, North always attempted to sweeten the pot for Hezballah when a deal was imminent. He had been nudging the Kuwaitis to make a gesture on behalf of the seventeen prisoners. His intermediary was 'Spiro', the man who made arrangements for Terry Waite in Beirut. 'Spiro', using his connections with the Kuwaiti princes, persuaded the Kuwaitis to allow the prisoners to write to their relatives in the Lebanese capital.

On 15 May, North met Samir Habiby at his office in Washington. North mentioned the letters and discussed ways of getting them to Beirut. He was also hopeful that the Kuwaitis would agree to include some photographs of the prisoners: the captors in Beirut believed their relatives were being badly treated, and pictures would be a way of reassuring them. There were reports at the time that the prisoners were too ill to write. Letters and pictures were one of the things that Terry Waite, on a humanitarian level, had offered the captors.

North received three letters from the Kuwaiti prisoners addressed to their relatives in Beirut. They were written on Red Cross paper. North asked Waite to deliver them. Although it was a minor gesture it would indicate to the captors that he had not forgotten their demands. Waite went to Cyprus and was flown by helicopter to Beirut. North, with his fondness for code-names, had begun referring to Waite as 'Superman'. In his diary, he wrote 'Superman go to that location.' The operation was not without its risks. The last time Waite had been in Beirut the captors had warned him not to return. The intention, on this occasion, was for him to meet a trusted intermediary.

Having delivered his letters, Waite remained on standby. North, without disclosing his forthcoming visit to the Iranian capital, had told him that the release of hostages was likely. On May 25, North wrote: 'All quiet in BRT (Beirut). TW (Terry Waite) waiting/praying. Will take no further action/ fully cooperative.'

In the planning for the mission to Tehran, North envisaged a futher role for Terry Waite. North had his own optimistic timetable of events. Twenty-four hours after they arrived in Tehran the captors in Beirut would release the hostages. Eight hours later, 240 spare parts would be delivered to the Iranians. Four days later, a C-141 aircraft would deliver two HAWK radar systems to Tehran via Israel. Further spare parts would arrive by boat at the Iranian port of Bandar Abbas at the end of May. North was aware that the Iranians might not accept his timetable. It would involve them trading their assets before they had received all the arms. So he had an alternative. The hostages would be moved to the Iranian capital. Terry Waite would join them in Tehran and stay with them until the arms deal was complete. What Waite would have been told about why he was biding his time in the Iranian capital is unclear. There was also the risk that the Iranians might not honour the deal and Waite could have found himself added to the hostages. In any event the scheme was unrealistic. There was no evidence the Iranians wanted the hostages in Iran, as North was later to acknowledge in his testimony before Congress. 'One of our proposals was to take a European who had been engaged in this effort, the humanitarian effort, and have him go to Tehran and have all the hostages received there. The Iranians said: "For heaven's sake the last thing in the world we want is all the hostages here." This is not our doing. These people [the captors] have a philosophical loyalty, but are not necessarily in control in Tehran.' Whatever his later reflections, North was about to witness for himself the potential for duplicity and misunderstanding in trading with the Iranians.

The Congressional committee which investigated the Iran—Contra affair described the mission to Iran as 'heroic and very foolish'. McFarlane, North and Teicher were party, between them, to many of America's intelligence secrets and would have made invaluable hostages. They had no guarantees of safe conduct from the Iranian government, and the State Department in Washington didn't even know of the visit. Later, Ghorbanifar was to reveal that the man in Iran who was handling their visit had also been responsible for the kidnapping of the CIA agent William Buckley.

When they arrived at Tehran airport confusion reigned. There was no one to meet them. They waited for over an hour while Revolutionary guards eyed them nervously. McFarlane, who had been expecting to be received by high-level Iranians, cabled Washington on the scene he encountered. 'It may be best for us to try to picture what it would be like,' he said, 'if after a nuclear attack, a surviving tailor became Vice President; a recent grad student became Secretary of State; and a bookie became the interlocutor for all discourse with foreign countries.'

Matters did not improve when they reached the Hilton Hotel. McFarlane insisted that the hostages be freed first, before any spare parts were handed over; but the Iranians wanted to have the weapons first. They claimed there had been no agreement that the initial move should be made by the captors in Beirut. And so it went on. For two days the Americans were dealing with low-level functionaries.

McFarlane was furious and withdrew from the discussions, leaving North, Teicher and Cave to handle the negotiations.

Like age-old hagglers in a bazaar, the Iranians came up with a whole new set of conditions. They had been in touch with the captors in Beirut, who had demanded the following: 'Israel to withdraw from the Golan Heights and south Lebanon. Lahad must return to East Beirut, the prisoners in Kuwait must be freed, and all the expenses paid for hostage taking.' The Americans were taken aback. None of these demands was in their gift and, even if they were, they could not be agreed to. As regards paying the captors' bills, it was an extraordinary piece of cheek.

McFarlane threatened to leave. Several hours later the Iranians reported that the captors had dropped all their demands except for the release of the seventeen prisoners in Kuwait. McFarlane refused to intervene with the Kuwaitis, saying that US policy was to respect the judicial process of other nations. North was less resolute. His notebooks reveal his desperation. He listed arguments that might appeal to his Iranian hosts. Among them was: '– Great admiration for courage of Iranian fighting men. – Because I am a Christian I understand and believe that when one dies in faith he will spend eternity in a far better place.'

But North recognized that these blandishments would not be enough. The problem of the Kuwaiti prisoners would have to be addressed. 'We must try,' he wrote, 'to get guarantees that the Kuwaiti prisoners will be released in the future.' Later, at four in the morning, North returned to the Iranians with a form of words which he hoped might satisfy them. 'The United States' would be willing to issue a statement to the effect, that they would make 'every effort through and with international organizations and other third parties in a humanitarian effort to achieve the release of and just and fair treatment for Shi'ites held in confinement as soon as possible.' North went further than he was permitted; even so, it was not enough.

Faced with a breakdown of the mission, the Iranians kept changing their story. The captors, they said, could not arrange the release of the hostages in time. A short while later they returned with a compromise: they would release two hostages immediately. McFarlane rejected the compromise and boarded the plane for Israel, pausing only to tell the official that 'the lack of trust will endure for a long time.'

The mission to Tehran should have been a moment of truth for the administration. Ghorbanifar, the Iranian intermediary, had proved duplicitous. Both sides had been lied to. The idea that a group of Iranian moderates was interested in better relations with the United States was exposed as wishful thinking. The Iranians wanted weapons for their war with Iraq.

The mission also revealed misunderstandings and a lack of trust between the Americans themselves. General Dick Secord, who had attended many of the pre-mission meetings, claimed: 'There was no Iranian agreement to produce all the hostages at the time of the meeting in Tehran.' Yet that was the clear impression of at least two of those involved. Before the trip, Howard Teicher had enquired of North what the plans were for a rescue mission if the Iranians detained them. 'Don't worry,' North told him. 'Everything is sorted out.' Later, Teicher discovered that nothing had been arranged. There were no rescue plans. North had brought suicide pills for himself and McFarlane, but no provision had been made for the others. 'He lied to me,' said Teicher ruefully.

McFarlane, who until this moment had regarded North like a son, believed he had tried to negotiate with the Iranians behind his back. When he returned to Washington he wrote to Admiral Poindexter, 'In Ollie's interest I would get him transferred or sent to Bethesda for disability review board.' Bethesda was the naval hospital where North had gone in 1974, suffering from emotional stress after serving in Vietnam. But North had made himself indispensable, and he remained in charge of the hostage issue.

Terry Waite had stayed out of sight in the American embassy compound in East Beirut whilst North had been haggling with the Iranians. He hadn't told his colleague, Samir Habiby, about returning to Lebanon. Habiby, who was abroad at the time on Church business, learnt about it later. He was very unhappy and served notice on his friend that if it happened again he would 'no longer have my cooperation'.

The discovery of Waite's travels marked the moment of greatest doubt for Habiby. Although he liked and trusted Oliver North, he didn't want Waite dealing directly with the White House. He felt strongly that, if the Episcopalian Church was managing his mission, then North should pass all requests through him. Although he was politically close to North and shared many of his instincts, Habiby was beset by a nagging fear that he might involve Waite in an operation that could embarrass the Church.

On 23 June, Habiby went again to see North at his office in the Executive Office Building in Washington, to 'ensure the independence of the Church'. 'We should have known about this,' he told North, referring to Waite's secret trip to Lebanon. The White House official looked hurt, his eyes widening into an expression of injured innocence.

'Samir,' North said, 'there are times when these things happen. This was an exception.'

'In future,' said Habiby, 'I want these things routed through me.'

North agreed, assuring Habiby of his concern to protect the Church. He was a man who cared deeply about his faith and the Church. He cared, too, about serving his country. Occasionally the two would conflict, but he had a personality which coped with contradictions. It made him sincere but dangerous. Within a few weeks he would be needing Terry Waite again.

12

'GUESS PRAYER WORKS!'

During his nineteen months in captivity, Father Martin Jenco had found his guards unpredictable. Some were mere boys, aged eighteen or nineteen, hardened by war but strangely innocent. Their education had been minimal and they willingly agreed to watch over a ragbag collection of foreigners for $25 to $50 a month. Father Jenco detected an embarrassment at having to detain a priest. 'Some of them really needed to be stroked,' he said.

Father Jenco, who had headed the Beirut office of the Catholic Relief Services, was middle-aged, with a grey beard, thinning hair, and a face lined by the tribulations of long years of missionary work. His kidnapping in January 1985 had been a mistake. The captors thought he was Joe Curtin, an American relief worker. Their error only briefly concerned them. Jenco was also an American and therefore, in their view, equally suspect. There could be no greater example of the void in understanding between the Shi'ite militants of Beirut and the West that they regarded this spiritually tough yet self-effacing man as a CIA agent.

At first he had been chained to a wall and blindfolded, but his guards had been kind — even gentle. But after another hostage, Jeremy Levin, escaped on Valentine's Day 1985, friendliness turned to savagery. They became threatening, violent. 'Guns were everywhere,' said Jenco. The hostages were moved from one building to another. When he commented on some makeshift wiring he was told the building had been primed with explosives. Haunted by the fear that the Americans might launch a rescue mission, the captors locked Father Jenco in a clothes closet for two months.

'They didn't know how to take care of old people,' he said later. 'We had needs they couldn't even comprehend, like going to the toilet. You had to go to the toilet when they told you to go, but your body sometimes doesn't function that way. And you try to explain that to them.' For almost two months Father Jenco wasn't able to wash himself. The only clothing he was given was two sets of underwear.

The nature of their captivity was to change again after the death of William Buckley in June 1985. Although the CIA thought their Station Chief had been tortured to death, Father Jenco believes Buckley died through neglect. For days he was vomiting and delirious, his cries of agony mixing with absurdly lucid recollections: Jenco recalls him calmly ordering a poached egg on toast. The guards were unmoved by his suffering, less out of callousness than ignorance. Blind-folded, Jenco and two other hostages listened to Buckley die. 'There was a moment when the note of the coughing changed. We all knew he was dying.'

The guards did not acknowledge Buckley's death but their attitude changed. A doctor visited and they became more considerate. The hostages were moved into the same room and their morale improved. 'Once they put us all together we had a kind of force,' said Jenco. 'Whenever there were confrontations we could band together.'

On 25 July 1986, the guards entered the room and told them they were going to be transferred to another prison. They gave the curious reason that conditions had become unhealthy. It was true that his room had been sealed and there was little air, but it had been that way for some time.

'They brought in new clothes and told us to dress and to take nothing with us. No utensils, no water bottle, no urine bottle.' Father Jenco managed to slip a Bible inside his jacket.

His fellow hostages, David Jacobsen and Thomas Sutherland, filed out first. As Father Jenco fell in behind them he was pushed to one side and they let Terry Anderson follow the others.

'When the guards came back into the room,' recalls Father Jenco, 'they said: "Sit down." My first response was: "Are you going to kill me?" They said: "No, you're going home."' Having told him he was going to be freed, the guards left the room.

Jenco sat back numb, as if by thinking he risked the guards

changing their minds. Then, as the reality of liberty dawned
on him, he recited from the Psalms. 'I love the Lord because
he hears my prayers and answers them . . . Death stared me
in the face. I was frightened and sad. Then I cried: Lord save
me! . . . Now I can relax. For the Lord has done this wonderful miracle for me. He has saved me from death, my eyes
from tears, my feet from stumbling. I shall live!'

As he waited, the air grew hotter. It was high summer and
he was being held at the top of a nine-storey building. He
wondered whether his captors had left the building, but he
hadn't heard the whine of the elevator and he suspected they
were still there. He was afraid to move in case he incurred
the anger of the guards. Some time later they reappeared.
They had been video-taping David Jacobsen reading a prepared statement.

Father Jenco asked them why he was being released. 'We're
setting you free,' they told him, 'because we know your
health is not good.'

They opened the door of what had become his cell, took
him down in the elevator, bundled him into the back of a
van and drove to a garage. It was three in the morning and
the guards told him to sleep. He lay down on a piece of
cardboard. Two hours later he was woken. A guard named
Said told him to take two Dyazide pills for high blood
pressure.

'They're not going to do the same thing again,' Jenco
thought. He remembered an earlier journey when he had
been bound from head to foot with tape. The guard repeated
his instruction to take the pills.

'They're diuretic,' said Jenco. 'They'll make me go to the
toilet.'

'Who cares?' said Said.

'I knew what was coming,' recalls Jenco. 'They tape you
up like a mummy, starting from the bottom.'

As they began winding the tape around him, Ahab, one of
the younger guards, came over and pressed a small cross into
the palm of his hand. It was a gesture of humanity, a shard
of kindness in the midst of stone-hearted cruelty. Fundamentalism bred its own schizophrenia. Hostage taking, they
believed, furthered the Islamic Revolution and brought

closer the day of justice. But every so often, as if during an interval in the chanting, they seemed to glimpse their own barbarity and wanted to make amends.

'They tape your mouth until it's sealed up,' said Jenco. 'The only place from which you can breathe is from your nostrils.'

He was slid into a compartment near the bottom of a truck, where they store the spare tyres.

'It's a very frightening experience. You're beneath there, you have no control over your body. You fly all over the place. When you hit bumps the gas comes in and the fumes. You feel as if you're going to be asphyxiated.'

During the six-hour journey, Father Jenco used his cross like a knife and cut the tape. He was able to free his hands and prevent his body bouncing against the side of the truck. But the road was rutted and uneven, and he was too frail to protect himself against every bump. His body flew up and crashed against the ceiling of the compartment. His nose started to bleed and the blood began coagulating, making breathing even more difficult. He began reciting the pilgrim's prayer, 'Lord Jesus have mercy on me.' He discovered the words helped control his breathing.

'If one panics in that kind of situation I think one would die,' he said.

Eventually he was pulled from beneath the truck and his bindings were removed. He was transferred to the back of a car and ordered to lie on the floor. They drove for about ten minutes and then dumped him beside the road.

During captivity his guards had sometimes asked, 'Father, is there anything you want?'

'I would say: "Yes. I want a taxi cab to go home."'

That July morning they gave him the equivalent of $2 in Lebanese pounds and said, 'Here, catch your taxi. You can go anywhere you want.'

Jenco asked them, 'Which way do I go? Put your hand over my head and point. I won't look.' The captors pointed to the left, to a small village, and then were gone.

'I sat there for a while,' said Father Jenco. 'I hadn't seen the sky or the earth. So I just sat and enjoyed God's lovely gifts.' His first moments of freedom seemed like an eternity.

When he got up he decided, incredibly, to try and catch a bus back to Beirut. He had a plan to reach the Vatican embassy.

'I started walking down the road and cars were going by. I didn't realize what I looked like – I still had cotton on my head, tape hanging off my body and my zipper was broken. I was carrying a little plastic bag with David [Jacobsen's] video tape.'

Father Jenco approached the village and asked in Arabic if there was a church, because he thought a priest would help him. A man pointed up the hill and he started to walk. After months cooped up Jenco moved awkwardly. A group of children were coming down the slope and he enquired again whether there was a church. They nodded shyly and ran off. Shortly afterwards, a car came by and offered him a lift. The driver spoke English. Father Jenco gave no explanation for his appearance, neither did he say he was a freed hostage. He just asked to be dropped at the church.

'Why do you want to go to a church?' asked the driver. 'There are no Christians here. They've all fled.'

Jenco became apprehensive, recalling how villages had changed hands during the civil war. He thanked the driver and continued walking. Using some of the money the captors had given him, he bought a Pepsi and began asking the villagers how he could catch a bus or taxi to Beirut. They either didn't know, or they chose not to give assistance to a bedraggled stranger. Near the church he did meet a Christian who was passing through, and asked him to help. The man said no, got back in his car and left.

Jenco was becoming desperate as he stumbled around the village, and begged a young Moslem to assist him. The man didn't want to talk, but indicated that Jenco was to accompany him.

'It was very strange because he wouldn't allow me to walk side by side with him. I had to follow him. And he brought me down to the police station.'

Father Jenco had been released near Lake Karaoun in the lower Bekaa valley. The police didn't know what to do with him. For an hour and a half he just sat there, his anxiety growing. They allowed him to use the station toilet, and it was then that he realized what he looked like.

'I just burst into tears,' he said. 'The utter frustration of it all. For a man to cry publicly, you know, they just can't cope with that. So they brought me in this lovely Shi'ite woman and I told her my story. And she says: "Father, you don't have to worry, you're safe." And within five minutes the Syrians were there.'

To his surprise, the Syrian soldiers were expecting him. They took him first to the headquarters of Syrian military intelligence in Aanjar, and then shortly afterwards they left for Damascus. As he was passing through the checkpoint on the Syrian border, one of the officers was reading a newspaper. He came over to the vehicle. 'Look,' he said, 'here's your picture,' pointing at the paper. 'You look different.' Word of his release was out.

'What does it say?' called out Jenco.

'You've been released because of poor health.'

Jenco was keen to be delivered to the American embassy, because the captors had warned him not to allow David Jacobsen's video to fall into the hands of the Syrians. The bond between the hostages was such that Jenco would have done anything to protect the tape. The captors had also told him to tell the Syrians that Hezballah didn't appreciate them very much. Father Jenco decided it best to forget that instruction.

Coincidentally, Peggy Say, the sister of Terry Anderson, one of the other hostages, happened to be in the Syrian capital at the time. She had been tireless in her quest for news of her brother to the point that officials in Washington had come to dread her call. She soon heard in Damascus that a hostage had been freed. When Father Jenco learnt that she was in the city, his first question was 'Where's Terry Anderson's sister?' Jenco embraced her warmly, but his exuberance, which she wanted to share, was like a cruelty to her.

Jenco had been worried about the Syrians taking the videotape because the captors had said to him that if it was not aired on television before sunset the hostages would die. Despite his best efforts the Syrians had found the tape. After much pleading it was handed back to the American Ambassador. He had no means of playing it, and, not being certain

Above: Benjamin Weir after being freed 19 September 1985.

Below: Terry Waite with Father Jenco in London 1 August 1986.

Left: Oliver North arriving at Larnaca airport in Cyprus 2 November 1986.

Right: Waite and Jacobsen arrive in Wiesbaden from Cyprus 3 November 1986.

Below: Terry Waite at a press conference in Wiesbaden saying he would not return to Beirut 3 November 1986.

Above: Waite with the Archbishop of Canterbury and the released hostages (*from left to right*) Jenco, Jacobsen and Weir in London on 17 November 1986.

Left: A pensive Waite in Beirut on 12 January 1987.

Right: The net closes in, Waite with his Druze guards the day before his disappearance.

Above and below: Terry Waite with then Vice-President Bush

Left: Oliver North being sworn in before the Iran-Contra Committee July 1987.

Right: Bob Dutton

Below: Samir Habiby

Left: Eugene Douglas

how to get the tape transmitted, phoned the Associated Press. Time was now short and AP asked the representatives of the American networks to gather at the Sheraton hotel. They soon discovered there was a problem. The tape had been recorded on a different system to that used in Damascus and would have to be copied before it could be sent to the United States. As the evening approached, producers and television engineers became increasingly desperate as they failed to find the necessary piece of equipment. All of this was observed by Peggy Say who was as anxious as everyone else to see the tape, believing it might contain news of her brother. Finally it was decided that they should go to the satellite station where the tape could be transmitted directly to the United States. When the pictures came up there was David Jacobsen reciting the captors' mixture of threats and demands. One of those at the station recalls turning round and seeing Peggy Say sitting by the stairwell, heartbroken.

After Father Jenco had finished a round of Syrian courtesy calls, and had his photograph taken with beaming Syrian officials, he was taken to the home of the American ambassador. The Syrians were always keen that freed hostages left Lebanon via Damascus. There was international credit, they believed, in their being seen as having helped in a hostage release; it was a useful riposte to those who branded Syria a terrorist state. Some Americans thought the Syrians were so keen on these public relations opportunities that they would frustrate a release unless they were guaranteed a role. Much as American hostages had become a commodity to be traded, so there was value in their releases. A variety of parts had to be choreographed. Credit had to be awarded to those whose role had been minimal, while the real players had to be placed in the wings out of sight.

That evening the Ambassador's wife and her staff arranged a celebration picnic for Father Jenco and invited a few friends. 'It was nice,' said Jenco, 'to see for the first time in nineteen months women and children. I think that's what I really needed – a picnic.'

That evening Terry Waite arrived from Jordan, where he had been attending to another matter. He had become involved with the Palestine hospital in Jordan, which was trying to establish a centre for neuro-surgery. Three years earlier the Primates of the Anglican Communion had formed a committee to raise funds for the centre which would treat, among others, children and refugees from southern Lebanon. Terry Waite had undertaken to act as a fundraiser. The previous year he had become honorary chairman of the YMCA's development wing, raising money for feeding centres in Sudan and Ethiopia, for training projects in India, and for supporting schemes which brought Lebanese Christians and Moslems together. It was to be one of the tragedies of the hostage affair that his mission would ultimately end in captivity and controversy when he and the Church had built important links to the Palestinians and other disadvantaged groups in the Middle East.

At the time of Father Jenco's release, Waite and Ambassador Eugene Douglas were in Jordan celebrating the anniversary of the hospital. Waite had been contacted by Oliver North and told that a hostage release was likely. If it happened, he wanted the Anglican envoy to move immediately to Damascus. North had learnt of the impending release from Amiram Nir who had been tipped off by Israeli intelligence. The extent of Iranian control over the captors in Beirut was demonstrated in a series of cables, one of which was sent hours before Jenco's release. The Israeli Defence Forces intercepted a cable, timed Thursday July 25, midnight. It was from Headquarters Revolutionary Guards (intelligence) to HQ Revolutionary Guards Syria/Lebanon. 'To Mr Mehdi Najad: act immediately in the matter of ret.box which was given as the deposit of the subject of your mission; report immediately to center on the execution of this order.' If there was ever any doubt as to Iran's influence over the Western hostages, this cable dispelled it.

As soon as North knew that Father Jenco had been released to the Syrians, he called Waite and asked him to travel at once to Damascus. The US embassy in Amman arranged his travel details and his visa for Syria. When he arrived at the Ambassador's residence in Damascus he and Father Jenco embraced. But the priest found the conversation puzzling.

'That evening Terry shows up,' recalls Father Jenco,

and he said that he was waiting for me in Jordan and it was an interesting thing because he said to me: "You believe me, don't you?" Well, at that point in my life I would have believed anybody but I just wondered why the question was even being asked. You know, we had asked him to come and help us, so why shouldn't I believe him? It's a question that's always bothered me. It was just the wrong question at the wrong time, I suppose.

Over the next few days Father Jenco's appearances were to be elaborately stage-managed. Oliver North was anxious for Terry Waite to 'get in every picture'. It was decided that, before returning to the United States, Father Jenco should visit the Archbishop of Canterbury and the Pope, and that Terry Waite should accompany him. It would appear to the world that his release had been secured by the intervention of the Church.

Father Jenco became aware of the attention to public relations. 'One of the most important visuals that Terry wanted,' said Father Jenco, 'was a visual of himself as a religious person. That he'd been sent by a leader of a religious faith on humanitarian grounds.'

Waite and Jenco flew together from Damascus to the United States air force hospital at Wiesbaden in West Germany. On his arrival, Jenco said how much he was looking forward to returning to his home state of Illinois: 'Chicago is a windy city, and I want to feel the wind on my face again.' At the hospital he was joined by eleven of his relatives. His brother John embraced him, saying through his tears, 'I love you, and please forgive me for anything that I have ever done wrong to you.'

Terry Waite also met Jenco's relatives. It was not an easy occasion. They wanted to talk about the months in captivity, but Waite was against such conversations. 'He was cautioning my family constantly to say nothing,' said Jenco. 'Sometimes he did get angry with them.' Eventually Father Jenco became a little paranoid with his own family, which marred the homecoming.

For a man who had just spent nineteen months in captivity Father Jenco had a hectic round of public engagements. He celebrated his first mass in freedom with the Servite brothers at St Mary's in London. Afterwards he saw Dr Runcie, the Archbishop of Canterbury, and the press was invited. He was publicly reunited with Ben Weir, the hostage who had been released the previous summer. Then he and Terry Waite flew to Rome, where they had an audience with the Pope.

Father Jenco mentioned that apart from David Jacobsen's video message, he also had something to tell the Pope. Waite understood this to be a message from the captors, and asked the priest to say there was also a message for the Archbishop of Canterbury. He explained that this would enable him to make an appeal to the captors. Jenco, although surprised, agreed and duly referred to it at a press conference.

Waite then announced that confidential messages sent to the Pope and the Archbishop of Canterbury had been received with 'sympathy and understanding'. He refused to comment on their content. He went on to appeal to the captors to continue a direct dialogue with him. A solution could be found, he thought, 'based on the tenets common to Islam and Christianity'. He was ready to return to Beirut at any time. Although it was a way of appealing to the captors to meet him again, it also left the impression that he had been involved in Jenco's release.

In Beirut, the captors were baffled by these references to messages. Islamic Jihad put out a statement saying: 'We gave no messages to anybody, either secretly or openly.' They were clearly irritated by pious-sounding appeals, and threatened to kill the hostages unless their demands were met. They mentioned the prisoners in Kuwait. When questioned about the captors' statement, Waite said, 'What is clear is that Father Jenco had messages which he delivered.' The argument about messages he thought was the captors' way of keeping the hostage issue on the front pages.

Within the administration there was some debate as to how Father Jenco's release had been achieved. No arms shipment had preceded it. Some thought it was the work of Syria: a few weeks previously the Director of the CIA, William Casey, had had a secret meeting with President Assad of Syria at which the hostage crisis had been discussed. Oliver North was content to attribute Jenco's freedom to the ill-

fated mission to Tehran, and wrote to Robert McFarlane:
'The bottom line is that this is the direct result of your mission and neither the Syrians nor a nonexistent Casey trip had
anything to do with it.' Admiral Poindexter believed that the
Iranians had finally been convinced to make a 'humanitarian
gesture'.

But it wasn't that simple. While Father Jenco was receiving
medical attention in Wiesbaden, Oliver North was a few
miles away meeting Ghorbanifar in Frankfurt. It soon
became apparent that the Iranian middleman had had to
make various promises to get the Iranians to order Jenco's
release. Without authorization, he had told Tehran that if a
hostage was freed Washington would deliver the remainder
of the weapons that were part of the deal discussed during
the Tehran mission.

When Poindexter heard of this undertaking, he dismissed
it as a 'story cooked up by Ghorbanifar'. 'Of course,' he
wrote in an internal memo, 'we have not agreed to any such
plan.' But after his meeting in Frankfurt, North argued for
agreeing to Ghorbanifar's deal. 'Despite our earlier and current protestations that we want all hostages before we deliver
anything, this is clearly not the way they wish to proceed,'
he wrote. 'They see clearly the ball is now in our court.'
What North was suggesting was precisely what McFarlane
had turned down two months previously – a sequence of
hostage releases in exchange for weapons deliveries. North
once again won the battle with the argument that had proved
so powerful at the start of the year. 'Bottom line,' he wrote,
'is that if we want to prevent the death of one of the three
remaining hostages, we are going to have to do something.'

There was little speculation in the press about why Father
Jenco had been released. Most papers, seeing Waite and the
freed priest together, drew the obvious conclusion. 'Hero
Waite helps free priest,' said one headline. 'Thank God for
Mr Fixit Terry Waite,' said another. Other papers were more
cautious, observing that less information than usual had
emerged about the Anglican envoy's role. In fact, there is no
evidence that Terry Waite played any part in Father Jenco's
release.

The American administration was cynically using an envoy

of the Church of England to disguise an arms deal. Robert
Oakley, who was Director of the Office for Counter-
terrorism at the time, said, 'It was convenient in that people
tended to focus their attention upon Terry Waite rather than
upon other sorts of negotiations or dealings that were going
on.' Michael Ledeen thought North was delighted to have
discovered Waite and to have seen that he could play this
role. 'In so far as it was always possible to give credit for
hostage releases to Terry Waite, it made it much easier for
North to conceal the actual operation that he was running.'

Terry Waite did ponder on why the hostages were being
released. In a conversation with Samir Habiby and Marion
Dawson he speculated that something else must be going on
behind the scenes. They even wondered whether the Israelis
were supplying the Iranians with arms in exchange for securing the freedom of Jews living in Tehran. They didn't realize
how close to the truth they were: there was a trade going on,
but at the instigation of the Americans.

After Jenco's release, Terry Waite was pointedly asked at
a news conference what had secured the priest's freedom.
Waite paused, looked down, and said, 'Wouldn't you like to
know?' and then chuckled. What he didn't do was dispel the
widely held belief that his efforts had been responsible. When
questioned about his own role, he said, 'For security reasons
I cannot comment.'

Why, then, was he willing effectively to take the credit?
He often said that it took many levers to free a hostage and
it was difficult sometimes to determine what was the deciding
factor. It is quite possible that he believed the captors had
decided to make a humanitarian gesture and that his efforts,
in some indeterminate way, had played a part.

He also felt that it would enhance the reputation of the
Anglican Church, enabling it to become involved in other
crises and areas of conflict. He had a vision of an activist
Church, having worldwide concerns. Ambassador Douglas,
who was with him in Jordan before Father Jenco was
released, believes this may have been his prime motivation.
'He was engaged in a larger exercise ... of creating,
revivifying in our time the role of the Church and the Anglican Communion. If there was a hostage being released, Waite

wished to be there, to be seen as someone who cared.'

It was a vision built on shaky ground. Inevitably, sooner or later, the real reasons why hostages were being released would emerge. When it became clear that the Church's role had been largely cosmetic, its reputation – far from being enhanced – would suffer, and he himself risked being seen as a dupe or a publicity seeker. But a greater danger lay with the captors in Beirut. They knew he had not been involved in Jenco's release. They had received instructions from Tehran. They must have puzzled over his role and his relationship with the American government. These doubts would later count against Terry Waite.

Father Jenco, after his tiring round of Christian photo opportunities, arrived at the White House. After the religious leaders, Ronald Reagan would get his thanks as well. While there, Jenco bumped into George Shultz, the hard-headed Secretary of State. He paused on seeing the freed hostage. 'Guess prayer works, huh?' was his only comment, and he walked away.

13
THE ANGLICAN DR KISSINGER

When Father Jenco flew to the United States, Terry Waite left his side. The picture of the Anglican envoy with American politicians was one 'visual' not needed. A few days later Waite flew to San Francisco with the Archbishop of Canterbury for a Church conference.

By now he was a celebrity. The television pictures of him with Father Jenco had brought him 'name recognition'. In American terms, he had arrived. At the airport he was surrounded by reporters and camera crews from local television stations. Despite the fact that he was in the company of the Archbishop as well as the Presiding Bishop of the Episcopal Church, the press's sole interest was in Waite and the hostages. It was an example of just how much the Church's reputation had become tied up with his mission. 'I want to make a direct appeal to Islamic Jihad,' he said on his arrival, 'to let the Christian Church continue to participate in finding a solution to the problems which face the people of Lebanon . . . I believe that by faith in God this problem will be solved.' This statement, which only repeated what he had said on many previous occasions, was faithfully reported. There was no response from the captors in Beirut.

While in San Francisco Waite asked a colleague from the Episcopal Church whether he could recommend a restaurant. After a few telephone calls, the Reverend Charles Cesaretti made a booking at Stars, a fashionable venue overlooking the city. They were, however, over half an hour late in arriving and all the tables were taken. 'We obviously needed to throw ourselves on the mercy of the maître d',' said Cesaretti. 'As soon as we walked in, I realized that this was not a problem at all. He recognized Terry at once. We were immediately seated. I felt rather sorry for the people who lost their booking.'

It wasn't only the restaurant owner who recognized Waite.

People dined there in the hope of seeing 'stars', and signed photographs of the famous lined the walls. That evening the diners were not disappointed. 'People would come over to the table,' said Cesaretti. 'It is both a fascinating and disturbing phenomenon. It was awfully difficult to get through one's meal with people coming over wishing him well.'

In these mealtime expressions of support, Cesaretti glimpsed the deep reservoir of love and concern that the American people had for the hostages. It was the constituency that Ronald Reagan understood and whose instincts he shared. Terry Waite had gone to Lebanon on behalf of the hostages, and the American people appreciated that. Their processions to the table were not just indicative of a national obsession with fame; it was as if by befriending Terry Waite they were expiating America's failure to bring their fellow citizens home.

Waite handled the attention graciously, but Cesaretti became more thoughtful as the evening wore on. He realized just how much the Church had invested in the envoy's mission. If it were to go wrong, the consequences could be disastrous. Cesaretti was a very different person from Waite. He was an aesthete, an intellectual, a liberal theologian uncomfortable with the macho policies of the Reagan administration. Waite's close relationship with Oliver North troubled him, and he decided to mention it.

Cesaretti talked about the invasion of Grenada, the bombing of Libya and the arming of the Nicaraguan Contras. The Episcopal Church had taken a strong stand against each of them. These operations were run not by the State Department but by the White House, by the very people with whom Terry Waite was dealing. 'I shared it [the information] with Terry because it was possible he did not understand the nuances of the American system.'

Waite was guarded. He knew that Cesaretti had always been opposed to the Reagan administration, and told him so. As regards the Contras, Waite was on record as opposing military aid to them. He had also argued with Oliver North about the issue. Cesaretti pointed out that there was growing interest in Congress in the activities of North and the National Security Council. The Church had to be careful.

But Waite insisted that talking to White House officials didn't mean he supported their policies. He said what he would repeat many times in the future, that he was in charge of his own agenda. Cesaretti worried about the quality of advice the envoy was receiving; he thought the Church should provide more support and analysis. The conversation strained the relationship between the two men, and they would not meet again until November, after the Iran–Contra scandal had broken.

Terry Waite was receiving almost no advice from outside the small circle that assisted him; he was very discreet about discussing the hostage issue. One of his closest friends was Philip Turner, a professor at a New York seminary. 'I knew him as a friend and a very deep friend, but he kept things very close to his chest.' At his office in Lambeth Palace, Waite took no one into his confidence. His secretary, Stella Taylor, had only the vaguest knowledge of his activities. After he became a hostage, his diary had to be reassembled with the help of airline ticket stubs. Although he reported to Dr Runcie, the Archbishop was not involved in Terry Waite's day-to-day meetings; he had no idea how close his envoy had grown to Oliver North. The Anglican Church has only a skeletal staff and is ill equipped to support and supervise a wide-ranging brief such as Terry Waite's.

Through the Archbishop's office, Waite had access to the Foreign Office and would occasionally ask for a briefing on Lebanon. Officials quite deliberately kept their distance. British diplomats were told to be careful not to embarrass him by being seen with him. Senior officials in the Foreign Office had learnt by the summer of 1986 that arms were being traded to Iran. A British official in Washington had demanded an explanation from the administration, but no one thought of warning Waite. It is apparent from North's notebooks that the British Secret Intelligence Service, MI6, knew even more about the hostage deals, and were aware of Waite's role. They were not, however, in the habit of giving judgements on the advisability of close relationships with an official on the National Security Council staff.

Those who met Terry Waite were often baffled about his role and his authority. Brian Jenkins was a consultant to the

Rand Corporation and advised the Catholic Relief Services on the case of Father Jenco. When he met the Anglican envoy he was intrigued to know what he actually did.

'I once asked him,' said Jenkins. 'I said "What is it that you do, Terry?" He said, "I am the Archbishop of Canterbury's Dr Kissinger." It was an extraordinary statement. I thought it conjured up a man that had certainly no shortage of confidence in his own capabilities and his own knowledge of world affairs.' Jenkins knew that the Catholic Church was a major actor on the world scene and could boast of a Secretariat and a figure who really was a Foreign Minister or Secretary of State. He doubted, correctly, whether the Anglican Church had those resources.

In Britain Terry Waite was in demand as a celebrity: every good cause wanted his blessing. He soared above Trafalgar Square in a hot air balloon to launch an appeal for peace; earlier, he had parachuted into the grounds of a theological college for charity. He was a Christian action-man and the media embraced him. When he traded in his battered car for an MGB roadster, which had been specially rebuilt to cope with his large frame, it made the papers.

A television company asked him to host a six-part talk show. He agreed: having been interviewed so many times himself he regarded the task as 'a small diversion'. On his first programme the guest was Princess Anne; it was not a success. 'Would you say you were a good mother?' he asked deferentially. 'Is the monarchy as popular as it's ever been?' he probed on tiptoe. The reviews were savage. One paper called him 'a bearded blancmange'. Another described the programme as 'wholesome and substantial as sweet porridge oats and just as dull'. But some of the critics detected an obsession with himself and his own adventures. 'Self-effacement is not one of Waite's strong suits, we soon learned. He talked as much about himself as about his interviewee,' wrote one. Another column followed the same theme: 'Looking like a great St Bernard which had lost its brandy-barrel, Waite inspected his hands and started talking about himself.' When he interviewed the climber Chris Bonington, he kept making comparisons between climbing mountains and negotiating with terrorists.

The unflattering comments Waite laughed off. But some of his Church friends were disappointed at this departure into television. One clergyman, who had known Terry Waite when he was a young lay preacher, counselled against it. 'This is not for you, Terry,' he told him.

His yearning for a larger role was reflected in his vision of the Church offering an alternative diplomacy, independent of the narrow interests of nation-states. The idea was big, ill-defined and far removed from the parochial concerns of filling the empty pews on a Sunday. Many Church matters he found petty, small-minded and irritating. But the hostage issue was not just an open sesame for his dreams – it offered him a grand cause, a cause to which he became deeply committed.

The distress of the hostage families moved him. When he encountered official weariness with the subject, he championed the rights of the captive individual. People couldn't be written off or dismissed, he insisted, by comparing them to the daily toll from traffic accidents. The detention of priests and missionaries, as many of the hostages were, he saw as an insult to the Church, a challenge to the freedom of religious figures to move in troubled places free from harassment, a challenge to his own vision of the Church in the world. Brian Jenkins, who had been surprised by Waite's description of himself as the Archbishop's Dr Kissinger, was impressed, however, by his dedication. 'On a personal level he was certainly a man of deep conviction. He was dedicated, absolutely dedicated to getting those hostages out.'

This commitment was matched by Oliver North's. His determination was obsessional, driving him beyond the point of exhaustion. The hostages were an assignment, like one of the many missions he had been given in Vietnam. It was part of the Marine code that you never returned until the task had been completed. You owed that to your unit, to the Marines and finally to yourself. Loyalty – unswerving, occasionally blind – had been drilled into him. The hostages were but another mission: the continuation, in a different theatre, of the battle in Vietnam. Islamic Jihad belonged to the same dark, threatening, incomprehensible world as the Vietcong: foes who were anti-imperialist, barbaric, careless of life, their ideology sustaining itself on its hatred of the West.

North told a friend that he saw the hostages as 'Missing in Action'. They weren't soldiers, but they were citizens of the United States seized by an enemy. The MIAs had become the emotional touchstone for thousands of Vietnam veterans who, in emotional disarray over the war, were haunted by the thought that some of their comrades had been left behind. Private operations had been launched into the jungles of Laos, as if the finding of one prisoner of war could erase the failure of the conflict itself. The hostages were a reminder of impotence, the lack of resolve, the decline of American power. North knew that their release was of the highest concern to President Reagan, his Commander in Chief. He would do anything in his power to complete the mission.

Though North's commitment sprang from very different roots from that of Terry Waite, the Anglican envoy felt he had found a soulmate. North's enthusiasm matched his own. He was a living example of the activist that Waite wanted to be: dynamic, committed, principled, and with access to power – a man who could make things happen. Ambassador Eugene Douglas watched the relationship between North and Waite deepen. 'I think, in some ways, it was close; a meeting of two very strong personalities, two deeply committed people . . . An emotional intensity was one of Oliver North's most endearing characteristics. It just happened to be one of Terry Waite's most pronounced characteristics. He feels deeply about things, about people, and if he feels deeply then he feels it's his obligation to act.'

By the summer of 1986, time was running out for Oliver North. It was becoming increasingly difficult to keep the supplying of the Contras in Nicaragua secret. North's network had developed too many tentacles. For a covert operation it was accumulating an embarrassing array of assets: it had six aircraft, warehouses, maintenance facilities, ships, boats, leased houses, vehicles, ordnance, munitions, communications equipment and a runway. Staff on Capitol Hill, who had bitterly opposed President Reagan's support for the Nicaraguan rebels, began picking up rumours in Central America that the operation to arm them was being run out of the White House. *CBS News* and the *Washington Times* began featuring Oliver North. Even the Soviet paper *Izvestia* reported on the private war of the colonel from the White House. In June, Robert McFarlane had warned Admiral Poindexter, 'It seems increasingly clear that the Democratic Left is coming after him [North] with a vengeance.' Poindexter half-heartedly tried to relieve North of his duties and his involvement with the Contras.

North, rather melodramatically, even offered his resignation. 'Under these circumstances, and given your intention that I extricate myself entirely from the Nicaraguan issue, it probably would be best if I were to move on as quietly, but expeditiously as possible.' But North's letter was a disguised plea to keep his job. 'I want you to know,' he wrote to Poindexter, 'that it is for me deeply disappointing to have lost your confidence, for I respect you . . .' Poindexter replied, 'Now you are getting emotional again.' The matter was allowed to pass.

Negotiations with the Iranians were proving almost as problematical. During the summer North had begun exploring a 'second channel' to the leadership in Tehran. The National Security Council had detected a change of mood among the mullahs. Pragmatists like Ali Akhbar Rafsanjani, the powerful Speaker of the Iranian Parliament, were expressing concern about Soviet intentions and unease that Iranian fortunes in the Gulf War might be ebbing. Washington thought it detected a clear signal that Tehran was open for business.

Members of North's private network began meeting one of Rafsanjani's relatives, his nephew. North was encouraged. They seemed to have established an independent channel to Tehran, exclusive of the Israelis and the untrustworthy middleman Manucher Ghorbanifar.

On 8 August, North had another meeting with Ghorbanifar. The Iranian was in poor spirits. The mullahs had discovered that they had been cheated, that the prices they had been charged for the previous deliveries had been outrageous. Ghorbanifar proposed that a thousand TOW missiles be shipped in compensation. North was evasive. He was in a difficult situation: he could not afford to make an enemy of the man without risking the whole operation becoming public.

While North was thinking this over, Ghorbanifar told him that he knew of the 'second channel'. He warned North that it would be a mistake to cut him out of future deals while his debts were unsettled. His friends in Tehran wouldn't understand. North realized that by changing intermediaries he was straying into the perilous politics of the Islamic Republic. Already various mullahs and their supporters were positioning themselves for the post-Khomeini power struggle. Access to American weapons, for the continuing war with Iraq, carried with it political advantages. As news of arms deals began to circulate in Tehran, some of the factions began trying to cut their own deal with the White House. Vince Cannistraro, an official on the National Security Council, was sought out by an intermediary acting on behalf of Ayatollah Montazeri. He was shopping for spare parts for F4s. Not every petitioner could be satisfied. Those who came away empty handed knew they could always discredit their opponents by disclosing their contacts with the West. It was clear that the secret of the arms sales would not be safe for long in faction-ridden Iran. It was made even less secure by leaving men like Ghorbanifar wounded. He proposed, rather tentatively, one more arms deal as a way of keeping the Iranian off his back. But North's hopes for ending the hostage crisis had transferred to his new contact, with whom he was already negotiating a much more comprehensive deal.

After the conference in San Francisco, Terry Waite had stayed on in the United States. He had met some of the hostage families and wanted to see Oliver North before he left. When he called North's office, his secretary, Fawn Hall, said that Ollie was in London but she would try and reach him. North was returning the next day and in due course suggested they meet his flight in New York; they could have a brief meeting before he flew on to Washington. Parker Borg from the State Department would join them.

Waite was staying with Samir Habiby at his home in Greenwich, Connecticut. It was one of America's oldest communities, established, prosperous and exclusive. Habiby's house had a view of the waterfront, and at night the lights of New York City glowed on the horizon.

Waite loved it; a refuge from his own peripatetic lifestyle.

For their meeting with Oliver North they collected Samir Habiby's assistant, Marion Dawson. The three of them drove down the interstate highway to La Guardia airport where they picked up Parker Borg. They then dashed over to Kennedy airport to meet North, but his flight was delayed so they went to the nearby Viscount Hotel for a sandwich. Parker Borg had not seen Terry Waite for nearly nine months, and they talked generally about the hostage situation.

When North finally arrived he was in a great hurry because he had to catch the last shuttle back to Washington, so they all crowded into Canon Habiby's Buick and raced back to La Guardia. North seemed exhausted – there were black bags under his eyes. That morning he had had a meeting with Ghorbanifar in London. He had appointments at the White House early the following day. For months it had been this way, a desperate scramble to keep track of his network. He was sleeping for no more than three or four hours a night, sometimes on the couch in his office. A colleague at the time had tried to persuade North to take a break, telling him that a close friend had gone to a health farm.

'Why? What's the matter with him?' North had asked.

'His blood pressure is 180 over 145.'

'That's not bad,' North had replied. 'Mine's 205 over 180.'

The colleague looked in North's eyes. 'The blood vessels were nearly breaking from the pressure. It was just off the scales,' he recalled.

North's notebooks reveal that dealing with the Iranian regime had become a nightmare for him. He depicts the leadership as riven by factions, competing in their dislike for the United States. Under the heading 'Problems in Tehran', he lists the following:

> Good guys/bad guys
> two who want to give host (hostages)
> Rafsanjani – wants to milk US

* * * *

> Musavi hates US
> Revolutionary Guard budget – overspent

Prime Minister is taking $ from Rev. Guards/Army to pay for airforce.

Despite his schemes to buy the hostages, North had a moment of clarity. 'Ronald Reagan,' he wrote, 'should not be misled.'

– Criminals are leading Iran; they hate US.

– this last should not end with any advantage for Iran.

– If it does the radicals will be in power forever.

The list of problems covers several pages of his notebooks. His conclusion contained a note of despair. 'The longer this goes on – the worse things will be.'

Terry Waite tried to talk to North as they drove the short distance to La Guardia, but the American's thoughts were on his connection. As he checked in, the Church party noticed he was carrying an unusually shaped briefcase. It was secure communications equipment, North said; he never travelled without it. To airline security it resembled any other laptop computer. But it came with its own dish, transmitter and batteries. North had become a kind of one-man National Security Council.

While waiting for the flight, North indicated that the captors might be willing to release another hostage. It was important, he said, to signal to them that their demands had not been forgotten. They reviewed all the schemes they had tried in the past. Father Jenco had reconfirmed the importance of the Kuwaiti prisoners. Jaded as he was, North was a fountain of ideas. He proposed that Samir Habiby's brother Armand, who had excellent contacts with the Saudis, try to use them to reach the Kuwaitis. He was hopeful that three more letters might be received from the seventeen prisoners. If that were so, he thought Waite should deliver them to Dr Adnam Mroueh, whose clinic he had used for his first meeting with the captors. Waite said he would appeal again to the Kuwaitis to let him see the prisoners.

North was also trying to resurrect the plan to get General Lahad to release some of the Shi'ite prisoners. This time he would enlist the help of Syria to put pressure on Islamic Jihad to free some of the hostages in return. He believed that Syria had some influence with Sheikh Fadlallah, the spiritual leader of Hezballah. In his notebooks North wrote, 'Syria can put squeeze on Fadlallah.' He also wrote that he would get 'Miller' to contact Waite. 'Miller' was the codename for Amiram Nir. If the Syrians had been willing and able to influence the captors, Terry Waite would have been used to enter 'negotiations' with General Lahad.

While they were talking, North learnt that his flight had been cancelled: there was a technical problem. North spoke to the crew, explaining that he was a White House official and had to get back to Washington. There was nothing they could do, they told him. North asked whether they couldn't fly in a spare plane, but it wasn't possible at that time of night – it was now past eleven o'clock.

He was becoming agitated. They began phoning other airlines but no flights were available. An official told them there might be a special flight leaving during the night which would be taking the crew to Washington. The five of them hurried to the desk; there was no one to check him in. North wanted to ensure he had a seat. He hadn't eaten, so while they waited they began scouring the halls in search of food. Finally an official was found who confirmed that a flight would be leaving at 2.30 in the morning.

The party decided to go to the nearby Marriot Hotel, where they sat at the bar and ordered beers and a snack. While the pianist played late-night music, Samir Habiby said grace: he prayed that God would grant them strength to finish what they had begun. Even in the half-light North couldn't disguise his weariness. He was in a pensive mood, telling the others that he didn't know how much longer he could continue. He had neglected his family – the only time he saw them was at church on Sunday. Each day, he said, he entrusted them to God, but the absences were painful. The next afternoon he hoped to go away with his son to a fathers-and-sons Bible camp in Yosemite National Park. But he believed that God had called him to this work. On several occasions in Vietnam he had faced death; he believed he had been spared for a reason.

Waite commiserated. He missed his family, and his son in particular. He spoke of the strains of being an envoy, of living out of a suitcase, of not leading a normal life, of being on call twenty-four hours a day. North nodded. There was a camaraderie in the sacrifices they were all making.

An air of unreality hung over the evening. They were a band of Christians who believed they were engaged in momentous events – events that justified the disruption of their lives. Yet each of them, in his own way, had become divorced from the counsel of others. Oliver North had excluded the career officers of the State Department and the seasoned analysts of the CIA. Incredibly, this worn-out individual wandering round a New York airport with his communications equipment was orchestrating key elements of American foreign policy. Terry Waite was an envoy of a Church that scarcely knew where he was or the many roles that he was playing. Samir Habiby, with his contacts in the Middle East, was given a free rein by his Church. All of them would pass through red lights beyond the reach of those who might have restrained them.

Brian Jenkins had worked on the periphery of the hostage question. He detected that they all had imbibed the 'heady potion of being at the centre of events'. 'There's a certain excitement,' he said, 'that goes along with secret negotiations, meetings with nefarious characters in exotic settings. It is awfully easy to get caught up in it to the point that one's judgement becomes impaired.'

At two in the morning they left the bar. Oliver North departed for Washington – another night with only a trace of sleep. Terry Waite and Samir Habiby drove back to Connecticut, determined as ever to play their part.

The next day when Waite returned to London, *The Times* ran an editorial entitled 'Mr Waite's Fine Line'. The paper had heard conflicting stories about Father Jenco's release and the reasons behind it. The paper didn't elaborate but it questioned whether the enormous publicity surrounding Father Jenco's release might make hostage-taking more attractive. It also noted how the Church of England's involvement with hostages had extended beyond Christian missionaries to ordinary Americans. The editorial concluded, 'It is to the credit of the Church of England that it has been able to sponsor this most unusual ministry. But it would be wise of it, too, to consider how best to wind it up. The line between being useful, and being used, is a fine one'.

A week later Waite unexpectedly announced that he was considering giving up his role as envoy and leaving Lambeth Palace. 'The dangers and pressures,' he said, 'have made me think it's time to evaluate things. The past few years have been incredibly rewarding, but the pressures and strains are beginning to take their toll.' His recent visit to the United States had convinced him that he had taken his work with the Church as far as he could. Other opportunities were being dangled before him, like taking a post with the United Nations or heading a relief agency. In his comments, there also was a hint of a souring in the relationship between himself and the Archbishop: 'I've enjoyed working with the Archbishop, but partnerships have to change eventually.' Although he said he would like to leave immediately, he ran a six-month diary and he acknowledged there was a great deal of work left to do.

14

A POLITICAL SCANDAL

In Beirut, David Jacobsen had been buoyed up by Father Jenco's release. For the hostages it was evidence of progress: it was comforting to know in their isolation that there were unseen forces working on their behalf. In time they, too, could expect freedom. But Jacobsen's optimism was short-lived.

After Father Jenco had been separated from the others, Jacobsen had recorded a video message which the priest took with him when he was freed. It was a *cri de coeur*: 'Please forgive me if I give the impression that I feel I'm one of General Custer's men, or one of the men at the Alamo waiting for help to arrive. You know the end of their stories. Pray that ours will be happier.' On the tape Jacobsen had also sent his condolences to the wife and family of William Buckley, without realizing that Buckley had never married. When his message was reported on Lebanese television the announcer pointed out the mistake. The guards were incensed. They believed that Jacobsen had deliberately tricked them and that, through his 'error', he had sent out a coded message. They yelled and screamed and threatened him with punishment. The days after Jenco's release were the most frightening since Jacobsen's kidnap on 28 May 1985.

On that day he had been walking from his apartment to his office at the American University when six men seized him. At first he was tied up, put on the floor and told to remain silent. 'Though I was chained by my right ankle and right hand,' he said later, 'I was able to turn and do push-ups and even leg lifts.' Sometimes, after he had been taken to the toilet, he was able to run on the spot for a couple of minutes. Conditions were rigorous, if not harsh. 'My clothes had been taken from me during interrogation, so I just had my underwear and a cotton tablecloth that served as a blanket.'

Unlike some of the others, he was never held alone. The long hours passed most swiftly when all five of them were together. 'Each day, we were allowed to go to the toilet one by one,' he recalled. 'We had fifteen minutes to take a shower, wash our clothes, empty our urinals, get fresh water and clean our plastic bowls, spoons and cups. The guards got very unhappy if it were sixteen minutes, because there were five of us, and the whole procedure took up at least an hour and fifteen minutes of their time.'

Jacobsen thought his captivity would be brief: he was convinced he would be free within a month in time for his son's wedding. That day, however, he spent chained to the floor. 'To help myself through the hours,' he later wrote,

> I spun an elaborate fantasy. I pretended I was with my family, getting ready to go to the wedding and doing all the things the father of the groom has to do. In my mind I went to St Bonaventure's church on Springdale Street and saw my future daughter-in-law coming in. In my mind I drove down to the Huntington Harbour Club for the reception. I spent the whole day lost in my fantasy of what was happening thousands of miles away.

There were long periods when his mind couldn't conjure up the images from the world outside his room and he succumbed to the numbing tedium of captivity. 'Imagine yourself as being paralysed from the neck down, and being conscious but not being able to do anything. There you are, stretched out, just being able to move your eyes and to think, twenty-four hours a day, day after day. It takes a man of great inner strength and belief in the Lord to be able to survive that.'

His moment of greatest joy was when he saw the moon. On three occasions he had been taken outside, but always blindfolded. Then one day the guards allowed him on the roof during the middle of the night. 'I just can't describe it in words,' said Jacobsen, 'to see the moon and the stars. It was just a thrilling moment, a moment that I will never forget. At that time it was almost fifteen months not to have seen out of doors, in fact, not to have seen anything further than twelve feet away.' Before he was taken inside again a purple flare lit up the sky and then died away. It had been fired by one of the Christian militias to illuminate the Moslem positions. The civil war was continuing around him, and yet what had once been so familiar now seemed strange, like a television clip from one of the world's remote conflicts. But as he thought about it he realized how insignificant was his detention compared to the interminable suffering of the Lebanese people. It was a depressing thought.

In September 1986, five weeks after he had been abused for his mistake in the video recording at the time of Father Jenco's release, he was asked to write a letter to President Reagan. The guards had watched, with interest, as the President negotiated the release of Nicholas Daniloff, a journalist detained in Moscow. Despite protestations that the United States would not submit to Soviet blackmail, Daniloff had been exchanged for a Soviet diplomat detained in New York. The guards saw an opportunity to revive the hostage issue in the United States, so they told Jacobsen to write a letter demanding to know why the administration was ignoring their plight when it was willing to help a journalist. Within an hour of his finishing the letter, the guards returned.

'It's no good,' one of them said. 'We don't trust you. We are going to rewrite it. You are going to write it down exactly as dictated. You are going to spell it like we tell you. You are going to punctuate it like we tell you.'

Jacobsen wrote down what was dictated. 'Don't we deserve the same attention and protection that you gave Daniloff?' the letter enquired of President Reagan. The guards examined it word for word, sentence for sentence. Jacobsen warned them that the outside world wouldn't believe it was his work: there were too many errors.

'Sure enough, when the letter made its way into print the news media circled all the grammatical mistakes, and my captors accused me of deliberately misleading them.'

It was impossible to explain. The guard who had dictated it remained silent, allowing the others to believe that Jacobsen had once again tried to fool them. He was not helped by an American television reporter speculating that the message had been coded. 'The captors saw that speculation. They were absolutely convinced that I had sent out a coded message, that I was a member of the CIA, and they knocked the heck out of me.' He was taken to another room and his feet were beaten with a rubber hose. Jacobsen pleaded with them, his cries of pain eventually persuading them to stop, but the guards remained suspicious. They put him in isolation in a cramped room six foot square. It was completely dark except for a shaft of light that pierced the sheets of metal they had placed around the window.

Jacobsen was cut off from the other hostages. What news he heard was depressing. On 9 September, Frank Reed, another American, was kidnapped; he was director of the Lebanese International School. Three days later Jacobsen overheard a radio report in Arabic mention Joseph Cicippio, controller at the American University and one of his friends. Jacobsen, not understanding Arabic well, thought he had been killed. It was only later that he realized that Cicippio, too, was a hostage. In a matter of days the captors had replenished their stock of hostages, making a mockery of a year's deals and negotiations.

The captors were not only angry at Jacobsen for his perceived treachery, they were growing impatient at the lack of progress on their demands relating to the seventeen prisoners in Kuwait. The CIA learnt, at this time, that Imad Mugniyah, the man they believed responsible for some of the kidnappings of Westerners, was threatening to kill the hostages. Charles Allen, who headed the agency's Hostage Location Task Force, wrote that 'No threat from Mugniyah should be considered idle. He is a violent extremist capable of impetuously killing the hostages.'

In Washington, Oliver North was under pressure not only from the rumours emanating from Beirut but from the hostage families who wanted to see him about the Daniloff affair. Why, they demanded, was the administration not giving the hostages the same attention? They were convinced a deal had been made. 'Some, like Jacobsen's son Paul,' wrote North, 'accused us of being callous to the LepNap [Lebanese] victims and unwilling to pressure the Kuwaitis because the issue had slipped from the public eye and that we were willing to make deals for Daniloff because it was more important to the President because of his visibility.'

How ironic that Oliver North should stand accused of being reluctant to make deals over the hostages; he could only hear the bitter complaints of the families in silence. Yet others shrewdly observed that the willingness to bargain over Daniloff could only give heart to the captors in Beirut. The administration was a victim of its own contradictions: it was neither consistent in its response to blackmail, nor had it a coherent policy. The ambiguities seemed to pass North by, but the pleas of the families distressed him. What he was unable to share with them was the knowledge that another deal was in the offing.

North and close colleagues like Dick Secord and George Cave were increasingly enthusiastic about the new channel they had opened up to Iran; for the first time they believed they could negotiate directly with the leadership in Tehran without going through Ghorbanifar. Their contact was Ali Hashemani Bahremani, a nephew of the Iranian Speaker Rafsanjani. The White House group dubbed him 'the Relative'.

On 19 September the Relative was invited to Washington for a two-day visit. North gave him the red carpet treatment. The first meeting was held in his office in the Old Executive Office Building. What the Iranian made of the assorted maps and aerial photographs of the Bekaa valley and Nicaragua is hard to say. Afterwards, North took him on a guided tour of the White House. According to one of North's colleagues, the tour 'covered every corner' including the Oval Office. Before they left the building, North paused, presidentially, before a portrait of President Theodore Roosevelt. He told the young Iranian how Roosevelt had arbitrated an end to the Russo–Japanese War of 1904–5. The United States, he announced grandly, would now be willing to arbitrate an end to the Iran–Iraq conflict. Later, the concerns were less lofty. According to Secord the CIA was enlisted to scour Washington's escort agencies for a suitable young woman to go to the hotel where the Relative and his entourage were staying.

At the meetings it was apparent that arms were top of the Relative's agenda. He had come with what the Americans later called a 'wish list', such was its ambition. He didn't just want the spare parts that had been promised in previous deals; he wanted offensive weapons such as artillery. For the Americans it was a difficult request, for artillery was a critical weapon in the Gulf War. In sufficient quantity it could even be used to soften up Iraqi ground forces as a prelude to an attack on Baghdad. The Iranian also wanted a sampling of intelligence on Iraqi troop positions and 'technical assistance' in the use of missiles, and proposed that the United States send a technician to Iran.

North baulked at the suggestion, knowing how difficult it would be for the United States to become so directly involved on one side in the Gulf War, but he did not reject these requests outright. He said the President would find it very hard to help Iran while the obstacle of the hostages remained. 'It would be very difficult to explain to our people,' he said. The message North was giving the Iranians was that if the hostages were released then almost anything was possible.

The Relative told him that Iran did not have complete control over the groups holding the hostages. Nothing mattered more to those groups, he said, than the prisoners in Kuwait. North reminded the Relative that the United States could not intervene in Kuwait, but he predicted that Kuwait would free the prisoners in phases 'if the government of Iran goes privately to Kuwait and promises them no terrorism'. He encouraged the Relative to approach Kuwait. There is no evidence that North had any basis for this assertion: he had not been in touch with the Kuwaitis, and subsequent events were to show them unmoved by bland assurances from Iran. It was evidence of North's 'creative thinking' during negotiations.

Following the discussions, both sides needed to refer. North sought authorization from Poindexter to attend another meeting in Europe. He had thought of a way whereby the United States could comply with the Relative's request for intelligence without giving Iran an advantage in the war. He suggested that a 'mix of factual and bogus information could be provided'. Poindexter agreed to a further meeting.

On 6 October the two sides met again in Frankfurt. North

was joined by General Secord; Albert Hakim, an Iranian expatriate and Secord's business partner; and George Cave, a former member of the CIA and an Iran specialist. The Relative was accompanied by an intelligence official from the Revolutionary guards whom Secord named 'the Monster' because of his dour expression. He had been imprisoned under the Shah and was a committed Moslem. The Monster was there to protect the interests of the Revolution.

Before discussions began there was an exchange of gifts, as if this meeting in a hotel bedroom were between heads of state. North presented the Relative with a Bible inscribed by President Reagan with a verse from Galatians: 'And the Scripture, foreseeing that God would justify the Gentiles by faith, preached the Gospel beforehand to Abraham, saying, All the nations shall be blessed in you.' For the moment when he made the presentation, North had dreamt up a story. 'We inside our government had an enormous debate,' he told the surprised Iranians,

> a very angry debate over whether or not my President should authorize me to say we accept the Islamic Revolution as a fact ... The President went off one whole weekend and prayed about what the answer should be and he came back almost a year ago with that passage I gave you that he wrote in the front of the Bible. And he [the President] said to me: 'This is a promise that God gave to Abraham. Who am I to say that we should not do this?'

The story was a complete fabrication, but North wanted to give the impression that his various undertakings had the backing of the President, even though Ronald Reagan had no knowledge of these extraordinary negotiations.

The Relative responded by presenting a copy of the Koran, which, he explained, was a gift from Rafsanjani for the President. The young man muttered that 'We are all Peoples of the Book,' and that he regarded President Reagan as 'a true man of God'.

The pleasantries having been dispensed with, the haggling began. The Iranians' position had hardened and North immediately began offering concessions. The Monster asked

North to 'show me the way' to gain the confidence of the captors in Beirut. North replied dramatically, 'Let me give you some ammunition for your guns.' If Kuwait decided to release the seventeen prisoners, he told the Iranians, then the United States would not object. This had recently been conveyed to the Kuwaitis. Furthermore, the administration would try and assist in the freeing of the prisoners. North's undertaking went much further than any other statement previously made, and was contrary to American foreign policy.

He also made a concession on the sale of offensive weapons. The 'only' limitation would be that the sales would not include items that would allow the Revolutionary guards to 'seize' Baghdad. There were plenty of Iranian operations short of taking the Iraqi capital that would benefit from American weapons.

The Iranians brought up an issue they had referred to in Washington. They wanted American backing for the removal of the Iraqi President, Saddam Hussein. North was in accommodating mood: 'It's become very evident to everybody that the guy who is causing the problem is Saddam Hussein.' This was the view of the government in Washington, he said. He also wanted to convey President Reagan's view of the Iraqi leader. 'Saddam Hussein is a shit.' Hakim, who was translating, was reluctant to use the phrase, fearing it might cause offence. 'Go ahead,' urged North. 'That's his [the President's] word, not mine.' North later admitted that this story was one of his lies.

At the heart of the deal was an arms sale. The United States would sell five hundred TOW missiles at once and fifteen hundred later. In exchange, North expected at least two hostages to be freed. He sensed this might be his last deal – his opponents were closing in on him in Washington. His salvation lay in the pictures of freed Americans being reunited by their families.

The Iranians withdrew to think about the proposition, and returned with a series of much tougher proposals. Only one hostage would be released after the first delivery, and they would 'only promise' to gain the release of two others if there was progress on the Kuwaiti prisoners. North was exasperated. He said the differences were so great that the United States and Iran were destined 'to pass each other like ships in the night'.

Before the meeting had finished, North had to return to Washington; there was a crisis with his other major operation in Central America. A cargo plane, carrying military supplies for the Contras, had been shot down over Nicaragua. Three of the crewmen were killed but a fourth, Eugene Hasenfus, an American from Wisconsin, had been captured. The flight had been arranged by General Secord's network, and the American press was demanding to know who had financed it. Already there was speculation that the operation was linked to high-ranking officials in Washington.

Before North departed to extinguish the fire in Central America he authorized Albert Hakim to continue the negotiations. An incredulous Congressman was to remark that an Iranian expatriate had been left to play 'Secretary of State for a day'. Hakim rapidly reached agreement with the Iranians; obstacles melted away. They drew up a nine-point agenda which later became known as the 'Hakim accords'. Hakim was prepared to concede even more than North: he promised to develop a plan for the release of the Kuwaiti prisoners. The Tower Commission, which later investigated the affair, said that North and his partners 'committed the US, without authorization, to a position contrary to well-established US policy on the prisoners held by Kuwait'.

North thought the agreement a bargain and was convinced that two hostages would be freed; he persuaded Poindexter to go along with it. There were two further meetings with the Iranians in Europe. On 29 October they met in Mainz to go over the logistics of the first missile delivery and hostage release. But the Iranians had ominous news. A faction in Iran, opposed to the 'dialogue' with the Americans, had printed and distributed five million leaflets describing North and McFarlane's visit to Tehran in May. Worse still, a group in Lebanon had learnt of the story. The realization that his nemesis was approaching seemed to inspire North to greater efforts. He told the Relative that he had 'already started' on the plan to release the Kuwaiti prisoners. He claimed that he had 'met with the Kuwaiti Foreign Minister, secretly, in my spare time between blowing up Nicaragua'.

North was aware that the deal remained problematical. In his notebooks he jotted down a list which he thought would finally persuade the Iranians to resolve the hostage issue. Among them was reconnaissance cameras for Iranian F4 aircraft; spare parts for Iranian Phoenix missiles; a further 1500 TOW missiles and the offer of technicians to help fix the Phoenix missiles on release of two of the hostages. North appears to have had little regard for the effect these concessions might have had on the military balance in the Iran–Iraq war. Rather he was desperately seeking the deal that would bring all the hostages home. 'Hashemi Rafsanjani,' he noted, 'was interested in using these parts/cameras as means of ending all hostages.' Even though he knew difficulties remained, North was convinced some hostages would be released within a few days.

While in West Germany, North began making arrangements to receive them. He flew to Lebanon with Dick Secord to inform the American embassy that they should expect developments. He telephoned Terry Waite in London and asked him to meet him in Cyprus. In his notebook for November 1, North scribbled, 'Get Waite to Beirut ASAP.' With rumours circulating in Beirut about North's activities, secrecy was more important than ever.

The three of them met in Larnaca and flew in an American military helicopter to East Beirut, landing at a secure helicopter pad down the hill from the American embassy compound. They were met by Ambassador John Kelly, who had been informed by the White House situation room of their arrival. The State Department was not told – an omission that would lead to a public reprimand for the Ambassador.

Terry Waite and Oliver North appeared at ease in each other's company. Waite complained, good-humouredly, at how little notice he had been given to leave London. Privately, North was racked with doubts about the operation. Its successful outcome had become so important to him and the administration that he was nervous about every detail. The Ambassador considered him 'disorganized and hyperactive'. North did not know where the hostages would be freed, so he asked Secord to assemble a small force of embassy guards to be ready to cross into Moslem West Beirut to fetch them. He was concerned that some other group might seize a disorientated Westerner before they could get to him.

North was also worried whether Islamic Jihad would realize that they were supposed to release the hostages that weekend. He had the idea of using Terry Waite to remind them, and proposed sending the Anglican envoy into West Beirut to tour the streets. The captors would soon hear he was back. He would not have to stay long: after visiting a few neighbourhoods he could hold a brief press conference to announce he had returned. The local radio station would quickly broadcast the news and the captors would get the message.

Waite was extremely dubious; he thought it far too dangerous to drive around West Beirut. North offered him the protection of some of the armed mercenaries who guarded the embassy compound, but this was declined. It would not be understood by the Moslem militias, Waite said; there could easily be a clash and he could end up a hostage himself. After further discussion they all agreed it was much easier for Waite to call the press and tell them he was back.

In the Ambassador's office, Waite and North worked out what he should say. Waite then called Associated Press in Beirut. 'I'm back,' he announced. 'Things are moving. You keep an eye, just keep an eye.' Within hours reporters and camera crews were travelling to Cyprus, the nearest point to Lebanon – West Beirut itself was considered too dangerous to fly to. North was later to regret the telephone call, for American reporters, who had gathered at Larnaca airport, spotted him as he shuttled between Cyprus and Lebanon and began to question what was behind the hostage release.

Having made the call, North said Waite should stand by in Cyprus. It was always possible that the hostages would be taken to Damascus, and it would be much easier to fly to the Syrian capital from there. North would instruct his people on the island to look after him and keep him out of sight.

The Ambassador decided to cut the size of the diplomatic mission in order to make room for the hostages, and twenty-four embassy personnel were flown to Cyprus. It led to reports that the United States was reducing its presence in Lebanon as a gesture of goodwill to Islamic Jihad. A spokesman had to announce hurriedly: 'The diplomats are coming back. We're not closing down the Embassy.'

North returned to Germany – he wanted to be available to the Iranians if there were any last-minute hitch. Dick Secord went to London. The logistics of the operation were handled by Bob Dutton, one of Dick Secord's partners and the man responsible for running the operation to supply the Contras.

Dutton was in Italy with Rafael 'Chi Chi' Quintero, a Cuban-American who was a veteran of numerous covert CIA operations. They chartered a Lear jet to Cyprus and parked on the far side of the airport. CIA personnel met them and took them to the Golden Bay Hotel in Larnaca, a popular resort complex. Dutton was carrying a KL43, a secure communications system; he was able to talk to North, Secord and the White House situation room. He would coordinate the operation on the ground. That evening he called North to let him know he was in place and ready for further instruction.

A CIA official on the island informed Dutton that the next morning he was to go to a hotel in the capital, Nicosia, and walk round to the back of the building. There he would be met and taken to Terry Waite who had recently flown back to Cyprus from Beirut on an American military helicopter. 'It comes almost out of a story book,' Dutton recalled. 'I was met by an American who later turned out to be a CIA representative and taken to the safe house where I met Terry Waite.'

The Anglican envoy was in his boxer shorts; he and the Agency personnel had had a late night. There was a practical problem, Waite explained. His suitcase had been mislaid during the original flight to Cyprus and he had no change of clothes. A CIA official was despatched to buy a suit for a man six foot four inches tall.

Waite wanted to know who Dutton was and what his role would be. Dutton explained that he would be in charge of logistics, and it was his understanding that Waite would be handling the press releases and publicity. They discussed the latest information, and Dutton promised to inform Waite when it was time to move.

Dutton then drove back to Larnaca. At the hotel he was told he would have to vacate his room. 'The world's press had arrived because of developments in Lebanon,' he was informed. Dutton protested, without being able to explain that he was the lynchpin in the very operation that the journalists had come to cover. After some negotiations it was agreed that he could stay, although the flight crew of the Lear jet was moved to an adjoining hotel.

David Jacobsen had an overpowering feeling he was going to be released. 'It wasn't a dream, just a tremendous, powerful feeling that I was going to get out . . . It was so powerful that when I went to bed on Saturday night, I knew that I was going to be home in several hours.' He had just fallen asleep when he heard a noise in the guards' room, followed by a shuffling of feet. A man entered. 'Mr David, we're happy you're going home,' he said. Jacobsen had kept up his spirits in captivity by telling himself every week that he was going to be released the following Sunday. As each week passed he faithfully told the other hostages that next Sunday would be the day. It was only fitting, therefore, that his release should come on a Sunday.

He was driven down to the seafront, still blindfolded. 'When you get out,' the guard told him, 'walk straight to the seawall. Face the wall for three or four minutes. Then remove your blindfold, turn left, and you will see the old US embassy building.' Jacobsen counted the minutes, being generous in the time he allowed his captors to depart. He then started walking, looking neither right nor left. Suddenly he was tapped on the shoulder. 'You've walked a hundred yards too far.' One of the captors had been observing him. 'It was my first act as a free man,' said Jacobsen later, 'and I fucked it up.' Retracing his steps, he found the embassy annexe was still functioning. Surprised officials phoned the embassy in East Beirut and announced they had a freed hostage.

As soon as it was confirmed that a hostage had been released, Terry Waite was driven to Larnaca in the back of a black Mercedes. He picked up Bob Dutton from his hotel;

Waite sat well back in the car to avoid being seen by the scores of reporters who were now in the town. The two men were driven to the secure side of the airport where they boarded an H60 US military helicopter for Lebanon.

On the short flight across the Mediterranean there was no discussion about what had prompted Jacobsen's release. Dutton knew about the arms shipments to Iran, but he never talked about them with Terry Waite. They speculated as to whether more than one hostage would be freed. Dutton was hoping that Jacobsen would have information on the other hostages. As he talked with Waite he detected disappointment on the part of the Anglican envoy that he wasn't more directly involved. 'My sense was that he wanted to do more, that he wanted to play a more central role in possibly going in and doing direct negotiations to see if he couldn't effect a release that nobody else could get done.' But on the flight it already began to look as if there would be no negotiations.

When they arrived at the helipad in East Beirut they were put in embassy cars with armed guards sitting either side of them – it was some of the tightest security Dutton had ever seen. They drove up a steep and winding road to the embassy; on every corner there were guards with automatic weapons and rocket launchers. The American diplomatic presence in Lebanon had taken on the appearance of a frontier outpost in the Old West.

They were welcomed by Ambassador Kelly. 'David is here,' he said, as they went inside. Moments later they met David Jacobsen. He hugged Terry Waite, his eyes close to tears with gratitude. 'God bless you,' he said. 'You gave us hope.' Everyone watching was moved. Such was the warmth between them that Bob Dutton assumed they had met before on one of Waite's previous missions. In fact Waite had never been allowed to visit the hostages, but he had become a symbol of liberty to them to the point where they felt they knew him. To Bob Dutton, seeing the elation of a freed man made all the efforts worthwhile. 'If I could do it again to see that, I would,' he said after the whole affair had been marred by controversy.

Jacobsen went into a debriefing session which lasted four or five hours. It was conducted by an official who Bob Dutton presumed was from the CIA; the Ambassador and Terry Waite were also present. The debriefing went into the greatest detail about the circumstances of his release, the condition of the other hostages, the mood of the captors and the prospects for other releases. Jacobsen showed no fatigue during the questioning – he was a man invigorated by freedom. 'It just flowed,' said one of those present. He was driven by an overpowering obligation to do everything to help the others who remained in captivity. But it became apparent during his debriefing that further releases were unlikely.

He had brought with him a letter from the captors. It was the usual extortionist's brew of threat and tantalizing hope:

We announce to world opinion, to the American people, and to the families of the hostages the release of the American, David Jacobsen. We hold the American government responsible for the consequences of not benefiting from this opportunity by continuing what it, the American government, has begun, through proceeding with proposals that may lead, if continued, to the solution of the issue of the hostages. We remind the American government . . . that we will follow an entirely different course in the event the American government does not complete these proposals in order to attain the desired result. We pledge to everyone that we will continue the Jihad until the establishment of Allah's rule on earth, the destruction of idols and tyrants, and the victory of the oppressed and the downtrodden. The will of Allah be done. Islamic Jihad Organization. Nov. 1986

It was apparent on the first reading that the captors, as cautious as ever, were not going to throw away their assets; they were going to extract the maximum price out of each release, and America's agony would be prolonged. Additionally, in the weeks prior to Jacobsen's release three new hostages had been taken. Furthermore, the letter revealed that the captors had been informed about the undertakings given at the meetings in Europe, as far as they related to the prisoners in Kuwait. They were now expecting that the proposals, which had no foundation in reality, be 'proceeded' with. Oliver North's promises were returning to haunt him.

When North heard that only one hostage had been freed he was sure there had been 'a mistake'. He had been convinced, after the meeting with the Relative, that at least two would be freed. He and George Cave, the former CIA official who had taken part in the negotiations, began scouring Europe for the Iranian intermediary – but to no avail. North, a master of deception himself, was strangely willing to believe the best of the Iranians. He later told Peggy Say, sister of Terry Anderson, the other hostage whom he had expected to be released, that he had 'cried like a baby' when he realized it was not going to happen. North, however, thought that if he could only keep the story quiet then there was still a chance. He had intended to fly to Beirut that evening to brief David Jacobsen, but, using the excuse of poor flying conditions, he continued trying to contact the Relative.

In relaying the captors' letter to North and the White House situation room, Dutton had added the comment, 'Dave [Jacobsen] does not feel they intend to give us any more on this trip and my guess is they want the next delivery before we get another.' To Bob Dutton the memo was a memento of a special occasion and he asked Waite and Jacobsen to sign it. It is impossible to know whether Terry Waite read the words 'the next delivery' and pondered their meaning.

Because North would not be arriving that evening the Ambassador announced they would be going up to the house for the night. Dutton imagined they were going to walk to a building a couple of hundred yards behind the embassy, but a convoy of cars and a small militia formed up outside. The Ambassador and David Jacobsen were put in one car, Terry Waite and Bob Dutton in another. The guards hung out of the windows up to their waists, their automatic weapons sweeping the roads. The convoy drove at high speed for forty-five minutes. Advance cars, in radio contact, went ahead.

Dutton thought he knew about living with protection, having worked in Iran for two and a half years under the Shah. 'I really thought I understood that life,' he said, 'but this was the PhD course in survival.' When another vehicle approached, one of the guards leapt out, forced the driver to stop and pointed a gun at the windshield.

'You ever shot anyone?' Dutton enquired nervously.

'Dead right,' came the reply.

They arrived at the foot of a hill which was guarded three deep. A chicane of concrete blocks had been planted to prevent any suicide bomber from driving his vehicle at the Ambassador's residence. The house was beautiful and tranquil, an anomaly amidst the ruins of the Lebanese capital. But appearances were deceptive. Only two weeks before, one of the militias had fired a 'Stalin's organ' at the building and over twenty rockets had landed. It was a point of pride that all traces of the attack had been removed within days.

David Jacobsen had his first drink in eighteen months. He normally drank wine, but that evening had a Scotch. He impressed everyone with his normality. 'I found him very secure,' said Dutton, 'very much in control and outward-going.' He also had a sense of humour. When the Ambassador offered to show him to his room, Jacobsen said, 'Would you mind terribly if I slept on the floor? I think I'd be more comfortable.'

Before they went to bed the Ambassador explained the routine if there was a rocket attack during the night. The lights would go out. No one was to move. He would come and find everyone and lead them to a bomb shelter under the building.

At dawn the next morning Oliver North flew in by helicopter. The previous night at Larnaca airport he had been spotted getting into the back of an embassy Mercedes. He had tried to shield his face, like a criminal leaving court, and the curiosity of the press only grew. American journalists knew that he was involved in Central America and began to question what lay behind the release of the hostages and how much was due to Terry Waite's humanitarian efforts.

North hugged Jacobsen, his eyes moistening. No one had worked harder, had risked so much, for his release. Despite all the disappointments, another captive was going home. He briefed Jacobsen on what was going to happen that day. He confided to Terry Waite that, although there was little prospect of another hostage being freed immediately, he should strike an optimistic note about the others. North believed it was only a question of talking to the Relative for the deal to work out.

For Waite there would be no negotiations to engage in; his role would be to handle the publicity, and he was disappointed. 'He was the front man,' said Dutton. 'If he was uneasy, it certainly didn't show . . . As I saw him, he was as big as the world. I mean he's a big man. He talks big and he's just a very wonderful man who took that role very well. It almost came naturally to him.'

North, Waite, Dutton and Jacobsen flew to Larnaca that morning, landing on the far side of the airport. North and Dutton remained out of sight while Waite and Jacobsen spoke to the press. Jacobsen said he felt great, and was effusive about Terry Waite: 'This man did something that we really appreciated. He gave us hope that we would be free men again. We love this guy.' Waite said he was optimistic that the five remaining Americans would soon be released. 'This is a good and a promising time. Efforts will continue with the same force and vigour as they have in the past few days.' He hoped to hear within twenty-four hours from contacts in Lebanon whether it was worthwhile for him to return. Eight thousand miles away in California, the Presidential spokesman, Larry Speakes, walked into the Santa Barbara Sheraton and issued a statement to the White House press corps, expressing the President's thanks to Terry Waite.

Some of the Middle East correspondents who knew Waite well found him as jovial and ebullient as ever. He asked one of them to pass on a couple of messages to London. Then he returned to the tarmac with David Jacobsen and boarded a Lear jet for Wiesbaden in West Germany. Oliver North joined them. By the time they arrived at the American military hospital Jacobsen was red-eyed and exhausted. He was close to tears when he told reporters, 'I can't tell you how very, very happy I am here today. But it is with really mixed feel ings as the other guys are in hell and we have to get them out.'

He appeared on the balcony of the hospital with his family. The Stars and Stripes flew behind him, and the song which his son had recorded to draw attention to his captivity played over the loudspeakers. Jacobsen, a deeply patriotic man, was moved to call on his fellow Americans to vote in that day's Congressional elections because it was 'the greatest privilege in the world'.

When reporters began shouting more searching questions at him his composure broke. 'I know you all have questions to ask,' he began, and then, his voice choking with tears, he said, 'I just wanted this to be a day of joy with my kids.'

What had prompted the reporters' questions was a story in an obscure Lebanese paper, *Al Shiraa*. It claimed that Robert McFarlane had secretly visited Tehran and had discussed arms. In Washington, the administration immediately denied there had been a deal. But, having seen Oliver North in Cyprus, some journalists were sceptical.

When Terry Waite held a news conference in Germany his demeanour had changed noticeably in the twenty-four hours since leaving Cyprus. The press had always liked him. They found him accessible and ready with a quote even when nothing had happened. Among the Middle East press corps he could count many friends. But as he entered the room they all noticed the difference. Whereas in the past he had been relaxed, candid and occasionally humorous, he now appeared wary and cautious. During the conference he seemed uncertain and confused, as if his confidence had been shaken.

'Quite frankly,' he said, 'speculation as far as I'm concerned is so dangerous because it's putting further risk to the lives of the hostages in the Lebanon. There are a lot of people trying to make political capital; there are a lot of people trying to sabotage honest and straightforward efforts. There are a lot of people muscling in on this whole thing for a variety of reasons best known to themselves.'

Some recent claims, he said, had to be taken with a pinch of salt. But in his comments there was a new note of uncertainty. It was 'entirely possible', he said, that negotiations had taken place without his knowledge. After these brooding remarks he seemed to rediscover his old certainties. 'At the moment the two people specifically in my sights are Terry Anderson and Tom Sutherland . . . That is where our best chance lies.'

Before he left Wiesbaden, Waite went to say goodbye to Oliver North. The White House official appeared untroubled by the stories which were now circulating: they were unfortunate, he said, and complicated the situation, but he gave no hint of the political storm ahead. Waite didn't challenge him about the reports. North was hopeful there would soon be good news on the other hostages but he needed time. He asked Waite to provide him some time by publicly talking about 'new difficulties'. In his notebook for November 4, North wrote 'Message to Waite re delay "new obstacles"; can he drop out of sight for a few days?' North promised Waite that he would be in touch if anything was moving. He ended by saying, 'God bless you, Terry, and thank you.' The two men were not to meet again.

In Washington, reports persisted that arms had been traded for hostages. The Speaker of the Iranian Parliament, Ali Akhbar Rafsanjani, had elaborated on the story. He said five American officials had flown to Iran. In his words they were 'bearing gifts'. There was a cake in the shape of a key, a Bible inscribed by the President, the promise of Colt automatic pistols for top Iranian officials, and a planeload of US weapons. 'We did not rise to the bait,' said Rafsanjani mischievously. 'We told them we do not accept the gifts and had nothing to talk about with them.'

On 13 November, President Reagan addressed the American people. He said the secret 'diplomatic initiative' to Iran included 'only small amounts of defensive weapons and spare parts' that could fit into a single cargo plane. It was an admission, but also untrue. The President went on to insist that 'we did not, repeat, we did not trade weapons or anything else for hostages, nor will we.' However, each statement only added to the confusion. The administration seemed at a loss as to how to handle the crisis. Even former President Nixon, who had been forced to resign over the Watergate affair, was asked for advice. North and his colleagues on the National Security Council began to draw up their version of events. Over a fifteen-day period they produced a dozen different chronologies.

One of the freed hostages, Benjamin Weir, added to the administration's discomfort by saying he was 'deeply distressed and angry' by the reports. His Church was opposed to the arms race in the Middle East. President Reagan quickly wrote to him: 'I was saddened to learn from press reports,' he said,

> that you may have accepted at face value speculative stories in the media alleging arms for hostages. Let me assure you that no ransom was paid for your release. The longstanding policy of our government has been to make no concessions to the demands of terrorists. I firmly believe in that policy. To do otherwise is to encourage additional acts of terrorism and place many more Americans at risk. All of the extensive efforts the government has undertaken to obtain your release and the release of all the other American and foreign hostages in Lebanon have been fully consistent with that policy.

Oliver North, too, was looking to the hostages for his salvation. In the week since the story first appeared in a Lebanese paper he had intensified his efforts to get more hostages released. On 8 November, he, Secord and George Cave met the Monster in Geneva. Both sides were looking to each other to save them from political embarrassment. The Monster was concerned that the real role played by Rafsanjani's relative would become public. North assured him it would remain secret. He, in turn, said that details of the arms deal were damaging to the Reagan administration and that the improved relationship between the United States and Iran was now in jeopardy. The only thing which would preserve it was the release of further hostages. North was telling the Monster that, if Iran wanted future supplies of weapons from the United States, then it had to deliver the hostages now to help the administration. Ironically, North was pleading with Iran to help save an administration that had branded it an international pariah, a 'terrorist state'. If he had wanted to, Ayatollah Khomeini could have uttered a few words and helped Ronald Reagan, his sworn enemy. He remained silent.

The Monster said the problem remained the Kuwaiti prisoners. The captors had grown tired of words and empty promises. If the Kuwaitis would release the prisoners, then he could guarantee that the hostages would be freed. North was exasperated. After over a year of deals and discussions they were still thwarted by these little-known prisoners in Kuwait. He said he had spoken to the Kuwaitis secretly and would try again. In this North was sincere; he began making plans for a personal visit to Kuwait in a last-ditch effort to persuade the Kuwaitis to show some flexibility. The Monster told him that Iran couldn't just order the captors to release the hostages; this time the Americans believed him. The captors had been resolute in their central demand. North had tried every ploy to persuade the captors that if only they would free the hostages, freedom for the men in Kuwait would follow. Far from being persuaded, the captors had grown more stubborn. The hostages were their only card, and they were hardly likely to give it away. All North could say, rather lamely, was that he would work on it.

General Secord gave the Monster a KL43, a secure communications device, so that they could stay in touch. The Monster installed it at the headquarters of the Revolutionary guards. In the following weeks the Iranian and George Cave would try and arrange another deal. It was a sign of how desperate North and his partners had become that they committed a top-secret device into the hands of the Revolutionary guards, the stormtroopers of the Islamic Revolution. North was looking for a miracle – anything that would justify his extraordinary efforts of the past year.

Steven Emerson, in his book *Secret Warriors*, says that North even tried to resurrect the idea of a military rescue. Apparently, Joint Special Operations Command at Fort Bragg began preparing a mission to free the hostages. But time was not on North's side. Congress and the press were in full cry and they would not be drawn off the scent.

The administration was becoming increasingly ensnared in the tangle of details emerging over the arms sales. On 19 November, President Reagan held a disastrous news conference, littered with factual inaccuracies. His aides attempted to blame the errors on the conflicting versions prepared by the National Security Council. They had, the aides insisted, 'confused the Presidential mind'. North, however, was sanguine: many of the more sensitive documents had been quietly shredded. On 23 November he told Robert McFarlane, 'It's been a rocky three or four days, but I think everything is going to be all right.'

Unknown to North, the previous day investigators had stumbled on the most sensitive aspect of his activities. The Assistant Attorney General, William Bradford Reynolds, had been examining files in North's office when he came across a memo which said: '$12 million in profits from the Iranian arms sales [will] be used to buy supplies for the Nicaraguan Resistance Forces.' Reynolds was flabbergasted. He knew immediately that the diversion of funds to help the Contras was illegal and an attempt to bypass laws passed by Congress. The memo was explicit. It said the material was needed to 'bridge' the gap until 'congressionally approved lethal assistance . . . can be delivered'.

This was a far more serious matter than the arms sales. Two days later, on 25 November, President Reagan again addressed the nation. Admiral Poindexter, he announced, was resigning. 'Lieutenant Colonel Oliver North has been relieved of his duties on the National Security Council staff. I'd deeply troubled that the implementation of a policy aimed at resolving a truly tragic situation in the Middle East has resulted in such controversy.'

Within two days Oliver North had been barred from his office, but not before large amounts of paperwork had been destroyed. President Reagan was to telephone him and thank him, calling him 'a national hero'. America was divided. To some he was the loyal Marine who had sliced through bureaucracy, resisted Communism in Central America and worked tirelessly for the freedom of his fellow Americans. To others he represented a threat to democracy – part of a small group, within the government, which had conducted secret operations outside the law. From being a dedicated White House official he fast assumed the reputation of being a GI Joe action-figure, a romantic inhabiting a world of ex-CIA men, arms dealers and far-right adventurers. Association with Oliver North had become an embarrassment, as Terry Waite was soon to discover.

CAUGHT IN POLITICAL CROSSFIRE

While in West Germany with David Jacobsen, Terry Waite had not been altogether reassured by his conversation with Oliver North. When he arrived back in London he was still on the defensive, denying to reporters that he had acted on behalf of governments and complaining that people were trying to sabotage his efforts.

'Do these people who write such speculative comments realize that such comments could cost me my life?' he asked angrily. 'Is it realized how sensitive this situation is?' He recounted how, during his visit to Lebanon the previous Christmas, he had been given twenty-four hours to leave the country. A reporter asked him whether, in the light of this, he would be returning to Beirut. 'Yes,' said Waite defiantly. 'I am absolutely committed to these people.' It was to prove a fateful undertaking, but one which he would become more determined to honour in the following weeks.

After his return Waite lay low, watching the revelations tumbling out of Washington. Initially, there was no speculation about his role in the release of the hostages. The British press printed its customary eulogies. 'Another success for the Archbishop's Angel of Mercy,' trumpeted one paper. An editorial was even more effusive: 'Terry Waite does not wear his collar back to front. He is not an ordained priest. Nor does he allow himself to get bogged down in paperwork and protocol. He is not a professional diplomat. But Terry Waite does more credit to his church and to his country than any number of prattling prelates or Foreign Office functionaries . . . Carry on, Mr Waite. The best wishes of Britain are behind you.'

Samir Habiby had watched events from his office in New York. He was, in his words, 'thoroughly shocked'. He spoke on the telephone to Oliver North, who agreed it was a storm but promised, 'We'll weather it.' Habiby had expressed the hope that North was not involved. The White House official was evasive but thought 'they [would] be able to take care of it.' Habiby was not so sure. He was a Republican and knew how frustrated the liberal press had been at their failure to challenge Reagan successfully. The dogs would not be called off until they had drawn blood. The liberal Establishment, in his view, was rooting for a replay of Watergate. He had no doubt the water would lap round the Church's door as well.

Habiby and Terry Waite conferred on the phone. 'We're not involved,' said Waite. 'We're clean.' Neither man was surprised to learn that something else had been securing the freedom of the hostages. They had had their suspicions. Waite was insistent that the scandal did not involve the Church, but Habiby remained uneasy. The Democrats had done well in the mid-term elections and controlled both houses of Congress. This, he told Waite, changed the political landscape. They would want to examine every corner of this affair. Anyone who had been associated with North was likely to be tarred. Habiby warned Waite to expect trouble.

Within days Waite had his first intimations that he was being tied into what was being called Irangate, and that his role as an independent negotiator was under scrutiny. A British newspaper, in a report from the United States, said, 'It emerges that Waite has been used, wittingly, as the front man in top-secret US efforts to spring the hostages . . . His role has, in fact, been that of a huge shadow.'

Whether the paper intended to use the word 'wittingly' is unclear. The article provided no evidence, but Terry Waite was appalled and angry. It was not true, in his view, that he had been a mere cover. He had frequently said that many levers were needed to free a hostage, and he was only one of them. He had worked tirelessly on humanitarian initiatives to help the hostages, but he saw now that these would be discounted and misunderstood. His frequent public appearances and press conferences would be seen as cosmetic, a distraction for the media. His achievements would be in doubt; the kudos and respect heaped upon him misplaced;

his reputation as an honest broker in jeopardy. Worst of all, the Anglican Church, on this, its first sortie into world affairs, could be seen as naïve and inept.

The Archbishop of Canterbury, who had given his envoy such latitude, was becoming concerned. On one occasion he expressed the view that matters relating to Terry Waite were 'out of control'. Dr Runcie, however, accepted the assurances of his envoy that he had not been involved in anything improper. What could not be avoided, however, was the realization that the hostages had been freed as a result of arms sales rather than through the intervention of Terry Waite; and yet the Church had taken the credit. Waite had never claimed that his efforts alone had freed the hostages, but by appearing with the hostages at their moment of freedom the impression had been given that he was an ingenious mediator. Dr Runcie had watched his envoy grow famous and the Church applauded for its humanitarian efforts. Now he had to face the possibility that the Church of England had been cynically used.

Dr Runcie called a crisis meeting at Lambeth Palace. It was felt necessary that the Church should make a statement declaring that its activities had been purely humanitarian. As President Reagan had done a few days earlier, the Church looked to the hostages for an endorsement. The three who had been freed during the period of Terry Waite's involvement were invited to London. Although two of them were disillusioned with the US administration, they were unanimous in their gratitude to the Anglican envoy. It was indisputable that he had risked his life on their behalf.

On 17 November, the Reverend Benjamin Weir and Father Jenco arrived at Lambeth Palace. Shortly afterwards they had a meeting with David Jacobsen – the first time they had seen their fellow hostage since his release. They all embraced, revealing the special bond bred in captivity. As one of them said, 'We're all brothers from the Church of the Locked Door.' As the three hostages revelled in their freedom, Terry Waite stood to one side, beaming. It was the picture that appeared in the papers the following day.

But even from the men whose freedom he had striven for there were questions and doubts. Father Jenco confronted

Waite directly. 'One of the questions I asked Terry was, "Did you sell arms for my release?" And he said: "No, I did not. I've always stayed on the humanitarian role and I've stuck with it." I accepted his word.'

After the pictures had been taken, Waite read out a detailed statement. Working for the release of the hostages, he said, was only a small part of his work. He spoke of his visits to South Africa and his projects in Sudan. The Church had become involved with the American hostages in response to 'the desperate pleas from relatives' and because 'we do believe in the ultimate value of the individual human life.'

His tone was measured and serious. He acknowledged that there were risks in the Church being involved with American hostages. 'This time last year,' he said,

I found myself exposed to crossfire whilst caught in the middle of a street battle in Beirut. This year one is exposed to political crossfire. I know that the problems of the Lebanon must be viewed at several different levels. At the international level governments have always, and no doubt will continue, to strike bargains both in secret and in public. My experience over the years has taught me that in the Middle East at the end of the day there are no secrets. As a representative of the Church, I would have nothing to do with any deal which seemed to me to breach the code to which I subscribe. Not only because I know that such actions would undoubtedly come to light one day, but more importantly, they could destroy my independence and credibility.

Towards the American administration he was charitable, saying that it had honoured and respected his position. Although, he said, the cry 'foul' was being levelled against the United States, the finger could just as well be pointed elsewhere. If he felt any anger or bitterness towards Oliver North he did not betray it.

He concluded by saying that the Church intended to continue with its humanitarian mission, no matter what the cost. 'But there is no doubt,' he said, 'that from this point onward the task has been made immeasurably more difficult.' In his statement there was an undercurrent of defiance. Afterwards, uncharacteristically, he declined to answer any questions. He, the former hostages, Canon Habiby and other Church officials posed for pictures. They all considered that the occasion had been worthwhile and would silence further questions about the Church's role.

Coverage of the press conference was rather disappointing. It did appear on the nightly news in Britain, but Terry Waite's statement didn't receive the attention they had been hoping for. Three days later it became apparent that the Lambeth meeting had failed to stem questions about his role. The *Listener* magazine, under the headline 'Was Terry Waite used as a pawn by the Reagan administration?' described him as 'ruefully licking his wounds, inflicted during his recent mission to Lebanon'. The article went on to say that his 'reputation as an independent, impartial, apolitical negotiator had been left somewhat battered.'

The article hurt Terry Waite deeply. Where once he had been praised so extravagantly, he was now dismissed as being a mere 'pawn'. His most precious qualities of independence and impartiality were being openly questioned. When, the following January, he returned to Beirut he was still talking about this article. For several days Waite did not talk to anyone. Colleagues in the Church commented that he had grown silent. Increasingly he felt that statements were not enough, that his mission had to be vindicated. He began thinking about returning to Lebanon that Christmas, seeing in this important festival of the Christian calendar an opportunity to reaffirm that his mission was humanitarian and independent of any government. He was encouraged in this by a telephone call that Samir Habiby had received from Oliver North.

North had called Habiby a few days before he was dismissed from the National Security Council; they had spoken for ten minutes. Despite all the problems in Washington, North said, initiatives were continuing. Habiby mentioned that Waite was considering returning to Beirut. North was surprised. 'I trust he'll take the proper precautions,' he said. Although he would not be talking to Terry directly, he said he would be grateful if Habiby would convey to him a message. The position of the US government as regards the Kuwaiti prisoners might be changing, said North. It would no longer have any objection to Kuwait releasing the prisoners. Habiby was intrigued. Up until that moment the official American policy had been to support Kuwait in resisting pressure and blackmail to free prisoners who had engaged in terrorism. North told him that if the Church were to launch a humanitarian initiative both to improve the conditions of the Kuwaiti prisoners and to re-examine their sentences, then the United States would not stand in its way. Indeed, through diplomatic channels it would support such an initiative. Habiby thought this latter comment especially significant. Both he and Terry Waite believed that the State Department had blocked their previous attempts to visit Kuwait.

North said, rather dramatically, that this would be his last call. Although he wasn't to know that he was shortly to be fired, he gave the impression that his days at the White House were numbered. A member of his staff would be calling, he said, and would handle contacts in the future. There was no apology, no explanation for the arms sales, no reference to the criticisms that he had used Terry Waite, no trace of remorse. He was a man who believed he had done what was right. He expressed his appreciation of the Church's concern about these issues. North asked that his best wishes be passed on to Terry, and then said goodbye.

Habiby cannot remember all the details of the conversation, but he is certain that North said 'there would not be any objection if the Kuwaiti government felt for humanitarian reasons that they wanted to reconsider the sentences. I can say that much about the conversation,' said Habiby, 'and I'm sure Colonel North would support what I've just said on that point.'

Habiby was in no doubt as to the importance of what he had heard and passed the information to Terry Waite, who was beginning to make his arrangements to return to the Lebanese capital. When Habiby was interviewed about his last telephone conversation with North he confirmed that he had told Waite that United States policy on the crucial question of the Kuwaiti prisoners had changed.

'And was that impression conveyed to Terry Waite?'
'Terry Waite was very much aware of that, yes.'
'That there was a change in US government policy?'
'Yes.'

Waite thought Habiby's news significant. At that point he was planning only a brief visit to Beirut, lasting perhaps no more than forty-eight hours. By his mere presence in those treacherous streets he hoped to demonstrate that his efforts were independent of the American government. Their initiatives might have been strangled by the Iran–Contra affair, but his was still alive. But the North telephone call sowed the seed that the mission could have other, bolder possibilities; that there could be real progress in the one area that really mattered to the captors – the Kuwaiti prisoners.

In fact there had been no change in American policy. North was clutching at straws. Even at the eleventh hour he was trying to con the Iranians into believing that if only the captors released the hostages then a deal could be done on the prisoners. During the first few weeks of December Terry Waite was labouring under a false impression.

The State Department was to learn during December that meetings with the Iranian intermediaries were continuing. Even after North had been dismissed, informal contacts were maintained through the secure communications channel which had been established at the Revolutionary guards' headquarters. The Iranians let it be known that they wanted to continue the relationship developed by North, Secord and Hakim. It was agreed that there should be another meeting, on 13 December in Frankfurt.

George Cave, who was conducting the conversations with Iran, realized that in the current political climate in Washington it would be impossible to keep such a meeting secret; the State Department would have to be informed. When Secretary of State George Shultz learnt of it he insisted on new ground rules. The American side would only be able to exchange information; they couldn't deal with matters of substance. The State Department insisted that one of their officials, Charles Dunbar, accompanied Cave to Frankfurt.

Even before the meeting took place there was an attempt

to modify the ground rules. CIA Director William Casey believed that such a narrow brief would not only anger the Iranians but make the meeting redundant. He agreed with the White House that the meeting should be allowed to discuss policy. Only later did George Shultz learn of the change. He complained bitterly that 'nothing ever gets settled in this town.'

In Frankfurt, the Iranians were represented by the Monster. Despite the revelations, the leadership in Iran was ready to proceed with the agreement they had worked out in October. The Monster began going through the nine-point agenda of the Hakim accords. Charles Dunbar, the State Department official who was present, was open-mouthed as he learnt of an undertaking to overthrow the Iraqi President and of a plan to release the Kuwaiti prisoners. Neither he nor the State Department had ever heard of it. He turned to George Cave and asked him whether what he had heard was true. Cave nodded.

Dunbar then delivered the message he had been given by the State Department. In future there would be no further sale of arms in exchange for hostages. Although the United States wanted a good relationship with Iran, it would have to be on a different basis. The Monster was thoughtful. He had come to the meeting with a shopping list, and among its items were TOW missiles. The State Department official had ruled that out. After a period of silence the Monster replied, quietly but with a touch of menace. 'That,' he said, 'would being us back to zero.' He urged Dunbar to consult to see if that was what the United States really wanted.

Dunbar returned to Washington, while Cave and the Monster continued talking for another day. Cave urged the Iranian to release a hostage; it was the only hope of keeping the initiative alive. But the revelations had narrowed the options of the Monster's boss. Ali Akhbar Rafsanjani, the Speaker of the Iranian Parliament, was having to fight for his political life. His enemies were using the revelation of his secret contacts with the United States to try and disgrace him, even to mount a coup against him. The Monster explained that Rafsanjani had to be able to demonstrate that the Islamic Revolution benefited from its dealings with the

'Great Satan' – and that meant weapons. What the State Department was proposing would force Rafsanjani to turn against the United States to ensure his own survival. Dialogue would cease.

The two men agreed to talk again. But for both the United States and Iran it was becoming politically impossible to continue such a relationship.

Charles Dunbar reported to George Shultz on the Frankfurt meeting. The Secretary of State was so shocked at the way American foreign policy had been hijacked by a group of largely self-appointed officials that he insisted on a meeting with the President. Shultz later testified that the President 'reacted like he'd been kicked in the belly'.

'And I told the President,' continued Shultz, 'the items on this [Hakim] agenda, including such things as doing something about the Kuwaiti prisoners, which made me sick to my stomach that anybody would talk about that as something we would consider doing. And the President was astonished and I've never seen him so mad. He is a very genial, pleasant man . . . very easy going. But his jaws set and his eyes flashed.'

This marked the end of an initiative which had been confused in its objectives and which had singularly failed to free the hostages. As many Americans were still held in Beirut as when the arms sales began. The Iranians took some time to appreciate that the Americans were serious about wanting to end the trade. During the remainder of December and into the beginning of January a series of messages were delivered to Iran underlining that decision.

For Terry Waite, the timing could not have been worse. He would be back in Beirut, sounding optimistic, precisely at the moment that the leadership in Tehran understood that they were going to get no further weapons from the Americans.

He was unaware of both the Frankfurt meeting and the fact that the Iran initiative had been killed. As Christmas approached, his determination to return to Beirut strengthened. He had met old friends and seen the questions in their eyes. To help organize the trip he turned to Kemal Khoury, a former Lebanese Cabinet Minister who lived in London and to whom he had been introduced a few months earlier. Khoury had left Beirut in 1984 but, like many Lebanese living in the West, he could not leave his flawed country behind and was in almost daily touch with family or friends. He was a Maronite Christian with an Anglican wife, but had excellent contacts in both the Shi'ite and Druze communities. A sophisticated and thoughtful man, Khoury longed for the day when Lebanon could be rebuilt as a society rather than existing as a series of mini-states divided along sectarian lines. He thought the Church could help with reconstruction and that Terry Waite, with his international profile, might have a role. Now, deprived of American assistance, Waite wanted Khoury to help arrange his security for him in Beirut.

Waite had confided to his old friend Philip Turner that he was very anxious about returning. 'He spoke about it several times,' said Turner, 'and he was worried primarily because his security arrangements . . . were no longer available to him.' Turner understood that Oliver North had helped make them in the past.

Khoury found Waite impatient to return to Beirut: 'He wanted to go immediately, he would ring every day.' There was a note of desperation in the calls. 'If I can just get there for twenty-four hours and make a statement on television,' Khoury remembers his saying, 'then I can clear myself.'

Although there remained a commitment to the families and the hostages, Waite was driven by the need to prove that he could act on his own and that he wasn't an American stooge. Khoury wanted to help, but at the same time was troubled by Waite's attitude. 'He was willing to take incredible risks,' he said. Khoury contacted an old school friend, Akram Shehayeb, who was the closest aide to the Druze leader, Walid Jumblatt. Akram was reluctant to help. West Beirut had become a much more dangerous place than when Waite had been there a year before. Protecting him would be difficult, but he would talk to Jumblatt. A visit by Christmas, however, would not be possible.

Waite was frustrated at the delay but told Khoury that he wanted to go as soon as possible in January. The Archbishop of Canterbury was uneasy about the visit. He had, belatedly, begun taking a closer interest in the Iran–Contra affair. Contacts in the Foreign Office advised him that it would be dangerous for his envoy to return. Dr Runcie expressed his reservations to Waite, who replied that he had a commitment to the families of the hostages and that he intended to fulfil it. 'It was something he convinced himself was right,' said the Archbishop after Waite disappeared, 'and so, on the basis of his past record and my knowledge of his contacts, it seemed to be a risk that could be taken.' Although the Archbishop could have ordered his envoy not to go, he did not want to face down a man who had become the best-known figure in the Anglican Church. There was, however, an understanding between them that this would be Waite's last mission and that he would be looking for a different job. On 2 January Waite said again that he was considering quitting the Anglican Church to work in the field of international affairs.

The Foreign Office also tried to dissuade Waite from returning to Beirut. They had heard of his plans and suggested that he talk with the British Ambassador to the Lebanon, John Gray. The Ambassador was home in Britain on leave, and Waite asked him to come to his office at Lambeth Palace.

On 23 December 1986, John Gray was received by Terry Waite in the pink drawing room. Gray, who was an Arabist, understood the Byzantine ways of the Lebanese militias. The situation in West Beirut had deteriorated, he said. Not only were rival militias competing for control of that half of the city, but there were freelance gangs conducting operations for the highest bidder. Gray said that Waite's meetings with Oliver North had been reported in Lebanon and that they might not be understood. Waite listened, but the Ambassador's words had not the slightest impact. 'He was very determined to go back,' said Gray. Towards the end of the meeting the Archbishop joined them, but he could tell from the sombre expression on his envoy's face that nothing would prevent his returning to the Lebanon.

Kemal Khoury's friend Akram had contacted the Druze leader, Walid Jumblatt, about providing Waite with protection. Jumblatt was as hesitant as his aide had been. They could only protect Waite, he said, as long as he stayed in the company of the Druze bodyguards. If he wanted to meet the captors, they could not guarantee his safety. Khoury sent word back that Waite's mission would only last a couple of days and that he would be visiting community leaders to reaffirm the Church's concern with the agony of Lebanon. He would not be seeing the captors. Reluctantly, Jumblatt agreed.

The Druze leader was at the time in the United States, where his son was receiving medical treatment. When Waite learnt where he was, he suggested that he join Jumblatt and fly back to Beirut with him. Khoury was appalled. It would be foolish, he said, to be seen arriving from the United States, the very place he was trying to disassociate himself from. 'You have to wait at least a week after Walid [Jumblatt] is back in Beirut to dispel any American connection,' advised Khoury. After further discussions they settled on 12 January as the date for Waite's return to Beirut.

While these travel plans were being finalized, Samir Habiby had been exploring whether there was anything more the Church could do about the Kuwaiti prisoners. Through his family connections he had come to believe that the Kuwaiti government was more amenable to a visit by Terry Waite. He believed they would understand that his concerns were humanitarian and independent of government. 'We did feel from these private conversations that his presence in Kuwait would be welcome – they would receive him.' The agenda would be limited to improving contact between the prisoners and their relatives, which remained poor. Not only could the delivery of letters be improved, but prison visits might be possible.

Habiby consulted Kemal Khoury, who had interests in a private school in Kuwait and knew members of the Royal Family. If it would help, said Khoury, he was prepared to go to the Gulf to sound out opinion. Waite was very keen on the idea. An audience with the Kuwaiti government would impress the captors, and it might even be possible to visit the seventeen in prison. He urged Khoury to depart at once. Waite's expectations about his forthcoming trip to Beirut began to change. From being purely a high-profile, goodwill mission there was now the germ of achieving something more substantial, more exciting.

Receiving almost no advice from government, Waite and Habiby were unaware that Kuwait's mood, far from softening, was, in fact, hardening. As it became known that the United States had traded arms for hostages, so the Kuwaitis had gone out of their way to emphasize their resolve. Visitors would be informed that Kuwait had the toughest anti-terrorist policy in the world. As regards the seventeen prisoners, they said, 'There is no change of policy.' In a sideswipe at the United States they asked, 'How can we compromise our principles?' There had been reports before the Iran–Contra scandal broke that Iran had been seeking a dialogue with Kuwait. That was now clearly impossible.

Since his conversation with North, Habiby remained convinced that the Church could make progress on the Kuwaiti prisoners. After North was dismissed he had stayed in touch with Commander Craig Coy, who had been one of North's aides on the National Security Council. Coy had initially shown some interest in Waite's plans to return to Beirut, but during December he had informed Habiby that from now on the hostage question would be handled by the State Department. During his conversations with State Department officials, Habiby learnt that the policy on the Kuwaiti prisoners had not changed after all and that the State Department remained opposed to the Kuwaiti government making any concessions.

Habiby discussed this seeming contradiction with Terry Waite; they were understandably confused. The two men thought it might only be the view of a State Department official who was unaware of other contacts and channels. That, after all, had been the way during the past eighteen months. The US administration had spoken with different voices. Over time Waite had seen that North and the National Security Council were closest to what was really going on. Habiby said that he and Waite had a 'feeling that the public view of the United States and what it wished to accomplish privately were two different things.' Eugene Douglas felt that Waite was getting increasingly out of his depth. 'As time went on and the hostage crisis deepened he found it very difficult to understand the layering . . . I think he had great difficulty in coming to grips with the compromises, if not the duplicity, of the black world, of the covert world, which had come, by that time, to be the paramount world.'

Neither Habiby nor Waite realized that, as a result of the Iran–Contra affair, power over foreign policy had reverted to the State Department and that the United States once more had a unified and coherent policy on the hostages. It was Waite's misfortune that no one explained to him the significance of the political upheaval in Washington. He was aware of what Habiby had told him, but it would become apparent from his statements in Beirut that he believed the Kuwaitis might be becoming more flexible. For most of his period as an envoy he had operated in a world of secrecy and subterfuge, where reality and appearance were hard to disentangle. At this crucial juncture he was without a political guide.

In December, while he was finalizing his plans to return to Beirut, more specific stories began appearing about his dealings with Oliver North. Robert Oakley, the former head of the State Department's Office for Counter-terrorism, was quoted as saying that North helped Waite by arranging planes, shelter and protection. At the time, Oakley's comments attracted little attention, but within a short period North's name would become a byword for covert operations, and association with the Colonel from the White House, however innocent, would invite suspicion.

But in early January 1987 the details of the Iran–Contra affair were still not widely known. The Tower Commission, which had been set up to investigate the matter, was still leafing through documents and would not report until the following month. Terry Waite did not know that Oliver North had not only lied to his own government but had misled the Iranians. North would later stand up and proudly declare, 'I lied every time I met the Iranians.' Although the State Department had learnt of the Hakim accords and the elaborate promises to free the Kuwaiti prisoners, Waite was not told. When the scandal broke, he was dropped like a stone. He was never really involved, so the word went – he was just 'ecclesiastical cover', as North had referred to him.

He had had a walk-on part and was expected to revert to being a humble aide in the Church of England. It was never expected that he would single-handedly try and revive the play, based as it was on deals and empty promises. For eighteen months he had striven on behalf of American hostages, talked to the captors and taken risks. But in the turbulence of the Reagan presidency's darkest storm he was forgotten.

During that January, when his intention of returning to Beirut was known, no one thought to take Terry Waite aside and spell out the perils of his mission. In a general way, the British Ambassador to the Lebanon had advised him to stay away; but no one from the American administration chose to warn him that both the Iranians and the captors had every reason to feel angry and cheated. As the person who had been encouraged to deal with the issue that most concerned the captors, he was likely to appear as the symbol of American betrayal. Because he was seen in Washington as the 'cellophane wrapping around the hostage releases', he was ignored. It was not understood that, much as those he had worked with were fighting for their reputation, so he was having to deal with the legacy of the affair in the only way available to him – by returning to Beirut. He was an isolated figure, bereft of information, setting out with a mixture of hope and illusion.

He was not totally unaware of the dangers. Three days before he left for Beirut he said there was 'a high element of risk. When I leave all my security behind . . . I'm entirely dependent on my reputation . . . I am absolutely vulnerable.' Although he thought that his reputation had been damaged, he believed he could explain everything. At a press conference in Italy he tried to clear the air by dealing with the stories about him and Oliver North directly. As an envoy he had known no more than part of what was happening. 'My job,' he said, 'standing as an independent negotiator in the middle, is to meet with a lot of people but to be in control of my own agenda and to be able, at the end of the day, to look anybody in the eye and say my dealings were honest and honourable, and if other people have tried to use me or attempted to use me, that, I'm afraid, is their problem.'

It was his only public reference to Oliver North; he was

never critical of the man whose dedication he admired so much. At the time of North's dismissal, Waite's only comment to Habiby had been, 'It's terribly sad for him.' Even though it was his association with North and the American's various schemes that had damaged his reputation, Waite couldn't bring himself to dislike the dedicated colonel from the White House. His methods may have been questionable, but his motives were honourable; and they were motives that Waite shared. Although Terry Waite was stung by the suggestion that he had been a 'front man', he did not blame Oliver North for having manipulated him.

While at dinner with Philip Turner a few days before his final mission, he had made light of what 'Oliver' had done. 'He didn't feel particularly used,' said Turner. Waite seemed to accept that in relationships people have different priorities. 'All kinds of people use each other,' he told his friend, 'for lots of different reasons, and the main thing to know is what is going on.'

During his conversation with Turner he revealed a deep foreboding about going back to Beirut. Publicly, he spoke of his commitment to the hostage families. Privately, he was a troubled man, compelled to salvage his reputation while at the same time tormented by the risk. Turner knew him as someone who thrived on dangerous missions. But as he listened to his friend speak he saw that the old zest was missing. 'The last time I saw him he had an enormous sense of danger . . . he kept saying, "You know, Philip, it's very, very dangerous. It's very, very dangerous." '

Even without the knowledge that the captors had indirectly been made promises that went unkept, Terry Waite knew from his conversations with Father Jenco and David Jacobsen that the captors had lost their faith in him. Furthermore, at the back of his mind was the warning he had received the previous Christmas, telling him not to return unless he had something concrete to offer. It was a measure of his bravery and his desperation to restore his good name that he planned to return to Lebanon at all. There would be no problem for him if he just worked the circuit of public officials, but if he was planning to meet the captors then he was gambling high.

A few days before he left for Beirut he spoke with 'Spiro', the man who had helped arrange his previous visits. Since the Iran–Contra affair had become known, 'Spiro' had had to take care, fearful that his links with the Americans would be revealed. Some of his contacts had been put in jeopardy. He was sorry, but on this occasion he could not help. 'Spiro' warned him that Imad Mugniyah, the man behind the hostage taking, believed he had been short-changed after the release of David Jacobsen and that the United States had not honoured its side of the deal. Waite thanked him for his advice. The conversation disturbed him, but it did not shake his resolve.

Samir Habiby flew to London to say farewell. Waite was now impatient to leave, to face the task he had set himself. Habiby expected him to be in Beirut for no longer than forty-eight hours, but in the meantime he would be working on arrangements for Waite to go on to Kuwait. Herein existed the seeds of a contradiction: on the one hand Terry Waite was not going to negotiate, yet on the other his colleague was pursuing the main demand of the captors. The trip to Beirut was to reaffirm his independence, but in the back of Waite's mind was the thought that he just might be able to secure the release of a hostage. If that happened, in a stroke he would have silenced his critics. The prize was tempting and dangerous.

Habiby arranged for a car to take him to Heathrow airport. As they parted he implored Terry Waite, 'Whatever you do, don't go alone.'

16

ONE MORE WESTERN HOSTAGE

On Monday, 12 January 1987, Terry Waite returned to West Beirut, a city which, he said, he feared above all others. It was now in the grip of militias, gangs and armed family clans; a very different place from the one he had visited twelve months earlier. Streets had become fiefdoms, sealed each end with roadblocks. A brief journey was like travelling through a series of mini-states where unpredictable guards checked papers and issued passes.

Waite was met by ten armed bodyguards from the Druze militia. Akram Shehayeb was struck by the envoy's seriousness. 'He was not the same Terry Waite. I sensed there was something wrong.' Waite told them he was fearful of being kidnapped. They drove him to the Riviera Hotel in the Ein el-Mreisseh district. The building could have overlooked a thousand Mediterranean beaches without provoking comment; it was a honeycomb of concrete balconies or cages, only partly redeemed by the cluster of palm trees on the street outside. The Druze had chosen the location because it was close to an enclave they controlled and some distance from the treacherous southern suburbs where the gunmen of Hezballah held sway. It had the sad, abandoned air of a seaside resort out of season, and Terry Waite was almost the only guest. Meals were sent to his second-floor room, and an armed guard stayed in the corridor outside.

In the past he had brought with him a press corps: cameras, boom mikes, tape recorders, an attentive throng and, towering above them, unperturbed, a bearded figure. That was the image of a Waite mission to Beirut. Now most of the foreign journalists had departed. Lebanon had always been a dangerous assignment; it was part of its strange attraction. But the kidnappers had raised the stakes too high. The major news agencies had come to rely on Lebanese stringers – local reporters who were paid by the story – rather than their own staff reporters. On his previous visits the press had not only provided coverage, they had also been a source of companionship; with several of the journalists he had formed close friendships. Now the familiar faces had gone, preferring to observe his mission from the safety of Larnaca or Damascus. In moments of stress or boredom he had enjoyed the gossip at the bar of the Commodore. This time all of that was absent, consumed by the savagery of the city. He was on his own, unable to leave his hotel room without an armed escort.

The American Ambassador, John Kelly, was surprised to learn of Terry Waite's return; he had not been informed beforehand. He thought it unwise and sent off a cable to Washington: 'Waite is back. It's very risky.'

As soon as he arrived at the Riviera Hotel, Waite set about distancing himself from the Iran–Contra affair. He denied that he had ever discussed arms deals. 'If I had done so, then I would be too afraid, and I wouldn't be back here now. So I have come here with a clear conscience and I will meet anybody.' His plan was to do the rounds of Lebanese leaders, many of whom he had never met before. He wanted to be seen back in West Beirut, untroubled by the revelations in Washington. The handshakes of the community leaders would be a riposte to those who thought he had been compromised. This was the mission as understood by colleagues like Samir Habiby, a restoration of trust. But it was apparent as soon as Waite arrived in Beirut that, deep down, he was hoping to see the captors. Even though he had been advised against meeting them, the prize of a hostage release was too great a lure. He described his mission as being on two levels, 'the general diplomatic level and the out-of-the-picture level'. Out of the picture was meeting in secret with the holders of the American hostages.

The morning after he had arrived, he witnessed first-hand just how dangerous the city had become. He had held an impromptu press conference in the hotel lobby and afterwards had agreed to walk along the seafront to enable the photographers to get their pictures. Among them were a few Westerners including Roger Auque, a freelance French photographer. Half an hour after leaving the Riviera Hotel Augue returned to his apartment with reporter Paul Marchand, who said later, 'I was near the lift of the building waiting for Roger when two gunmen, one with a pistol and another with a Kalashnikov, came to seize me. I started screaming and started to run away. One gunman fired in the air and as I ran I yelled to Roger Auque, who was coming down in the lift, to escape, but he did not. When he left the lift they took him.'

It was a setback before Terry Waite's mission had even begun. There was speculation that the kidnapping might be connected to his visit. Some thought the captors were using his trip to draw attention to the fact that their demands were not being addressed. Waite had to face the awful thought that by being in Beirut he was encouraging further hostage taking. That evening he began imploring foreign journalists to stay away. 'I wouldn't advise anyone to come back here at the moment,' he implored one American reporter who called him from London. 'I think everybody should keep clear.' When a British reporter, who also was a friend, telephoned him, Waite told him: 'Stay away. All sorts of people are roaming around here.'

The public meetings with Lebanese leaders, however, were going well. He had dinner with Walid Jumblatt, the Druze leader, and spoke with Hussein Husseini, the Moslem Speaker of the Lebanese Parliament. The following day he saw the second-in-command of the Amal militia, the General Secretary of the pro-Syrian Ba'ath party and Sheikh Mohammad Mehdi Shamseddine, Vice President of the Supreme Shi'ite Council. It was a roll call of Lebanese leaders. The meetings led one paper to comment that his visit was more like that of a 'visiting statesman than a secret negotiator'.

Terry Waite was well pleased with his reception. They all welcomed his mission and wished him success; the hostages were an impediment to resolving Lebanon's deep-seated problems. Most importantly, there wasn't the slightest hint that his standing had been diminished by the Iran–Contra affair. None of the leaders had referred to it. His spirits rose. He told one friend triumphantly that 'that business' did not seem to have had any impact over there. When Habiby called he found Waite tremendously excited, saying that they had 'made up ground lost by the problems in Washington'.

On Wednesday, 14 January he called a press conference and reported good progress. 'I am very glad that I am back. The time was right and the mood was right.' Revealing the optimism that he was now feeling, he said that he might visit other Arab capitals – a reference to Kuwait. 'There are plans,' he said cryptically.

In his telephone calls Waite was surprisngly concerned with the way his visit was being reported. 'What news have you got of me?' he asked one reporter. 'How is it reported in America?' he quizzed another. 'What was it like on the radio?' he enquired of a third. 'Have you seen any English papers?' he asked a journalist in Cyprus. Callers were peppered with questions.

When one caller said that a BBC report had been negative, Waite was dismayed. 'He's a so-and-so,' he said of the reporter. 'He's been a menace to me ... it doesn't do me any good at all.' The same reporter had earlier written of his visiting Beirut with Oliver North. 'It's not true I've been here many times with that fellow,' complained Waite. Later he returned to the subject, saying that he would like to prove the reporter wrong.

Waite suspected that his calls were being listened to and would occasionally use a conversation to underline his independence. In the middle of one call he surprised a friend by saying, 'I am not, repeat not, an agent of the British government or American government, and on this whole visit I've had no contact at all with the United States or Britain or any other governmental administration. I have not. Definitely not.'

If Waite had stuck to his original plan he would have left on the Thursday, having had two days of talks and having re-established his reputation as an honest broker. But he had made contact with Dr Adnam Mroueh, the man who had previously acted as go-between with the captors. Dr Mroueh thought a visit to see some of the hostages might be possible. According to Mroueh, Waite said he had information concerning Kuwait which he wished to tell the captors.

Mroueh promised to get back to him.

Waite was being drawn, inexorably, into going for the bigger prize; a meeting with the captors. The images of him in Beirut might convince the general public, but journalists who knew Lebanon well would ask more searching questions. He did not want the trip reported as a public relations exercise as some reporters were already doing. Through Dr Mroueh lay the chance of dispelling the questions once and for all.

While Waite sat in his hotel waiting for the captors' response, a new element of danger was added to his mission. On 13 January, the day after he arrived, there had been a chance arrest at a West German airport. A young Lebanese Shi'ite, Mohammad Ali Hamadei, had arrived in Frankfurt on a direct flight from Beirut. He was carrying what appeared to be three bottles of wine but which, on inspection, turned out to be methyl nitrate, a powerful liquid explosive. The Hamadei family, which was from the Bekaa valley, had strong ties to Hezballah. One of Hamadei's brothers was the party's chief of security; Mohammed Ali Hamadei was a friend of Imad Mugniyah. They had both taken part in the hijacking of a TWA plane in 1985.

A few days later Samir Habiby was telephoned by the State Department and warned that Hamadei's arrest could endanger Terry Waite. Habiby got straight on to Beirut. 'I have a message from friends,' he told Terry Waite. 'You know there was an incident in Europe . . .' he continued. It took some moments for Waite to decipher what his friend was talking about, but he had in fact heard of the arrest on his short-wave radio. Habiby urged him to be careful but Waite believed – wrongly – that it was unrelated to the people he was dealing with.

A warning was also conveyed to him in a bizarre call from a British diplomat. Aware of the sensitivity of a British official contacting Terry Waite, he introduced himself in Latin. 'Good afternoon to you. Look, I've got a little message which I've got to pass to you. It's a message from London. I want to be quite discreet. I'll introduce myself in guarded terms. *Linguam Latinam* [Do you speak Latin]?'

'Yes, I understand,' said Waite.

'*Sum Consulus Britannicus* [I am the British Consul].'

'Uh . . . right,' replied Waite uncertainly.

'*Nomen meum est Frank Gallagher* [My name is Frank Gallagher].'

'Yeah,' said Waite.

Having gone to the trouble of introducing himself in Latin, the British Consul in Beirut finished the conversation in English. He mentioned the arrest of Hamadei and said that he had a message from 'our people'. He proceeded to read out what was clearly a cable from the Foreign Office in London: 'Mr Waite will no doubt have this in mind in attending to his own security arrangements.' The Consul was most apologetic for having telephoned him, and rang off swiftly. Waite had been rather cool to the diplomat, mindful of how suspicious schoolboy Latin might sound to a poorly educated Lebanese. What made the call almost comic was that the incidental information was in Latin while the sensitive remarks were in English.

Terry Waite recognized that he would make an ideal hostage to exchange for Hamadei. The day after the warnings he acknowledged that 'some people here in Beirut might in retaliation try and seize someone as a bargaining counter and I would be a pretty good bargaining counter'. But the knowledge of extra danger did not deter him from hoping for a face-to-face meeting with the captors.

Soon afterwards, another foreigner was taken hostage. Waite was furious, and at the same time frustrated by outsiders continuing to travel to Beirut: it only complicated his mission. The new hostage was a businessman selling pharmaceutical products. Waite did not seem to have realized that he was a West German and that his kidnapping was directly related to the arrest of Hamadei in Frankfurt. 'No foreigner should travel here unless he has business which concerns life or death,' he complained to a friend on the telephone.

We cannot go on taking responsibility trying to get people out as hostages if people come here willy nilly, regardless of the risks. We've got enough to deal with. We can't take any more. Good God, say we're full. Full house. I don't know how many we are now. People coming here like that selling pharmaceutical products. I suppose he's selling condoms, trying to keep Aids down. But seriously, it's just asking for trouble. I can't see any need for him to be here.

On the Friday Waite spoke with Dr Mroueh again. There was no news. Waite's spirits seemed to sag. A note of resignation crept into his voice as he fielded calls from journalists. 'You can always be surprised,' he told one caller. 'We'll just see.' Although he remained optimistic that the problem of the hostages would be solved eventually, 'It won't be by the weekend,' he said.

Various people came to the hotel to see him: a delegation of Lebanese citizens whose relatives had gone missing; the wife of one of the American hostages; and the occasional reporter. But there were hours with nothing to do and no one to talk to. He asked one of the journalists in the city to bring him round some tapes of Mozart and Monteverdi. The isolation troubled him. 'You sit out here by yourself,' he told one of his callers. 'No guidance from anybody. You have to take every decision yourself. It's ludicrous in some ways. I've nobody to share with.'

When he was asked whether he had heard from the Archbishop his voice filled with scorn. 'By crikey, if he ever phones me up, that will be new, won't it! I haven't heard a thing from my office.' The question unlocked a whole series of grievances. 'I even [have to] get myself on the tube to the airport.' He recalled the morning of his departure. 'I was almost frantic that morning because I was trying to clear up everything in my office. I had to leave myself sufficient time to walk with my cases to the tube.' (Samir Habiby's recollection is different; he remembers ordering a car for him.) Waite was obviously bitter about the level of support his office was giving him. 'They don't even pay me,' he said. When his caller tried to cheer him up by joking that 'martyrs are never well paid,' Waite replied, 'They never get much fun out of life either.'

He was particularly irritated by a news agency report which said, incorrectly, that one of the Moslem militias had cold-shouldered him. 'Good God!' Waite exploded. 'I sometimes wonder whether I'm dealing with fools.' Any reporting that he regarded as inaccurate he fretted over. As the days passed he began losing patience with the reporters in Beirut. 'They're a stupid lot here,' he complained. 'They depress me. They're so thick. The bottom of the barrel is left here.'

The next day, Saturday, 17 January, he had an appointment with Sheikh Mohammad Hussein Fadlallah, the spiritual leader of Hezballah. The Americans regarded him as one of the godfathers of Shi'ite terrorism, believing him to have been directly involved in the bombing of the US Marine barracks and several other attacks on American buildings. In March 1985 Fadlallah had himself been the target of an assassination attempt, when a 2000 lb bomb had exploded outside his home. Sixty-two people had been killed and more than two hundred injured. The group who did it was allegedly trained and financed by the CIA. Others who knew the Shi'ite community well were less certain of Fadlallah's direct involvement in terrorism.

There was another reason, however, which made Sheikh Fadlallah important to Terry Waite. The former chief of his bodyguards was Imad Mugniyah, the man who was thought to he holding some of the American hostages, in particular Terry Anderson and Thomas Sutherland. Fadlallah and Mugniyah both sat on the Council of Beirut, the body which controlled Hezballah and its related groups. Another of its nine members was an Iranian.

Waite was driven by his Druze escort to Fadlallah's house in Bir Abed, a Shi'ite stronghold in the southern suburbs. His guards mingled uneasily with the bearded fighters of Hezballah who guarded the Sheikh's residence. Hezballah and the Druze had had occasion to fight in the past.

Fadlallah, wearing a black turban and a brown robe, sat on a hard wooden chair placed against the wall. He was overweight and his black beard was speckled with grey, but his eyes were alert, black and impenetrable. He gestured to Terry Waite to sit by the wall with an interpreter between them. As is often the case in the Middle East, Waite had to make his case before a small audience. There were others in the room waiting to see the Sheikh, and yet others unknown but possibly influential within the Shi'ite community. A visitor could never be certain who he was talking to.

Fadlallah rarely looked at Waite, preferring to gaze at a point in the middle of a Persian rug. Pointedly, he asked him why he had returned to Lebanon. Waite replied that it was time to end the hostage crisis, which had been going on too long and was causing suffering to too many people both within Lebanon and outside. He had come back as an envoy of the Church of England, independent of any government, on a humanitarian mission. He believed it important that a dialogue should be maintained with those holding the hostages.

Fadlallah, fitting a cigarette into a long ivory holder, said there had been a dialogue before, and promises. Waite, believing that to be a reference to the Kuwaiti situation, said he thought it was now possible for progress to be made over the prisoners in Kuwait. Fadlallah seemed doubtful and asked him for evidence. 'I have, at this moment, a messenger in Kuwait,' said Waite, 'who is expecting to hear from me.' Fadlallah showed no reaction to this news. Waite said he was willing to meet anyone who could help resolve this problem. Fadlallah replied that those who might be interested would know where to find him. He avoided any reference to the captors; he has always denied having any influence over them. He said that Waite, as a representative of the Church, was welcome in Beirut, and he hoped his visit would achieve a just solution. The two men shook hands and the audience was over.

Waite thought the meeting had gone well. Later that evening he had a three-way telephone call with Samir Habiby in the United States and Kemal Khoury who was, in fact, still in London. Habiby taped the conversation.

Waite: This evening I went to see Sheikh Fadlallah.
Habiby: Oh, excellent.
Waite: And we had a good conversation together and I'm going to wait on here maybe till Monday.
Habiby: OK, fine.
Waite: [I want to] see if anything's happened. If we can do something on the other front I think there's some enthusiasm.

Khoury: I'm moving immediately. I am off tomorrow.
Waite: Excellent.
Khoury: In the morning.
Waite: Excellent. Well done.
Khoury: I should be there in the evening. Sunday I should be working on it. I hope to get through early in the week.

'The other front' to which Waite was referring was his proposed visit to Kuwait. It is apparent from the call that no arrangements had yet been made. Khoury hadn't even left for Kuwait. In asking to see the captors Terry Waite was therefore taking a huge risk. They had warned him not to return without something concrete to offer them on the prisoners in Kuwait, and the prospect of a visit to the Gulf state was unlikely to convince them. Khoury thought he would make contact with officials in a few days, but he expected the discussions to take several weeks. He never imagined that the Anglican envoy would be able to travel on from Beirut to Kuwait. Terry Waite's final mission had become a quixotic mixture of bravado and optimism.

On Sunday, 18 January, Waite went for a stroll along the Corniche with his bodyguards. It was a photo opportunity for the press and an outing for himself. 'If I don't have any exercise,' he said, 'I'll die.' It was a relaxed occasion. He was in shirtsleeves and the guards took turns posing for pictures with him. A glass of beer was brought out on to the promenade and Waite sipped it in the winter sun. Beneath the smiles the guards were becoming increasingly anxious over the length of his visit. 'Why don't you leave?' they asked several times. They could not understand what he was still doing there.

During the weekend there was a further meeting with Dr Mroueh. The captors wanted to talk. Waite was delighted. 'My friends told me they definitely wanted to see me,' he confided to one of the few journalists in the city whom he trusted. 'So obviously they either want to talk or pick me up,' he added with a nervous laugh.

But there were obstacles. As he was preparing to leave for another meeting with Dr Mroueh, his bodyguards informed him that they would be unable to take him. A convoy of cars carrying the Chief Security officer of the Druze had been ambushed near the airport; he had been wounded and one of his bodyguards killed. Waite was exasperated: 'Every time we have difficulty.' Without his escorts he was hotel-bound, but the knowledge that the captors wanted to see him again was reason enough to postpone his departure.

By the Monday he was more optimistic than at any time during his visit. He told a news conference that 'the chances are good for the release of Terry Anderson and Thomas Sutherland.' Islamic Jihad had assured him that both were being 'well looked after' and were in 'generally good' condition. When he was questioned as to whether he had actually had face-to-face contact with Islamic Jihad, he said, 'Oh yes, definitely. Oh yes, we're talking.'

By the evening when the arrangements for the meeting he was really seeking still hadn't emerged, he began planning his return to London. He made a reservation for Tuesday, 20 January. He hoped, he said, to be back within three or four weeks. His Druze guards expected him to leave, as did Samir Habiby in the United States. Although a hostage had not been released, Waite felt he had achieved what he had set out to do. He had demonstrated his independence as an envoy and he had renewed contact, albeit indirectly, with the captors. If he got to Kuwait he was hopeful of achieving more.

The Druze's first intimation of a change of plan came when Waite asked Akram Shehayeb, the personal assistant of the Druze leader, to bring to the hotel three suitcases, each in a different colour. He also asked for warm clothing, a leather jacket and some dark glasses. He offered no explanation.

Some time on the Tuesday, the day of his expected departure, he received a message from the captors. They were ready to see him. They had become concerned that the morale of the hostages was low and deteriorating. There was a clear hint that he might be allowed to see them – something he had never achieved on any of his previous visits. To a man who had come back to restore his reputation as an independent envoy, it was the ultimate temptation: a visit to the hostages would erase all suggestion that he had been an American dupe.

He informed his guards that his departure had been postponed and he was going to meet the captors instead. They were very concerned. He asked them to take him to Dr Adnam Mroueh's clinic. There he was to be left. He was most insistent: there must be no cars tailing him, no watchers, no attempt to find out where he was going or who he was going with. The commander of the guards who had been attached to him protested strongly: they couldn't guarantee his safety if he left them, and it would be very dangerous. 'My job is full of adventures,' responded Waite. 'I have to do this.'

Before he left the hotel for the meeting Waite examined every item of his clothing and personal effects for any object that might make his captors suspect him of carrying a tracking device. He discarded his pen, and he showed his bodyguards that his watch had no batteries. He put on a raincoat and walked down to the lobby. A cameraman filmed him getting into a red Range Rover with three guards. It was 6.45 in the evening.

It was only a short drive to the clinic. Dr Mroueh was from a prominent Shi'ite family which published one of Lebanon's papers. The Americans suspected that on occasions he had visited the hostages when they were sick, although they were never sure of it. Waite had found him intelligent and honourable. Mroueh did not give the appearance of a man with dangerous acquaintances: he was short, in his fifties, with receding hair.

Outside the clinic Waite's guards urged him again not to go on his own. He shook his head. 'If you don't do as I ask, both I and the hostages may well die.' He thanked them for their consideration and said he would either see them back at the hotel or telephone when he needed collecting.

It was just before seven o'clock that he entered the clinic and was met by Dr Mroueh. According to Dr Mroueh, he told Waite that they would be contacted and taken to another building. Waite suggested that, as on his first visit to Lebanon, they should verify that the person in question was genuine. He pointed to a magazine on the table and said he would ask the contact to photograph one of the hostages holding it.

They had been talking for about forty minutes when Dr

Mroueh was interrupted by a phone call. There was an emergency at the hospital. A woman was having difficulty giving birth, and he was needed at once. Dr Mroueh claims he told Waite he would be back shortly. On no account was the envoy to leave the clinic without him.

When he returned an hour and a half later, Terry Waite was gone. There were no messages, no sign of a struggle. The magazine was missing. Dr Mroueh presumed that in the short time he had been away the contact had been able to take a picture of the hostages and persuade Waite to go with him. However keen Waite was to meet the captors, it is unlikely he would have left without seeing some evidence first.

The Druze have a different story. Despite Waite's insistence that he be left alone, they posted a man in the Haykal centre, an apartment block opposite. According to Akram Shehayeb, the man observed Waite and Dr Mroueh meeting with a figure who they thought was Imad Mugniyah. They believe Waite was taken out of the building through an underground passage that leads towards the university.

Several hours later, the head of the Druze bodyguards telephoned the clinic. 'Where's Terry?' he asked. Dr Mroueh sounded worried. He explained that Waite had left without him and he did not know where he was. Dr Mroueh said he had telephoned the contact who was due to meet Waite but the man hadn't seen the envoy, claiming that they had driven to the clinic to meet him but had found him not there.

The Druze were immediately suspicious but, mindful of Terry Waite's insistence that they should not try to find him, kept quiet for twenty-four hours. It was always possible, they thought, that he had been taken to a building in the Bekaa valley and would return the following day. By the Thursday, two days after his disappearance, they decided to investigate. Akram Shehayeb went to see Sheikh Fadlallah. The cleric appeared very concerned: he would be against anyone taking Terry Waite. Being in charge of the Druze leader's security, Akram had good intelligence on who was behind the hostage taking and demanded to see Imad Mugniyah. Fadlallah, aware of the reputation of the Druze as fighters, promised to make some enquiries and get back to him immediately.

Mugniyah himself contacted Akram the next day and suggested they should meet at once, at the Summerland Hotel. A few hours later they sat down together. Mugniyah denied any knowledge of Waite's whereabouts. He had not seen him, and he hadn't planned to see him. Several times during the conversation, which lasted several hours, Mugniyah reminded Akram: 'I have a brother-in-law in Kuwait.' He promised he would look into the matter and report to them in twenty-four hours. He never did. When the Druze tried to find him through Fadlallah they were told he had left town.

At first Lambeth Palace was unruffled by their envoy's disappearance. He was conducting 'quiet talks', they said quaintly. Even after six days their confidence was unshaken. 'Mr Waite is locked in secret negotiations with the kidnappers but is safe and well.' The Anglican Church, which had chosen to enter the hazardous business of diplomacy, soon realized the limits of its resources. The Archbishop turned to the Foreign Office. They were getting reports, principally from Dr Mroueh, that Waite was a 'house guest' and that he was being well looked after. As the British government began making appeals and sifting through reports of dubious reliability, they realized they were as impotent as every other government had been in retrieving their citizens. As Terry Waite himself had said, 'When I leave my security behind . . . I am absolutely vulnerable.'

For the Druze, the loss of Waite was a humiliation. They had extended their hospitality to him, and in the Middle East that carries with it the promise of protection. Failure involves shame. To Walid Jumblatt, the Druze leader, it was an insult, a slight against himself and his people. The detention of Waite, he said, was an 'act against Islam, against the rules of hospitality'. He ordered his party and its militia to leave no stone unturned in the hunt for the missing envoy.

Jumblatt went to see Fadlallah personally to beg for Waite's return. He knelt before the cleric, an act of humiliation for a leader of one of Lebanon's religious sects. 'Don't embarrass me,' he pleaded with Fadlallah. 'If you want, take me as a hostage – but I want Mr Waite to be delivered.' The Shi'ite leader promised to help, but the Druze doubted his sincerity. Jumblatt didn't leave without issuing a warning. If anything were to happen to Terry Waite he would take revenge. Between the militias that kind of threat is well understood, and it may have helped save Waite's life.

At one point the Druze thought they had located the house where Waite was being held. Jumblatt contemplated a rescue attempt or kidnapping one of Mugniyah's relatives, but, angry as he was, he wasn't prepared to initiate another round of fighting for the sake of Terry Waite. Within a few weeks Jumblatt would be battling for his survival in another murderous bout of Lebanon's civil war. 'There is now a political problem more important than Terry Waite,' he declared.

Rumours abounded. There were even sightings. On 5 February a taxi driver said he saw Waite walking in the southern suburbs with an escort of ten gunmen and four turbaned mullahs: 'I saw him smiling and waving to onlookers as he walked.' A second driver claimed to have seen the same event. Then Waite was spotted in a convoy of three vehicles in the Bekaa valley. It was possible that, for a period, he was still negotiating, but gradually these stories were supplanted by others. Within two weeks of his disappearance an unnamed militia leader in West Beirut spoke to Reuters. 'My information is,' he said, 'that Terry Waite will not be returning, as he is kidnapped. He has been added to the list of hostages. He became one the day he left without his bodyguard.' The truth was elusive, but time verified the statement.

17

'WHAT TREMENDOUS FOOLISHNESS'

For Terry Waite the timing of his mission could not have been worse. Events conspired against him. The day before he went to meet the captors there had been three arson attacks on Kuwaiti oilfields. The 'Revolutionary Organization of the Forces of the Prophet Mohammad in Kuwait' claimed responsibility. In the past Kuwait had discovered the hand of Iran behind acts of terrorism on its soil. They believed the seventeen members of the Da'Wa who were now their prisoners had been directed from Tehran. In the face of fresh attacks, the Kuwaitis were to respond defiantly. Their Foreign Minister reiterated that there would be no concessions to the seventeen. A Kuwaiti paper summed it up with the headline, 'No deal for 17 criminals and killers'. It was at the precise moment that Terry Waite was explaining to the captors that he had a messenger in Kuwait.

Furthermore, the Iranians, who still exercised a large measure of control over Hezballah, were concluding that the Iran–Contra affair had finally closed the door to further arms supplies from the United States. Three days after Waite disappeared, President Ali Hassani Khamen'ei of Iran stated at Friday prayers that they had 'rebuffed the final efforts by Reagan to maintain contacts. Our brothers at the Foreign Ministry encountered it with the same Islamic stand.' In fact there had been no such efforts by the US administration: the comment was a jab in the power struggle going on inside Iran. Khamen'ei, by claiming to have 'rebuffed' the Americans, was shaming his rival Rafsanjani, whose relative had conducted some of the negotiations with the Americans. The insinuation was to spur Rafsanjani into a virulent bout of anti-American behaviour. Officials in Washington and Paris believe that Rafsanjani personally sanctioned Waite's capture. The Iran–Contra affair had made him vulnerable, and in order to survive politically he gave his blessing to further hostage taking.

There were other events with ominous implications for the Anglican envoy. The US government was seeking the extradition of Mohammed Ali Hamadei from West Germany for his part in the TWA hijacking in 1985. It was a reminder to Hezballah that their previous misdeeds had not been forgotten by the United States. Mugniyah believed that the CIA was determined to avenge the death of William Buckley. Hamadei's arrest encouraged Hezballah to seize fresh hostages not only so as to bargain for his release but also to insure themselves against their enemies. Terry Waite, as he himself recognized, would be an ideal bargaining counter.

Most damaging of all to Waite was the Iran–Contra affair. Although he fretted, probably needlessly, over the damage it had done to his reputation in the West, he was not able to judge its impact on the captors until he met them. Although it was, no doubt, reassuring to learn that various Lebanese leaders still treated him seriously, in the end it didn't matter. What the Iran–Contra affair had revealed to the captors was that, while Iran had benefited from the release of the hostages, they had got next to nothing out of it. As Iran's client militia they had received funds, weapons and medical supplies, but they had not won the freedom of the prisoners in Kuwait – particularly Mugniyah's brother-in-law. In retrospect, Waite's long involvement in the hostage affair would have been seen as a way of placating them, stringing them along, while the United States and Iran dealt behind their backs. All the talk of progress, of improved conditions for the prisoners, of a regular exchange of letters, of a reduction in the sentences, of the 'blood money' idea must have appeared as empty words. And yet here he was, yesterday's salesman, back again offering more of the same.

Waite did not just remind the captors of promises broken; he aroused their suspicions. It had been revealed in the press that he had had meetings with Colonel North; in their eyes, therefore, he no longer qualified as a religious envoy but was part of the American team handling the hostage crisis. So what was the real reason for his return? An indication of how devalued his currency as an envoy had become was the speed with which, after his capture, stories began circulating about his previous activities. The Palestine Liberation Organization alleged that Waite had been carrying $2 million dollars at the time of David Jacobsen's release. Even Walid Jumblatt, the Druze leader, told a Beirut radio station that Waite had been 'carrying certain amounts of money' during his final mission, although he never provided any evidence.'

Tehran radio announced that Terry Waite was being held as a spy. The Revolutionary Justice Organisation was to claim that a small locating device had been found implanted under his skin. Improbable as the story sounded it was believed by the Syrian defence minister, Mustafa Tlass. He was to tell a British official that a device had been found and that it had been positively identified by Soviet experts working out of their embassy in Damascus.

Whatever the truth of the story it came to be believed by the captors and the Iranians. The West German hostage, Alfred Schmidt, said that his guards confiscated his glasses, telling him that they now had to be more careful since finding a device on Terry Waite.

Roger Cooper, a Briton who was held in jail in Iran for five years on spying charges, heard the same story. Soon after Waite was taken hostage Cooper was asked by one of his regular Iranian interrogators what links he had with Terry Waite. Cooper, mystified, said he had never met the Anglican envoy. His interrogator then declared that Waite was a spy. When Cooper mocked this announcement he was told that they had the evidence. A bug had been discovered on Waite that transmitted a radio signal. They told Cooper that it had been found hidden in his hair or his beard. This proved, as far as the Iranians were concerned, said Cooper, 'that Waite was trying to lure the captors to where the hostages were and then the CIA would be monitoring him and they'd be able to come in and rescue them.' Although Cooper caught his interrogators lying to him on other occasions, he was convinced they believed this story. 'They were excited by the news and returned to the subject on two or three occasions.'

Others were to pick up the accusation. Colonel Qadaffi claimed that Waite had deceived Libya and was 'related to the intelligence services'. The story of the device was not just believed in the Middle East. John Lyttle, the man chosen by the Archbishop of Canterbury to lead the search for Waite, said that people in the British Foreign Office had come to suspect that Waite was carrying a device.

Some of these stories were wild and improbable but Waite had become a figure around which conspiracies could be spun. The fact that a number were believed indicates how vulnerable he had become. Others, on the fringes of the Iran– Contra affair, were able to take the stand and dispel the rumours and accusations. The court of public opinion for Terry Waite was, tragically, to be a basement in Beirut. Worse still, although there was an agreement that Waite's name would be omitted from the Iran–Contra hearings and references to him in North's diaries would remain classified, the system was imperfect. North's comment about Waite being 'our only access to events in Lebanon' was not deleted. A succession of articles appeared referring cryptically to Waite's dealings with North. To captors, weaned on suspicion, these comments served only to confirm their hostage's guilt.

Brian Jenkins, who had been closely involved in trying to get the hostages released, believed it was extraordinarily dangerous for Waite to go back to Beirut. 'I think increasingly he was seen as somehow an agent of Western intelligence, a spy, not an honest broker but one who was being used, consciously, to obtain information about the kidnappers and the hostages themselves. He was viewed with growing suspicion and of course we're talking about people who tend to be somewhat paranoid anyway in terms of their dealing with the West.'

The real reason why Waite was taken may never be known. He probably doesn't know himself. No claims were made, no harrowing pictures of him in captivity issued, no video messages recorded, no emotional appeals made. Nothing. The silence baffled many people. What was the point, they asked, of seizing someone and demanding nothing in return? But increasingly hostages had become an insurance policy against the vicissitudes of Lebanese life. By threatening to kill him, a high-value hostage like Terry Waite could be used to prevent the Syrian army invading one of Hezballah's strongholds; he could be traded if one of their relatives was arrested; he could be ransomed for money if Iran ever tired of filling their coffers. The hostages were a long-term investment in some future pay-off. In the short term, the holding of Westerners enhanced the status of the captors. It made them a factor in any equation because they held a commodity that had a value to a foreign government. Hezballah, fighting for their existence in Lebanon, were in no hurry to cash in their investment.

The void suited the captors. The less information they gave, the more likely was it that rumours would abound, confusing and distracting the intelligence agencies on their trail. Terry Waite proved to be a rumour factory, with the press its willing publishers. He was variously reported to have been smuggled to Iran in a coffin, to be living in the Iranian holy city of Qom, to have been seen exercising in the Bekaa valley, to have been wounded in a shooting incident, to have been tried by an Islamic court, and to have been murdered because his captors thought his pacemaker – which he didn't have – was an electronic device.

In the early years after his capture, there was no hard evidence about what had happened to Waite, just occasional fragments of information. Dr Mroueh, who felt he was suspected of complicity in Waite's capture, reported that he was being well treated. The leadership in Iran, while professing their lack of influence with the captors, assured several visitors to Iran that Waite was alive. Sheikh Shamseddine, the Vice President of the influential Shi'ite council in Lebanon, declared somewhat bizarrely that Terry Waite was 'the most alive of all the hostages'. Then several of the freed French hostages reported glimpses of a man they thought was Waite. Roger Auque saw 'a very tall man with a grey beard and grey hair'. Marcel Fontaine thought he might have shared a cell with Waite, and Jean-Paul Kauffman saw a 'tall, large man' through a keyhole.

During 1987 there was serious doubt within the CIA as to whether Waite was alive. 'We lost him,' said one official. It was a real issue of debate within the Agency. Millions of dollars were paid out to potential sources. Later they had hard evidence that he was alive and shared it with the British government. By the end of 1988 the Americans knew where all the hostages were and the conditions under which they were being held. This was verified by papers found at the scene of the crash when the Pan Am plane exploded over Scotland. On board had been a member of the CIA stationed in Beirut, who was returning to the United States to report to the Hostage Location Task Force. Among his papers were detailed drawings of where the hostages were being held, the frequency with which the guards were changed, and the position of the guards at different times of day and night.

The first reliable information that Waite was alive came from the hostage, Brian Keenan, when he was released in September 1990. It was nearly four years after Waite had been seized. Keenan had not seen Waite, but through a gap in the door he had seen the feet of a large man. He knew the person was English because he had heard him asking for a candle and a glass of water. He also heard the guards address him as Terry.

Keenan reported that Waite was being held in solitary confinement, in a tiny cell with an electric generator for company. He believed that Waite had suffered. 'He is alive and unwell. But I'm convinced it is him. I could hear him crying in the night, saying "Oh, no".' Privately, Keenan's news was more disturbing. He had heard Waite sobbing and feared for his mental health. He believed that Waite had been tortured and had been treated worse than the others.

When, in August 1991, John McCarthy was freed, the news was better. Since December 1990, Waite and he had shared a cell. Waite's spirits had improved with company. With a release in prospect, the captors had cynically begun to improve their conditions. One former hostage described it as 'being fattened for freedom.' McCarthy said they had had access to a Bible, editions of *Time* and *Newsweek* and a radio. 'Terry is a real radio addict,' said McCarthy, 'you could almost superglue a radio to Terry's ear and he would be quite happy.'

Waite, who had suffered badly from asthma during captivity, was now receiving treatment. Since May 1991, he had received regular visits from a Druze doctor who was even able to pass messages.

When McCarthy returned to Britain he was questioned by Waite's family as to whether Terry felt they were doing enough in campaigning for his release. McCarthy reassured them. For even the attempts to free Terry Waite had been marred by controversy.

'Spiro', Waite's shadowy contact had begun quizzing his sources in Lebanon from the moment he disappeared. He soon learnt, to his satisfaction, that Waite was alive and was given a detailed account of the envoy's health – even though he had undergone a thorough interrogation, the details of which were sent to Iran. 'Spiro's' contacts in the Shi'ite community questioned him closely about Waite's relationship with Oliver North. Some of their questions he referred to Samir Habiby. 'Spiro' seems to have felt some responsibility for Waite: he approached Lambeth Palace and offered his services, but they were wary. They checked him out with the Foreign Office which, while denying any knowledge of him, suggested, half in jest, that they might like to get his fingerprints. MI6 would have needed no such clues. Lambeth Palace had had its fill of figures from the 'grey world', and declined 'Spiro's' offer.

Not long after Waite's disappearance, 'Spiro' received what he considered to be a ransom demand. It was put not in crude financial terms but in the form of requesting financial assistance for the relatives of the seventeen men imprisoned in Kuwait. A member of one of the families needed eye surgery outside Lebanon, and there were other medical expenses. 'Spiro' referred the demand to Samir Habiby, who considered it to be serious: 'I'm convinced that the request for financial assistance for the families of the seventeen came directly from the captors.' As 'Spiro' explored the idea, it became larger in its scope. His contacts wanted a relief programme for southern Lebanon, involving hospitals, schools and housing; the projects could cost millions of dollars. Habiby thought as much as $20 million would be needed to secure Terry Waite's release. Apparently other parties before them had made donations for development – a euphemism for making a cash payment to Hezballah. Habiby did consider setting up a development agency through which private capital could be routed to some of the poorer Shi'ite villages, but he recognized that some people would consider it to be ransom money, which would be unacceptable to the Church.

Terry Waite had left strict instructions that no ransom should be paid in the event of his being taken hostage. He had insisted that 'No effort at all should be made by any authority to seek for, or negotiate for, my release.' The words 'no effort at all' had been underlined. To do otherwise, he believed, would endanger envoys in the future.

At first, Lambeth Palace did little except seek information. They faced a dilemma, familiar to all governments whose citizens had been seized: how could they seek Waite's release without appearing to negotiate? The British government had moved quickly to rule out the idea that the Archbishop's envoy was a special case. 'We don't do deals,' a spokesman said. 'We must treat him as any other individual.' Yet the Church could not ignore its envoy, so Dr Runcie wrote to Ali Akhbar Rafsanjani, the Speaker of the Iranian Parliament, and asked him to use what influence Iran might have with the captors to get Waite released.

Rafsanjani was mistakenly regarded as a moderate who was working for the release of the hostages. He was more pragmatic than some of the zealous mullahs, particularly as regards dealing with the West, but he was also politically ambitious and determined to take over after the death of Ayatollah Khomeini. While appearing sympathetic to Western appeals he was, in fact, not prepared to order the release of the hostages unless he could demonstrate that Iran had got something for them or that he himself was politically secure.

A device was found that enabled him to avoid having to take any action. Iran, he claimed, had hostages too. If the Church could discover what had happened to four Iranians who had gone missing in Lebanon it would help in the matter of the Western hostages. All that was known was that the four had been seized by Christian Falangists on the road between Beirut and Baalbek in July 1982. One of them, Mate Vasellani, had been a commander in the Revolutionary guards. In Lebanon it was presumed they had all been killed.

Dr Runcie offered to use the Church's contacts with the Christian community to make enquiries; no information was forthcoming. The case of the four missing Iranians continued to be raised in all discussions with the leadership in Tehran. Most diplomats familiar with Iran believe that the oft-repeated cry, 'We have hostages too,' was a convenient way of deflecting criticism and of avoiding taking any action.

The Church's search for Terry Waite was delegated to John Lyttle, a man of political experience and worldly wise. He was inundated with calls from those offering to help or claiming to have some rare piece of information. All had to be examined patiently: the publicity seekers, the gossips, the well-meaning and the crackpots. In 1988 he was approached by two men who thought they could help get Waite released; they appeared to have unusual connections in the Middle East and were willing to pursue their contacts, but wanted the Church to meet their hotel bills and travelling expenses. Lyttle passed their names to the police but they had no information on them, so he went ahead and paid them £12,000. They immediately disappeared, only to be unveiled later as two con men – one a former scrap merchant, the other a failed bloodstock agent. It was a rare misjudgement.

With Syrian protection, Lyttle travelled to Beirut and met Sheikh Fadlallah. The cleric was, by now, irritated by enquiries about Terry Waite. He said he had investigated the matter before and had no information. Lyttle made several trips to Iran. After the Iran–Iraq War ended he detected a new mood of flexibility: they were eager for Western assistance in rebuilding their exhausted economy. He made it clear that the continued detention of hostages was an impediment to better diplomatic relations. There was a flurry. Diplomats met and relations improved, but like so many other initiatives it ultimately led nowhere. The hostage crisis had a dynamic of its own, unrelated to the West; the currents were dictated by the power struggle in Iran and the battle for supremacy within the Lebanese Shi'ite community itself. The Church would have to wait for those conflicts to resolve themselves before they would see Terry Waite.

There were, however, disturbing questions for the Church about Waite's role and how his capture had come about.

What was the Church doing working on behalf of American hostages? Had it thought through the role of envoy and the risks involved? Had the Church of England stumbled into playing a part it was ill prepared to perform? Was Waite given sufficient support and supervision? Had the Church allowed itself to be used by the American administration? Had the Church's reputation for independence been placed in jeopardy?

When Terry Waite joined the Archbishop's staff in 1980, the Church of England had no recent record of involvement in international affairs unrelated to the business of the Church. His job was to arrange the overseas visits of the Archbishop. When, in 1981, three Anglican missionaries were imprisoned in Tehran it was clearly a matter of concern for the Church. Waite proved an able mediator. His vision then seemed uncomplicated, in the best traditions of the Church. He was fond of quoting from Isaiah: 'The Spirit of the Lord God is upon me, because the Lord has anointed me to bring good tidings to the afflicted; he has sent me to bind up the broken hearted, to proclaim liberty to the captives, and the opening of the prison to those who are bound.'

When, three years later, Britons were detained in Libya, the Archbishop decided to become involved again, even though the men had no direct connection with the Church. Colonel Qadaffi was judged, correctly, to be more amenable to the petitions of Christians than to those of governments.

Waite revelled in his new role. It provided him with the challenge that more traditional Christian work had failed to offer. He began spending more and more of his time as a mediator, and with his successes, appeals for help poured in to Lambeth Palace. Dr Runcie was delighted. 'Terry Waite brings light where there is darkness and justice where there is injustice,' he declared. The Archbishop and Waite saw a new ministry emerging for the Anglican Church, one it had not undertaken before and one which would greatly enhance its international profile. It would stand alongside agencies like the International Committee of the Red Cross in offering mediation to the troubled corners of the world.

By 1984, Terry Waite was an obvious person for the Presbyterian Church in the United States to turn to when one of its missionaries, Benjamin Weir, was taken hostage in the Lebanon. For the Archbishop it was an easy request to accept. Weir was a clergyman and the Church would be going to the aid of one of its own, albeit from a different denomination. When Weir was released, Waite was given the credit and the other American hostages appealed to the Archbishop to help them too. Within a matter of days, without any great awareness of the magnitude of the step being taken, the Church of England was working for the release of all American hostages.

On the surface it seemed no different from other humanitarian missions that Terry Waite had undertaken. But the American hostages, unlike the missionaries in Iran and the Britons in Libya, weren't being held on trumped-up charges of spying which could easily be disposed of. The reasons for detaining them were far more complicated. On one level it was to bargain for the release of other prisoners, but on another it was a tactic in an on-going struggle by radical Islamic groups to drive the Americans out of the Middle East. Furthermore, the captors were financed and partly controlled by a foreign government which had its own interests. For Waite there were real issues to be negotiated, matters which required political decisions by various governments. The Church, whether it liked it or not, was involving itself in the politics of the Middle East. After Waite was taken hostage, the Archbishop said his conscience was clear about what they had been trying to do. 'We were not trying to act as politicians or diplomats,' he said, 'but were fulfilling the ancient Christian imperative of mercy towards a prisoner.' But the roles could not be so easily divided. It was not possible to separate the humanitarian from the political.

For his negotiations, Waite needed to know the position of the US government on, say, the Kuwaiti prisoners. That required him to talk to American officials. Their objectives appeared to coincide; they were both working for the release of the hostages. The danger was that, in pursuing the same end, Church efforts and US government efforts would become entwined. 'The risk for a Church envoy,' said one American official, 'is that they will be seen as the instrument of national government.'

In dealing with groups like Islamic Jihad and Hezballah, Waite had to be particularly careful that he remained independent of the US government. The militant Shi'ites had learnt their politics from Iran. The United States was a power of darkness, militarily strong, economically dominant, with a pervasive intelligence service that could set up and tear down governments at will. To retain the Shi'ites' trust, a Church envoy had to be seen as formal, even cool, in his dealings with American officials. He could not afford to give the slightest impression of being close to the American side. He needed to avoid rides on US military helicopters, accepting US travel arrangements, hotel meetings with White House officials, sharing information, and turning up in the Middle East at the behest of the Americans. To the paranoid, embattled fighters of South Beirut, symbols mattered and therefore became part of reality.

Lambeth Palace seemed blissfully unaware of how politically sensitive Terry Waite's mission had become. He was left to his own devices, being considered experienced enough to avoid any pitfalls. But if the Church of England was serious about playing the role of international mediator then it had to provide the back-up and support necessary to ensure the envoy's independence. The staff at Lambeth Palace was small, its resources meagre. There were no political advisers, no research staff, no supervision. Waite was never required to document his activities. Dr Runcie had only the vaguest idea of what his envoy was doing and whom he was seeing. Above all, the Church had to have the financial resources to pay for private flights, if that were necessary, rather than use government transport. On one occasion, in Beirut, Terry Waite was so short of money that the Associated Press agency had to pick up some of his bills, although the Church repaid the money later.

The Church of England had also developed no coherent policy on how to deal with hostage takers. It believed it could attend to the humanitarian concerns of the individuals involved without any regard to the problem of how to discourage hostage taking in the future. Governments faced a similar dilemma. By negotiating with the captors, they raised the value of the hostages, thereby encouraging the captors to seize others. If, however, the hostages were ignored, then in theory there would be no purpose in keeping them. Such resolve had proved politically difficult: governments in the West were castigated if they ignored the plight of their citizens.

In the United States such was the attention given to the hostages that successive presidents became virtual prisoners of the crisis itself. Terrorism and hostage taking assumed the dimensions of theatre: a small, often insignificant group could command the attention of a vast audience, achieving a platform it could never hope for otherwise. The media staged the play, transmitting every moment of the drama: the captors' demands, the sufferings of the relatives and their emotional reunions. In 1980, while hostages were being held in Iran, American television even put up on screen each night the number of days they had been held. This policy generated emotion – and frustration – to the point where the issue became one of national pride and presidents and prime ministers were forced to deal with armed gangs. Publicity was doing the captors' bidding for them. 'It is extraordinary,' said Brian Jenkins of the Rand Corporation, 'that you have groups the size of gangs dealing with heads of powerful nations as if they were co-equals, like heads of respective Mafia families.'

Terry Waite came to be seen as adding to the drama. He encouraged media attention. He had his reasons: the press enabled him to send messages to the captors. But his missions flattered what were, after all, a group of kidnappers. With Waite in Beirut, young men from the city's poorer neighbourhoods could imagine themselves at the centre of the world stage. There were those who argued that such a public intervention by the Church both raised the value of the hostages and gave incentive to further hostage taking. The alternative was a quieter diplomacy, conducted in stealth, out of the glare of television lights – even if heroic efforts went unsung.

If the Church drifted into a role it was ill prepared to perform, and the implications of which it only dimly understood, governments acted even less reputably. The hostages were encouraged to seize more foreigners, Terry Waite among them, because of the willingness of governments to pay ransoms. The United States traded weapons, private parties in West Germany paid money to Hezballah, and France brazenly negotiated with Iran. Even Israel, which has chided Western nations for being weak-kneed over terrorism, has regularly traded prisoners in return for its own soldiers and airmen.

The French government believed that Iran held the key to the hostage crisis and, in a series of secret meetings, gave several undertakings. Firstly, it promised to restore diplomatic relations with Iran. Secondly, it undertook to repay $300 million outstanding on a loan negotiated under the Shah. Thirdly, the Iranians expected the French to reduce the sentence passed on Anis Naccache, a Lebanese imprisoned in France for attempting to assassinate the Shah's last Prime Minister. Over a two-year period all ten French hostages were freed, although Hezballah accused France of reneging for a time on the release of Naccache. In the summer of 1990 Naccache was allowed to leave France.

In dealing with the captors in Beirut, the French did not deceive themselves that this was other than trading with kidnappers. The French government despatched to Lebanon Jean-Charles Marchiani, a tough Corsican. He dealt directly with Hezballah. Before negotiations began he recited a list of their relatives who were living abroad. If anything happened to him, Marchiani told them, their relatives would be visited by his fellow Corsicans. It was language Hezballah understood.

Even the British, who publicly were so opposed to any concessions to terrorists, saw the Iranians in Geneva in November 1988. A British official with connections had a meeting with Rafsanjani's relative, the same man whom North had negotiated with initially. The official intimated that if the British hostages were freed then Iran would be permitted to buy a radar system from Marconi, diplomatic relations would be restored, and Iran would receive important credit to rebuild its economy with the help of British firms. Iran thought it a good enough deal to signal Hezballah to release the hostages, but the captors felt they had not benefited enough from the French deal and refused to cooperate. The payment of disguised ransom has ensured the lengthy detention of the other hostages because of the expectation that sooner or later the West will pay up.

The story of Terry Waite is not, primarily, about the role of the Church or the ethics of negotiating with hostage takers. It is the odyssey of an idealistic man in search of a calling, at a time when causes were unfashionable. He belonged in the past, when individuals carved out their destinies through exploration and empire-building. He had looked for adventure in Africa, while a missionary, and had come away unfulfilled. Hostage taking, the diplomacy of the deprived, gave him his opportunity. He became the champion of the innocent held captive. It was a big role, played out on a global stage, courtesy of television. Praise was heaped upon him excessively, blindingly.

In Oliver North he found a soulmate, a fellow Christian, a buccaneer dedicated to the release of innocent Americans. North lived in the epic manner, defying the constraints of bureaucracy. He financed brush-fire wars, planned invasions, traded arms with the enemy and hunted down terrorists. Never had such a junior official on the National Security Council achieved such power over America's foreign policy. He was an anachronistic figure, still partly living in the Old West where scores could be settled face-to-face. 'I'll be glad to meet Abu Nidal on equal terms,' he said, staring into the eyes of his Congressional inquisitors. 'Anywhere in the world, OK.' A memory haunted him: Vietnam. It left him determined that there would be no more retreats; no more pictures of Americans clinging to helicopters as they fled a country under fire.

Ronald Reagan, a man out of the West, promised to restore American pride, to revive the dream. The captors in Beirut intruded, recalling other humiliations. They were the mote in Reagan's eye, his tormentors. Every instinct told him to defy their threats, but the sufferings of the families moved him more. North gradually took charge of the task of ending his President's agony. The goal became paramount; other values, deeply held, were jettisoned. North was fighting the President's battle, which was yesterday's battle, too. In taking on America's enemies he was exorcising ghosts. He became single-minded, obsessed, willing to concede almost anything to his Iranian interlocutors if it ended the hostage crisis.

An Englishman, a religious envoy, shared his obsession. For Terry Waite, the release of the hostages became a humanitarian imperative. Idealism masked the obsessions of both men. North promised that in the great endeavour the Church would not be harmed. But lies were a weapon in his armoury – justifiable lies, wartime lies, untruths that soldiers understood. There was no trace of shame when he acknowledged his duplicity to Congress.

> *North*: I lied every time I met the Iranians.
> *Van Cleve* (Counsel to Select Committee re Iran–Contra affair): And you've admitted that you lied to General Secord with respect to conversations that you supposedly had with the President. Is that correct?
> *North*: In order to encourage him to stay with the project, yes.
> *Van Cleve*: And you've admitted that you lied to the Congress, is that correct?
> *North*: I have.
> *Van Cleve*: And you admitted that you lied in creating false chronologies of these events. Is that correct?
> *North*: That is true.

Waite had had his doubts, his misgivings, but in the excitement of the enterprise they were set aside. North was an actor, a master of B-movie performances like his President. He could play the innocent. Open-faced, with his Boy Scout grin and altar boy eyes, his was a vulnerability which melted probing questions.

As the Iran–Contra affair unfolded, and with Terry Waite in captivity, Samir Habiby had to face the painful possibility that the charming colonel from the White House had lied to Waite and him too. 'When I heard Oliver North say what he did [to Congress] it caused me personal grief because I said to myself, "Well, that's not the Ollie North that I got to know." . . . I don't think he ever lied to us. No, because I don't think we were in a position where he would specifically give us an untruth.' It is quite possible that North never actually lied to Terry Waite; he was content to manipulate enthusiasm, and the good name of the Church of England. A different man from Terry Waite might have seen the darker side of Oliver North. He didn't, and neither did most of North's colleagues on the National Security Council.

On November 25, 1986, with his world collapsing around him, North indulged in a few moments of reflection. He listed his priorities:

1. My country.
2. Presidency.
3. Family.
4. Hostages.
5. Others who helped.

Before the words 'others who helped' North had written 'self' but crossed it out. It was a list Terry Wait could have done with during the eighteen months he worked to free the American hostages.

North was unrepentant about his handling of Terry Waite. When challenged whether he felt any guilt over Waite, he replied. 'Guilt? I have a hard problem with the word.' That, of course, was true. For in Oliver North's world the interests of America had a moral imperative of their own. It enabled him to lie and cheat without remorse.

What North revealed to Waite was a world he had never experienced before – a glimpse of the hidden levers of government, the intelligence agencies, the back-door channels, the grey figures. Eugene Douglas observed Waite's growing fascination. 'I think that Waite knew all along that he was running a risk talking to and dealing with that part of life. But his sense of commitment, what he was about, what his own spirit impelled him to do, told him that he must take that risk upon himself and deal with it in judgement later, but deal with it he must.'

Oliver North and Terry Waite were both Christians, driven by the highest motives – the freedom of innocent men held hostage. In pursuit of that goal, North was to engage in deception on a grand scale. 'There is great deceit,' he said, 'practised in the conduct of secret operations. They are at essence a lie.' The tragedy for Terry Waite was that he became a victim of the very deception that was intended to free the hostages. For North's secret deals had damaged the envoy's credibility. On it everything rested – his past successes and his future plans. For Waite there were no televised hearings where he could banish the doubts and the question marks. For him they could only be answered in the streets of Beirut.

When Father Jenco came to understand what had secured his release he was appalled. If he had known about it, he said, he would have said no. 'Here I am, a single person. I have no wife, I have no children, and you're exchanging me for arms that are going to kill men, women, children by the thousands for one man. What tremendous foolishness.'

18

'23 HOURS AND
50 MINUTES A DAY'

In 1990, the tectonic plates of the Middle East shifted. Iraq, emboldened by its growing arsenal of deadly weapons, seized Kuwait. Saddam, who had shrugged off the world's feeble response to his previous atrocities, overreached himself. Even though Kuwait's wealth was resented in parts of the Arab world, Saddam's ambitions frightened the region. The United States, Britain and the West, determined to resist Iraq's aggression, found unexpected allies. The loyalties and alliances of the Middle East were changing.

Overnight, pariah states became allies. Syria, castigated by Washington as a sponsor of terrorism, sent forces to join the Coalition. Even Iran, which had despatched terrorist groups to drive America from the region, watched silently as the United States assembled its largest military force since the Vietnam War. Iran's religious and ideological differences with the 'Great Satan' were set aside in favour of seeing the destruction of its enemy Iraq.

'Desert Storm' changed reality. The military technology of the allies made a nonsense of the millions that Saddam had spent on building a military machine. In a matter of days his army was swept aside. The United States had reasserted its global power. Those in the region who resented American imperialism understood that the alternative of turning to Moscow no longer existed.

The war coincided with the disintegration of the Soviet empire. Within six months of victory in the desert, Communism was officially buried in the Soviet Union. Its discordant republics began breaking away to seek their own destiny. Soviet power had crumbled. No longer could the states of the Middle East depend on playing off one superpower against the other. President Assad of Syria, Moscow's closest ally in the region, was quick to understand that the old alliances no longer held good.

It was not just a recognition that power had shifted that brought about the freedom of the hostages. Both Syria and Iran, the two states with the greatest influence over the captors in Beirut, had compelling reasons for wanting to improve relations with Washington.

Syria had ambitions in the region that could best be realized by seeking an accommodation with the United States. Firstly, there was Lebanon. President Assad had a dream that the Lebanese state would belong in a Greater Syria. Even if the creation of such a state would never be realized, Lebanon could be placed firmly in the Syrian zone of influence. The United States, driven out of Lebanon by terror, had come to accept that a *Pax Syriana* was the best hope for stability in a country riven by conflict. Secondly, Syria wanted to retrieve the Golan Heights, lost to Israel in the 1967 war. Even if that goal was unlikely to be achieved in the short term, Assad knew that the territory would never be returned without the involvement of the United States.

Iran, too, started to come in from the cold. Since Ayatollah Khomeini's Islamic Revolution, Iran had been excluded from access to Western technology and arms. In the beginning it didn't matter. The Iranians were inspired with the teachings and exhortations of their Imam. In time, other older concerns began to intrude. The masses of South Tehran who, ten years earlier, had gathered at the gates of the American embassy to shout 'Death to America' now grumbled and cursed at the shortages in the shops. The pragmatists who had succeeded Khomeini understood that political survival in Iran, like in most countries, finally depended on being able to deliver a better life. Trading ties with the West had to be restored. The hostages were the greatest obstacle to improved relations and Tehran began signalling that it was ready to end its isolation.

Other impediments to ending the hostage crisis were gradually removed. The captors in Beirut had demanded the release of the 17 Dawa prisoners in Kuwait. Ironically their freedom was gained, not by some deal or pay-off, but by Saddam Hussein's invasion. When Iraqi forces entered Kuwait City the prison guards fled and there were mass escapes. During August

1990 the 17 prisoners made their way to Iran, possibly with the help of the Iraqis themselves. Imad Mugniyah, who had ruthlessly seized hostages to barter for his brother-in-law's freedom, had lost his cause. His relative was to play an important part in the hostage negotiations with the United Nations.

In the aftermath of the Gulf War, America chose to act as broker in yet another attempt to solve the heart of the Middle East problem: the Palestinians. James Baker, the US Secretary of State, cajoled and pleaded with the Middle East's antagonists to sit down with each other. In October 1991, they faced each other across a table in Madrid. Although ancient insults were traded, the talking continued. The fact that Israel turned up at all was seen as evidence that the United States was being more even-handed in its policy towards the Middle East.

Problems remained. Radicals in Iran denounced the meeting in Madrid, even hosting a conference of radical terrorist groups in the Iranian capital to coincide with the peace talks. It was a reminder that the more pragmatic leadership of Hashemi Rafsanjani had still to keep an eye on the fundamentalists and their abiding hatred of the West. Diplomats believed the leadership in Tehran sanctioned the conference as a way of drawing the sting of those opposed to ending the hostage crisis.

There were other incidents which, in the past, would have delayed the release of the hostages. Fighters from Hezballah launched a series of raids inside the Israeli security zone in Southern Lebanon killing several soldiers. Israel responded with some of the most sustained shelling of Shi'ite villages for many years. These attacks were set aside by all the parties, as if they belonged to a separate argument, for there now existed compelling reasons why even the captors in Beirut wanted to end the hostage problem.

Above all, the hostages had outlived their usefulness. They were taken at the height of an undeclared war between Islamic fundamentalism and the West. The hostages could help drive the infidel from the region; they could be traded for weapons or money or just simply held, a card to be played at an appropriate moment. But by 1991, the card was of diminishing value. The West, quite simply, was not going to trade. In the past when Western leaders had promised no deals, Hezballah had smiled. They had witnessed a procession of intermediaries, politicians, and envoys to their door. The West talked tough and then traded. But the captors understood that a cooler climate now existed in Westen capitals. The governments still demanded the return of the hostages but, if necessary, they were prepared to be patient. The captors also knew that their sponsors in Iran and Syria were seeking an end to the hostage crisis. The pressure on the captors was to conclude the affair on the best terms possible.

Before releasing the hostages the captors wanted reassurances that when the affair was over, Western intelligence or their allies would not come looking for them. Their abiding fear was that the CIA would seek to avenge the death of William Buckley, the CIA Station Chief who had died in captivity. Without a hostage they would be vulnerable. In discussions with the United Nations envoy, Giandomenico Picco they asked for guarantees that when the hostages were freed they would be protected; thereby seeking a guarantee of safety they had so cruelly denied others. The UN envoy could offer no such indemnity. But, privately, the United States told Iran and Syria that there would be no retribution. Whatever the scars, the hostage file was being closed.

The captors did have one condition. They wanted the release of a group of Shi'ite prisoners being held by the Israelis and their allies, the South Lebanon army. The Israelis regarded these several hundred men as prisoners and terrorists although most of them had never been tried. In Lebanon they were regarded as hostages. The holders of the Western hostages saw the freedom of these men as their last reward before returning to the more mundane existence of eking out a living in the slums of West Beirut. It was not just that these Shi'ite prisoners were fellow Hezballah fighters. The captors of the Western hostages wanted the Shi'ite community to be indebted to them for forcing the release of their relatives. It was a kind of protection.

So over a period of months a deal unfolded. It involved Iran, Syria, Israel and Hezballah and was brokered by the United Nations. The hostage crisis was being brought to an end not by the sale of missiles or by shady intermediaries or even by courageous Church envoys but by an official from the United Nations conducting quiet diplomacy. The discussions had begun in earnest in early summer. They were to lead to the release of John Macarthy, Jackie Mann and Jesse Turner. The Israelis released 66 Shi'ite prisoners and the remains of nine others. In exchange Israel received news and the bodies of some of its missing servicemen. Even though the releases were interspersed with silences, the process continued. The deal hammered out at meetings in Turkey and France was not only precise in its intentions but provided target dates for the next stage in the release programme. Iran, in particular, ensured that the timetable was adhered to even when the captors attempted to renegotiate the whole deal, as they did after every release.

In the third week of November 1991 one last obstacle to a conclusion of the hostage crisis was removed. It involved the bombing of Pan Am 103 over Lockerbie. The Scottish police and the American justice department simultaneously announced that they were seeking two Libyan intelligence agents in connection with the bombing.

The involvement of either Syria or Iran was ruled out. Officials said they had found no evidence linking the two countries to the bombing. Relatives of those who had died on the plane were sceptical. They had been told that Iran had wanted to avenge the shooting down of an Iranian airbus by the USS Vincennes and had hired the PFLP-GC (the Popular Front for the Liberation of Palestine – General Command) for the task. The PFLP-GC was based in Damascus. Bombs, with barometric devices, intended to destroy aircraft had been found with a PFLP-GC team in Germany a few weeks before Pan Am 103 was blown up. But the US and the UK governments both exempted Syria of any connection with the bombing. Whatever the truth, Syria and Iran were relieved of the stigma of sponsoring terrorism. Within days further hostages were freed.

It had always been assumed that Terry Waite would be the last hostage to be freed. Because of his high-profile he was regarded as the most valuable hostage. But, quite suddenly on 18 November, Islamic Jihad issued a brief statement. 'To complete what we have started with the United Nations

secretary general, Perez de Cuellar we announce the release of
1. Terry Waite, 2. Thomas Sutherland.' The message was
accompanied by an old black and white photograph of Terry
Anderson. Three hours later, after 1763 days in captivity,
Terry Waite was free.

That evening he reappeared before the world at the Syrian
Foreign Ministry. It was part of the ritual of hostage releases
that Syria received public thanks for its role in ending another
man's nightmare.

Like other hostages before him, Waite was thinner and his
skin pasty white from the years of darkness. His voice was
weak and he coughed several times but he spoke with dignity
and authority. He related how he had heard the news of his
impending freedom, 'This afternoon, when we were sitting
together in our cell, chained to the wall as we have been for
the last five years . . . one of our captors came in and told us
that Tom and myself would be freed this evening.'

His captor tried to apologize for the injustice of captivity, a
flash of remorse that had also been shown to Father Jenco. He
told Waite, 'We apologize for having captured you. We
recognize now that this was the wrong thing to do. Holding
hostages serves no useful purpose.'

What Waite and Sutherland made of this recantation they
did not say. They embraced their freedom and ignored the
cynicism of their guards.

Closing one's eyes and listening to Terry Waite it was as if
he had only been away for weeks. He was back again, addressing the world's media, bringing news that the entire hostage
chapter was drawing to a close. Then, his voice full of
emotion, he made a plea on behalf of all the hostages in the
region. It was a general appeal but it was directed at Israel.
'All hostages would plead with those who hold the people of
South Lebanon, innocent people being held as hostages, to
release them soon to put an end to terrorism and to find
peaceful, humane and civilized ways of solving the complex
problems of the Middle East.' In his voice was all the anguish
of five, wasted, frightened years. If the captors had been
listening they might have contemplated what a spokesman
Waite would have been for their own grievances if they had
not deprived him of his liberty.

When his fellow hostage, Tom Sutherland spoke, Waite relaxed, revealing that his humour had survived his ordeal. To his obvious amusement, Sutherland complained of how long it had taken Waite to free him. 'One thing I can say is that the British take a long time to get things done. Terry Waite came to rescue me, and after five years he is finally taking me home.'

Terry Waite was a man of compassion and faith; virtues sullied by the schemes of others. He is party to secrets that some would prefer remain untold. For he witnessed America trading in the hostage bazaar. His capture was an unnecessary tragedy born out of a flawed policy. If there was any hope to be drawn from his terrible ordeal it lay in the dignity of his return.

At the airbase in Lyneham he stood, ironically, under the wings of a Hercules tanker that had been deployed in the Gulf War; the catalyst for his own release. He told a story from captivity of a shaft of hope in his miserable existence. One day a guard delivered a postcard showing a stained glass window from Bedford depicting John Bunyan in jail.

'And I looked at that card,' said Waite, and I thought, 'My word Bunyan you're a lucky fellow. You've got a window out of which you can look, see the sky. Here am I in a dark room. You've got pen and ink, you can write, but here am I, I've got nothing and you've got your own clothes and a table and chair.

'And I turned the card over and there was a message from someone whom I didn't know simply saying, "We remember, we shall not forget. We shall continue to pray for you and to work for all people who are detained around the world."'

These simple words were lifeblood in captivity.

A few days before his release, Oliver North was reflecting on what he had done. 'The endeavours in which I was involved,' he concluded, 'were fraught with error and human frailty but I believe the goals were noble.' In seeking to liberate the hostages there was a price to be paid for error and human frailty. It was summed up by Terry Waite with a chilling statistic. 'We have been chained to the wall for the last five years, for 23 hours and 50 minutes a day.'

North was unrepentant about his handling of Terry Waite.

When challenged whether he felt any guilt over Waite, he replied. 'Guilt? I have a hard problem with the word.' That, of course, was true. For in Oliver North's world the interests of America had a moral imperative of their own. It enabled him to lie and cheat without remorse.

North said that he had never told Waite about the trading of arms for hostages. 'He never knew.' But that, of course, was part of the problem. It made sense while running a covert operation. It became questionable when it exposed a Church envoy to captivity. After some thought North conceded that some of what he did had been 'less than desirable.' He convinced himself that Terry Waite wanted to help 'in a selfless way'. In North's lexicon 'selfless' was the soldier who was prepared to sacrifice himself. Speaking of Waite's willingness to complete the mission he said 'it was a beautiful thing.' Christendom was at war and the end justified the means. Three weeks before Waite regained his freedom North said he was looking forward to renewing his friendship with the English envoy. One looked into his face to detect the slightest doubt that his friendship might be reciprocated. There was none. Waite had been Missing in Action. 'I only wish,' said North 'that I had been able to prevent him returning to Beirut.' Beyond that, no regrets.

SOURCES

CHAPTER 1. ON THE EDGE OF THE TARMAC

Page 2.   Parker Borg, who was Assistant Director of the Office of Counter-terrorism at the time, was a valuable witness to this North/Waite meeting and provided useful material for this chapter.

Page 4.   The phrase 'Clandestine meetings, in exotic settings, with the cast of Casablanca' was an observation made by Dr Brian Jenkins formerly of the Rand Corporation. He advised both the Catholic Relief Services and the Archbishop of Canterbury's office on the hostage crisis.

Page 5.   Ambassador Eugene Douglas's observation that Terry Waite had become fascinated with Oliver North's world was drawn from an interview he gave to BBC television in December 1988. Ambassador Douglas was one of Waite's unofficial guides to the political ways of Washington. After he left government Ambassador Douglas was to work tirelessly for Waite's release.

Page 5   North's comment re 'offering the Iranians a free trip to Disney . . .' was made at the Iran–Contra hearings in 1987.

CHAPTER 2. THE GENTLE GIANT

Page 8.   Dr Runcie, the Archibishop of Canterbury sent a letter to Ayatollah Khomeini in December 1980. The letter read, 'I wish to express my personal thanks to you for the generous response which you and the Iranian government have made to my urgent request that a pastoral visit might be paid to members of the Anglican Church at present awaiting their trial.'

Page 9.   The Colemans' accounts of life in prison were taken from an interview they gave with the *Daily Telegraph*, 23.02.81.

Page 10.   Waite's stories about his premonitons were taken from an interview he gave the *Sunday Mirror*, 22.06.82.

Page 11.   The interchange between Waite and the Libyan Foreign Minister was taken from a profile in the London *Observer*, 13.01.1985.

Page 11.   Excerpts from the conversation between Waite and Qadaffi were recorded by television cameras which were allowed to attend the early stages of the meeting.

Page 14.   'I think the key to this man . . .' This remark was made by Patrick Keatley, former Diplomatic Correspondent of the *Guardian*, in a television interview. Keatley's wife Eve is a member of staff at Lambeth Palace.

CHAPTER 3. AN AMERICAN HOSTAGE APPEALS

Page 17.   Benjamin Weir's account of his kidnapping was taken from his book *Hostage Bound, Hostage Free* which was co-written with his wife Carol. The author also met both of them and did a television interview with them in the summer of 1987.

Page 18.   The conversation between Carol Weir and the US Deputy Chief of Mission was taken from her own account in *Hostage Bound, Hostage Free*.

Page 18.   President Reagan had declared on 27 January 1981, during his inauguration address 'Let terrorists beware that when the rules of international behavior are violated, our policy will be one of swift and effective retribution.'

Page 21.   'Do I have to wait 444 days . . .'? That appeal was made by Carol Weir at a press conference in San Diego in March 1985.

Page 21.   The account of the meeting with George Shultz is taken from Carol Weir's account and a conversation with Fred Wilson who was also present at the meeting.

CHAPTER 4. THE INNER CIRCLE

Page 27.   The account of Waite's first meeting with North was drawn from conversations with the State Department official present, Samir Habiby and Fred Wilson.

Page 30.   The Rev Philip Turner's remarks about Waite's view of North were taken from an interview he gave to BBC television in the summer of 1987.

SOURCES

Page 31.   Samir Habiby was an invaluable source for much of the material for both a BBC film and this book. He gave generously of his time while working constantly on initiatives which he thought might secure Terry Waite's release.

CHAPTER 5. THE IDEAS OF SUMMER

Page 42.   The CIA memorandum was revealed in the documents made available to the Tower Commission during its investigation into the Iran–Contra scandal.

Page 45.   The assessment of the way the decision was taken to supply Iran with arms was taken from the Report of the Congressional Committees investigating the Iran–Contra scandal.

CHAPTER 6. ECCLESIASTICAL COVER

Page 47.   Weir's account of his meeting with Father Jenco, in captivity, was taken from *Hostage Bound, Hostage Free*.

Page 48.   Jean-Paul Kauffman's remark, 'How often I walked the roads . . .' was taken from an article in the *New York Times* magazine 1988 entitled 'Non vintage years'.

Page 48.   Weir: 'There are two reasons why you're being released . . .' Quotation from interview given to author in summer of 1987.

Page 51.   Fred Wilson's account of his phone conversation with North was taken from a BBC interview he gave in 1987.

Page 51.   David Jacobsen's comment about Weir is taken from *Hostage: My Nightmare in Beirut* by David Jacobsen with Gerald Astor.

Page 52.   Ledeen's remark about taking Weir back came from *Perilous Statecraft; an Insider's account of the Iran–Contra affair* by Michael Ledeen.

Page 54.   Waite: 'I have established through an intermediary . . .' 23 September 1985 at the Inter Church Centre in Manhattan.

CHAPTER 7. MEETING THE CAPTORS

Page 56.   The letter from the hostages was written on 8 November. Although it was addressed to the Archbishop of Canterbury, it said 'Copy to US Embassy or US State Department.'

Page 58.   'To the Rescue' an editorial in the *Sun*, 12.11.85.

Page 58.   The inscription in the front of the Pepys Diary was taken from an article in the London *Times* on 14.11.85.

Page 61.   Waite's description of his meetings 'I'm taken in a car to a deserted building . . .' Waite made these comments in an interview on Italian TV December 1986.

Page 64.   The information regarding the meeting where the 'tracking device' was discussed came from a source at the meeting and a senior official at the State Department who attended a later meeting where the idea was discussed.

Page 65.   The television interview with Ambassador Douglas was with the BBC. December 1988.

Page 66.   Father Jenco gave a firsthand description to the author of how the captors suspected him of carrying a communication's device.

Page 67.   After the Iran–Contra scandal was revealed, North's notebooks were made available to the Congressional committees investigating the affair. North himself removed some names and facts that he thought could compromise individuals or continuing operations. All references to Terry Waite were removed and have never been disclosed even when sections of North's notebooks were declassified. But, in the notebooks, there were frequent references to Waite. Many of these are now included in the manuscript.

Page 67.   North's statement 'I lied to the CIA.' Comment made to House/Senate select committee 7 July 1987.

CHAPTER 8. THE KUWAITIS

Page 76.   'Mr Waite would be welcomed here as a tourist . . .' Briefing given by Kuwaiti officials during visit of British Foreign Secretary. 15 January 1986.

Page 81.   David Jacobsen's account of hearing Dr Kissinger on the radio was taken from an article published in the *Observer*, 22.03.87.

Page 82. 'It was Christmas Eve . . .' This account by Father Jenco was taken from a BBC interview recorded in 1987.

Page 83. Shultz: 'We are signalling to Iran . . .' A quotation taken from notes made by Shultz's executive assistant during the phone call with Admiral Poindexter on 7 December 1985.

Page 83. North: 'Based on what we can conclude . . . this assessment.' An internal memo written by North on 4 December 1985 and revealed during the Tower commission investigation.

CHAPTER 9. OPERATION RECOVERY

Page 92. Details of the meeting between North, Secord and Ghorbanifar in the London hotel, which was given to the Congressional committee examining the Iran–Contra scandal.

Page 93. The Habiby interview re North's visit to Lambeth Palace was given to the BBC in the summer of 1987.

Page 96. North: 'With the grace of the good Lord . . .' Memo to Macfarlane, 22 February 1986.

CHAPTER 10. 'OUR ONLY ACCESS TO EVENTS IN LEBANON'

Page 102. 'I'm the man from Mr Goode . . .' Major Christensen made this statement in his appearance before the Iran–Contra committees.

Page 102. Major Julius Christensen's options were outlined in the Tower Commission report.

Page 102. 'Our only access to events in Lebanon.' On 8 December 1985 North had sent a memorandum to Poindexter and McFarlane. In it, he wrote: 'Terry Waite, our only access to events in Lebanon, readily admits that his influence is marginal at best.' Source: Tower Commission.

Page 103. Douglas: 'There were discussions about many . . .' Taken from BBC interview, December 1988.

Page 104. Stansfield Turner, 'I think you use people like T. Waite.' Taken from BBC interview, August 1987.

CHAPTER 11. THE SECRET TRIP

Page 106. Poindexter: 'There are not to be any parts . . .' This was contained in a memorandum, revealed to the Iran–Contra committees, which Poindexter wrote to North just before he went to Frankfurt to negotiate the trip to Tehran.

Page 109. McFarlane: 'It may be best for us to try to picture . . .' This was a cable sent by McFarlane to Washington shortly after his arrival in Tehran. Source: Iran–Contra committee.

Page 111. Secord: 'There was no Iranian agreement . . .' Testimony to the Iran–Contra committee.

Page 111. McFarlane: 'In Ollie's interst I would get him transferred . . .' 10 June. McFarlane message to Poindexter.

CHAPTER 12. 'GUESS PRAYER WORKS'

Page 113. Father Jenco's account of his captivity and release was drawn from a series of conversations with him in 1987.

Page 122. Waite's statement re a solution 'based on tenets common to Islam . . .' was made at a London press conference, 1 August 1986.
Islamic Jihad's statement 'We gave no messages' was delivered to a Beirut paper, 3 August 1986.

Page 123. North: 'The bottom line is that this is the direct result . . .' This was an internal memo sent to McFarlane on 29 July.
Poindexter: 'We have not agreed to any such plan.' Comment made in a memo to McFarlane on 26 July and revealed in the Tower Commission.
North: 'Despite our earlier and current protestations . . .' This view was expressed in a letter signed by North and George Cave following a meeting with Nir and Ghorbanifar on 27 July.

Page 124. Robert Oakley's remark: 'It was convenient in that people . . .' Comment made in BBC interview, Summer 1987.

SOURCES

Waite's comment 'Wouldn't you like to know,' was made at a press conference at the Episcopal Centre, New York, 8 August.

CHAPTER 13. THE ANGLICAN DR KISSINGER

Page 126.   Waite: 'I want to make a direct appeal . . .' Statement made on 5 August 1986 at San Francisco airport.

Comments by the Reverend Charles Cesaretti recorded at his home in New Jersey in 1987.

Page 129.   Waite's TV show: 'Self-effacement is not one of . . .' *Sunday Mirror*, 20 July 1986.

Page 132.   McFarlane: 'It seems increasingly clear . . .' Internal note to Poindexter, 6.10.86.

North re resignation: 'Under these circumstances . . .' July 1986, c.f. Tower Commission.

Page 134.   The account of North and his blood pressure was taken from *Guts and Glory, The Rise and Fall of Oliver North* by Ben Bradlee Jnr.

Page 137.   The editorial 'Waite's Fine Line' was the London *Times* on 9 August 1986.

Page 138.   Waite's statement re giving up as envoy was made on 15 August 1986 in London.

CHAPTER 14. A POLITICAL SCANDAL

Page 139.   Jacobsen's account of his time in captivity was taken from an article in the *Observer*, 22.03.87.

Page 140.   Jacobsen: 'I just can't describe it in words . . .' Interview given to author in summer 1987.

Page 142.   Allen: 'No threat from Mugniyah . . .' Message written on 8 September to Poindexter.

Page 142.   North: 'Some, like Jacobsen's Son . . .' Note to Poindexter, 9.08.86.

Page 144.   'If the government of Iran . . .' Assurance given by North on 19 September 1986 during the two days the 'Relative' was in Washington.

Page 145.   North: 'We had a very angry debate over whether or not . . .' Remarks made by North at meeting with Iranians in Frankfurt, 6–8 October. Details revealed to Iran–Contra Congressional committees.

Page 146.   North: 'It's become very evident to everybody . . .' Remarks made about Saddam Hussein were made at Frankfurt meeting, 6–8 October.

Page 147.   North: '. . . in my spare time between blowing up Nicaragua.' Remark made at a meeting in Mainz, Germany on 29 October 1986 in conversation with the 'Relative'.

Page 150.   Dutton: 'It comes almost out of a storybook . . .' Comments made in interview, December 1987.

CHAPTER 15. CAUGHT IN POLITICAL CROSSFIRE

Page 162.   Waite: 'Do these people who write such speculative comments . . .' Press conference, Heathrow, 5 November 1986.

Page 162.   'Terry Waite does not wear his collar back to front.' *Daily Star*, 3 November 1986.

Page 163.   'It emerges that Waite has been used . . .' Similar article appeared in the Washington Post on 17 December 1986. Quoting an informed US official it said, 'He was used in the sense that he didn't know the whole picture.' The same article reported, 'The Americans provided him with protection on occasion, with transport, and with secret lines of communication.'

Page 166.   'Was Terry Waite used as a pawn . . .?' *Listener* article, 20.11.86.

Page 169.   Schultz. 'Nothing ever gets settled in this town.' Statement to Congressional committees investigating the Iran–Contra affair, 1987.

Page 169.   Meeting in Frankfurt. Details from C. Dunbar and material made available to Congressional committee, 1987.

Page 170.   Schultz: 'Reacted like he'd been kicked in the belly.' Statement to Congressional committees investigating the Iran–Contra scandal, 1987.

Page 172.   Dr Runcie: 'It was something he convinced himself was right.' Interview with *Woman's Own*, 12.09.87.

Page 175.   North: 'I lied every time I met the Iranians.' Statement made by North to Select Committee of the House and Senate on 9 July 1989.
Page 176.   'Cellophane wrapping around the hostage releases.' Statement made in Congress.
Page 176.   Waite: 'A high element of risk. When I leave all my security behind . . .'
Waite: 'My job standing as an independent negotiator . . .'
Both comments made in an interview with Italian TV in December 1986.

CHAPTER 16. ONE MORE WESTERN HOSTAGE
Page 180.   Waite: 'If I had done so, then I would be too afraid . . .' As quoted in the *Daily Telegraph*, 13.01.87.
Page 181.   Marchand: 'I was near the lift of the building . . .' Statement made to news agencies in Beirut, 13.01.87.
Page 182.   Waite's telephone calls were made via an exchange controlled by the Druze. As he suspected they were recorded and, after his capture, edited versions were offered to visitors to Beirut.
Page 183.   Waite's conversation with a British consular official was first revealed in the *Sunday Express*.
Page 192.   Jumblatt: The detention of Waite was an 'act against Islam.' Statement made at Jumblatt's home in Mouktara on 1 February 1987.

CHAPTER 17. WHAT TREMENDOUS FOOLISHNESS
Page 196.   Tehran Radio announced that Waite was a spy. 24 March 1987.
Page 197.   Brian Jenkins 'I think increasingly he was seen . . . of their dealing with the West.' Statement made in television interview to BBC in August 1988.
Page 208.   North: 'I'll be glad to meet Abu Nidal . . .' Testimony before Select Committee of House and Senate, 7 July 1987. North went on to say: 'There's an even deal for him. But I am not willing to have my wife and my four children meet Abu Nidal or his organization on his terms.'
Page 209.   Habiby: 'When I heard Oliver North say what he did . . .' Interview, BBC, August 1987.
Page 211.   Jenco: 'What tremendous foolishness.' Interview with author, August 1987.

CHAPTER 18. '23 HOURS AND 50 MINUTES A DAY
Page 218.   The quotations from Oliver North came from an interview conducted with him by the author for BBC television three weeks before the release of Terry Waite.

ACKNOWLEDGEMENTS

In writing this account of the political intrigue that led to Terry Waite's captivity, there are many people who encouraged me to tell this story. Others gave generously of their time.

The project originated as a film for BBC Panorama; only latterly did it evolve into a book. I am indebted to the BBC for continuing with a project that often appeared beset by difficulties. In particular I am grateful for the patience of David Dickenson, Tim Gardam, Mark Thompson and Samir Shah.

I would also like to thank my producer Peter Molloy, who not only accompanied me to many extraordinary meetings in Washington, but came to believe that 'Terry Waite' was an important political story.

Over the years many others helped including Sue Robertson, Sarah Hann and Kiran Soni.

From the summer of 1987 I received invaluable help from John Lyttle of Lambeth Palace. As he learnt more about the sad circumstances of Terry Waite's captivity, he became convinced that the story should be told. A week before his death in May 1991 I was able to show him a version of the BBC film. He never flagged in his determination to secure Waite's release.

Most particularly I would like to thank Canon Samir Habiby, Terry Waite's colleague. No one I met grieved more over Waite's predicament. He worked tirelessly on projects that might end his captivity. I came to respect his honesty even when confronted with some uncomfortable truths. He was a man unjustly criticized by his Church after Terry Waite's capture.

There were many conversations with Eugene Douglas and Kemal Khoury. I came to respect their sincerity and dedication in trying to end this affair.

In the United States I met with countless officials, too numerous to mention. Many of the conversations were off the record. They bore testimony to the unhappiness that many felt about what had happened to a man who had worked with the American Administration.

David Ignatius of the *Washington Post* was particularly encouraging when he first heard of this story and my thanks to Steven Emerson of CNN who, at an early stage, shared some of his knowledge about the Iran–Contra affair. During this time my literary agent, Jim Reynolds died. He was always a source of encouragement, whatever the project. I am only sad he was unable to see this come to fruition. My thanks, too, to Kathy Rooney of Bloomsbury and Irv Goodman of Little Brown for their invaluable support in the hectic moments to complete this book.

Finally my love and thanks to Sally, Becky and Daniel who shared much of the turmoil.

INDEX